MW00527423

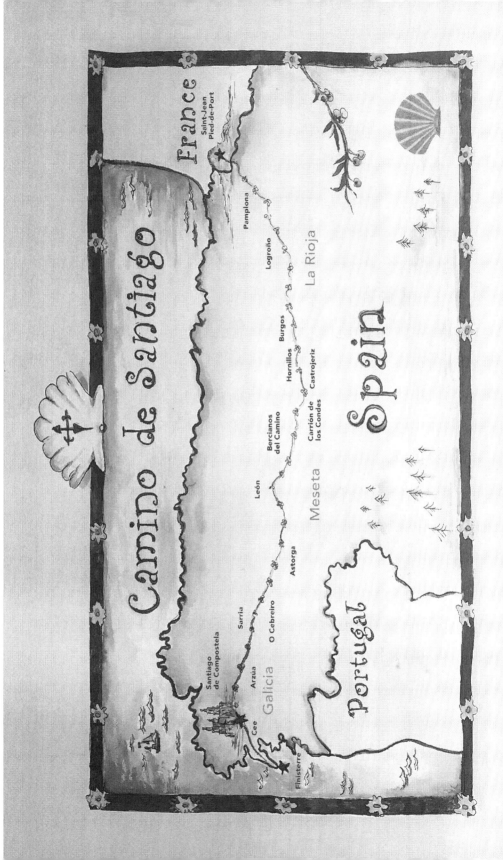

Slow Your Roll

Ruminations & Reflections
On My Walk Across Spain

MEG S. MALONEY

bobtimystic
BOOKS

Copyright © 2020 by Meg S. Maloney

Cover design by Olga Arseniev

Map & additional art by Sarah Marcum

Photos by Meg S. Maloney

Edited by Bob Makela

ISBN-13: 978-1-64999-153-9

Manufactured in the United States of America
First Edition

Slow Your Roll

Words and Music by Troy Verges, Barry Dean, Thomas Osborne and John Osborne Copyright © 2018 SONGS OF UNIVERSAL, INC., LOW Z MUSIC, CREATIVE PULSE MUSIC, PULSE NATION, BE BARRY QUIET, WC MUSIC CORP., ALL THE KING'S PENS, SONGSTEIN PUBLISHING and TRAMPY McCAULEY All Rights for LOW Z MUSIC Administered by SONGS OF UNIVERSAL, INC. All Rights for ALL THE KING'S PENS, SONGSTEIN PUBLISHING and TRAMPY McCAULEY Administered by WC MUSIC CORP. All Rights Reserved   Used by Permission
Reprinted by Permission of Hal Leonard LLC

Words and Music by JOHN OSBORNE, THOMAS OSBORNE, TROY VERGES and BARRY DEAN Copyright @ 2018 ALL THE KING'S PENS, WC MUSIC CORP., SONGSTEIN PUBLISHING, TRAMPY McCAULEY, SONGS OF UNIVERSAL, INC. and THESE ARE PULSE SONGS All Rights on behalf of Iself, ALL THE KING'S PENS, SONGSTEIN PUBLISHING and TRAMPY McCAULEY Administered by WC MUSIC CORP. All Rights Reserved   Used By Permission of ALFRED MUSIC

While You Still Can

Words and Music by Daniel Travis Meadows, Thomas Osborne and John Osborne Copyright 2017 BMG Platinum Songs US, Travis Meadows Music, WC Music Corp., All The King's Pens, Songstein Publishing and Trampy McCauley All Rights for BMG Platinum Songs US and Travis Meadows Music Administered by BMG Rights Management (US) LLC All Rights for All The King's Pens, Songstein Publishing and Trampy McCauley Administered by WC Music Corp. All Rights Reserved   Used by Permission
Reprinted by Permission of Hal Leonard LLC

Words and Music by JOHN OSBORNE, THOMAS OSBORNE, TROY VERGES and BARRY DEAN Copyright @ 2018 TRAMPY McCAULEY, ALL THE KING'S PENS, SONGSTEIN PUBLISH-ING, WB MUSIC CORP. and BMG PLATINUM SONGS All Rights on behalf of Iself TRAMPY Mc-NAULY, ALL THE KING'S PENS and SONGSTEIN PUBLISHING Administered by WC MUSIC CORP. All Rights Reserved   Used By Permission of ALFRED MUSIC

"Santiago," from the book *Pilgrim*, second edition, copyright 2014 by David Whyte, printed with permission from © Many Rivers Press, Langley, WA USA and www.davidwhyte.com.

"On Marriage" from Khalil Gibran's *The Prophet* available courtesy of current public domain laws.

Some names and identifying details have been changed to protect the privacy of certain individuals.

To order this book or to contact the publisher go to:

www.BobtimysticBooks.com

or Amazon.com

Suggested retail price: $13.39

For Jackson, Charlie and Mia

May you always have the courage to follow your dreams.

Take a little break from the rat race
Pour up a little heaven on ice
Pick it back up on Monday
Today I'm gonna testify
The lord's been talking through the weather
Sunday sermon in the sundown sky
Don't think I could say it any better
So I think I'm gonna take that advice
Slow your roll, slow your roll

(Lyrics from "Slow Your Roll" by Brothers Osborne)

Contents

Prologue

Every year countless people from around the world walk the Camino de Santiago, an ancient pilgrimage in Northern Spain. Over 325,000 "pilgrims" from nearly 200 countries completed the journey to Santiago de Compostela in 2018, according to the Pilgrim's Office near the stunning cathedral in Santiago—with travelers drawn to this mystical path for their own reasons. Every pilgrim has a worthy story to share and a lifetime's worth of motivations for taking this journey.

This is my story.

I'm sharing my experience for those who are considering embarking on this challenging trek. I'm sharing my story for those who have already experienced the Camino and want to relive it through another pilgrim's eyes. And I'm sharing my tale for those who may simply be curious about this perspective-bending pilgrimage.

On May 23, 2019, I began walking the Camino Francés route from Saint-Jean-Pied-de-Port, a charming small town in southern France, not sure what I'd find. The plan was to reach Santiago de Compostela on June 26, after 35 days of walking and one rest day. I would then walk for a few more days to reach the coastal town of Finisterre, the spot thought to be during Roman times "the end of the known world." If all went according to plan, I'd be finishing my 550-mile trek on July 1.

So what was *my* reason for walking?

That question was often bandied about among us pilgrims—often as a follow-up to "where are you from?" (Both innocuous and essential icebreakers that guaranteed meeting new pilgrims seemingly every day.) While I don't have a tragic or heartbreaking story behind why I wanted to complete the Camino—I didn't lose a loved one or quit my job or go through a painful divorce—my reasons are more subtle, more nuanced. And, I suspect, more common. Quite simply, I love the thrill of adventure. I crave the experience of being in new places and meeting interesting people. I love the outdoors and feel at peace when I'm in nature. And, at 55, I looked forward to the challenge of physically pushing my body. The spiritual part of this journey also appealed to me, and I liked the idea of exploring my religious beliefs.

Maybe most importantly though, I was also looking forward to time on my own. Without being responsible for anyone else. I was eager to reconnect with the person I was before I became a wife and a mother. I wanted to rediscover the younger version of myself and pay attention to the things that interested me and brought me joy. And I loved the idea of doing exactly what I wanted, when I wanted. What a concept!

Before I even set foot back in Spain, I felt an immense sense of gratitude for having the opportunity to take this time for myself.

The Camino also appealed to me for another reason: since I was a teenager, Spain has had a special place in my heart. I was a 14-year-old freshman at Paly High School in Palo Alto, California when I realized I wanted to study abroad during my junior year in college. These days that's not such an unusual desire. But in 1977, study abroad programs were not so popular. I was drawn to the promise of adventure though. I loved the idea of going to a foreign country, meeting new people and soaking up all sorts of new experiences. I don't remember exactly how I even knew about study abroad programs, but I vaguely remember hearing adults talking about these college opportunities.

With that in mind, I enrolled in a French class freshman year thinking I might like to go somewhere in France. But fate had another adventure in store for me. I detested my French teacher. She seemed like she'd rather be anyplace else than with a roomful of teenagers, so I immediately transferred into a Spanish class.

Señora Azevedo, born and raised in Spain, was a famously difficult teacher. She was exotic looking, with long flowing black hair. She appeared stern and serious, and everything about her demanded perfection from her students. Only Spanish was to be spoken in her class. She expected quality work and proper pronunciation. I loved Señora Azevedo's class. And I loved her. I continued taking Spanish classes with her for the rest of high school—and it was because of her that I decided I would spend my junior year abroad somewhere in Spain. As I prepared to write this book, I revisited my high school yearbook to look at Señora Azevedo's picture. I had to smile when I learned for the first time that her name was Margaret, or Margarita in Spanish, the same name I was known as during my time in Spain. Perhaps fate had a hand in the selection of my language teacher all along. Whatever the case, I felt a renewed sense of affection and appreciation for Señora Azevedo.

I'm not exactly sure why I was driven to experience life in a different country. Perhaps it was a reaction to seeing many of the families I grew up with taking trips to far away places. I yearned to have these experiences, too. But my parents divorced when I was 12 and my mother, after staying home to raise her three children, hadn't been in the workforce for almost two decades. She now found herself in the position of being financially responsible for three teenage kids—without any alimony or reliable child support from my father, who had moved across the country to New York to be with the woman who broke up my parents' marriage and eventually became his second wife.

Life was challenging for all of us.

My mother, an English literature major from Smith College, found work as an office manager for a group of doctors. But money was tight. She made enough to pay our mortgage and put food on the table, but there certainly wasn't any extra money for vacations or extraneous luxuries.

Growing up in affluent Palo Alto could be tough on a modest income, even before the birth of Silicon Valley and the ensuing staggering wealth of its future residents. Although the locals didn't flaunt their money, many of my classmates lived in elegant, tastefully furnished homes. They donned the latest fashions and spent their school vacations skiing in Vail or Park City, or soaking up the sun in Hawaii or Mexico.

I don't recall feeling resentful of my friends and classmates. Being a realist at heart, I accepted the fact that we were staying home during Christmas and Spring break. And I knew how it anguished my mother every time she had to say, "I'm sorry, but no, we can't do that" or "No, we can't afford that right now."

When I realized how tight money was, I decided I needed to get a job. But what can a 12-year-old girl do to make money? I convinced my friend Amanda, also living with a single mother, to start a housecleaning business. Somehow we managed to find a few families—complete strangers—to hire us. By cleaning toilets, dusting, vacuuming and doing laundry twice a week, I was able to make enough money to buy some new clothes for school and pay for nights out at the movies with my friends.

By the time I was 15, I found work scooping ice cream at Swensen's in downtown Palo Alto. Not long after that, I was approached by a photographer who introduced me to a few agents at the Grimme modeling agency in San Francisco. After looking at the photographer's pictures of me, Grimme decided to represent me. They landed me modeling jobs throughout high school, mainly catalogue shoots and advertisements for local department stores. I'd often show up in the Macy's ads next to Herb Caen's column in the *San Francisco Chronicle*. I was a high school kid who went from making minimum wage at Swensen's to $75 an hour modeling.

All of a sudden, I was able to pay for club ski trips with friends, buy myself a stereo with speakers, add to my vinyl record collection and purchase tickets to the *Day on the Green* concerts that were so popular during my high school years. And since we only had one car between my mom and my two siblings, I often had to take the train or bus to get to my various modeling gigs. By myself.

As a mom now, I can't imagine sending my young teenage daughter alone to some of these jobs. But I think my mom was under so much stress trying to keep our family afloat that she simply trusted I'd be okay. I had always been an independent child. According to my mom, I liked to do things myself without too much direction from other people. She always told me: "I never have to worry about you."

Of course, this rankled me at times. I wished she worried

about me just a *little*. She seemed to spend most of her time worrying about my sister, Sarah, who's four years older than me. Sarah was undoubtedly more aware of the growing tension between our parents and was hit hard by the divorce.

Then there was my brother, Bruce, who's two years older than me. My mom worried about him missing a father figure in the house. Bruce dealt with my parents' divorce by smoking pot and spending hours in our garage practicing guitar with his rock band. My mom came home early from work once and found one of Bruce's friends using a huge bong. Furious, she broke it and threw it in the trash. The friend, crestfallen, cried, "But Mrs. Johnson, that bong was expensive."

Throw a group of teenage boys together in a band, each dealing with their own angst, and the results can be quite powerful. And loud. The band's amps blared songs by Lynyrd Skynyrd, Led Zeppelin, Blue Oyster Cult and Eric Clapton. No wonder the neighbors often complained about the noise blasting from our house.

One of our neighbors got so fed up once, she called the police late one afternoon to complain. Since none of the band members could hear the doorbell, the police had to come around the side of the house and knock on the back door that led into our garage. Upon entering, the policemen detected a few large marijuana plants in plain view. My mom had never noticed them—and wouldn't have known what they were if she had. But the police did. Busted. For the next several weeks, Bruce had to attend "drug school" every Tuesday night, accompanied by our mother.

After my brother left for college, my mom started noticing the hose in our side yard was often uncoiled next to a ladder she rarely used. We didn't have a gardener or any other service people who might be using this hose, so she couldn't figure out why this was happening.

One evening after work, searching for an answer after finding the hose uncoiled yet again, my mom placed the ladder against the side of the house and climbed up to our roof. To her great astonishment, she soon found her answer. Several large, healthy marijuana plants basked in the sun, their verdant green leaves swaying in the wind. Bruce, away at college at Lewis and Clark in Oregon, had hired a friend back home to come by and water the plants while my mom was at work. My mother was absolutely outraged. Especially after having spent her Tuesday nights for weeks going to drug school with my brother the previous year. Bruce was crushed when he found out his stout plants were immediately destroyed upon my mom's discovery.

But Bruce was a devoted son, accepting the new man-of-the-house role with grace and a fierce sense of protectiveness towards my mother. He was a good brother to Sarah and me, and we all grew closer during the difficult time after our parents' divorce. He still loves music to this day, plays in two bands near his home in Texas, and is proud to watch his son perform in his own band.

When it came to me, my mother felt mostly relief. She was somehow under the notion that she didn't need to worry about me, the baby of the family. She believed I was handling everything just fine. And for the most part, I wanted to keep her believing that this was true. I didn't want to add to her stress level. My mom had enough on her plate.

In reality, I dealt with quite a bit of internal strife. But I kept all my feelings bottled up inside and didn't feel comfortable sharing these with anyone. I resented my father for leaving us, relinquishing his financial responsibility to his family, and forcing Sarah, Bruce and me to accept our new stepmother—even insisting that we be a part of their wedding party. I hated seeing my mom so stressed out and worried all the time about finances and how she was going to help us pay for college.

And I no longer had a private space of my own to deal with all of these feelings. After the divorce we moved into a much smaller home. We had a tiny three-bedroom house with one-and-a-half baths—which meant that my mom and all three of us teenage kids had to share one shower. Teenage primping time was to be kept to a minimum. Bruce, being the only boy, got his own room. And for the first time in my life, I had to share a bedroom with my sister. She was the messy Oscar to my neatnik Felix. We were the Odd Couple indeed, and you could see an invisible line down the center of our room clearly demarcating which side belonged to whom.

Sarah had turned to religion to cope with the divorce. Suddenly, I became a "sinner" due to my sneaking out at night and my underage drinking at high school parties. But at least Sarah didn't tattle on me, so my mom continued to think I was coping just fine. Sarah and I were dealing with the divorce in extremely dissimilar ways, so sharing a room was tough on both of us. But as I reflect on that time now, I find humor in the fact that we were forced to live together, each of us so very different, trying to figure out a way to make sense of our new lives. We became inextricably bonded. And throughout the ensuing years, we have forged a close and loving relationship.

As for my mom's hands-free approach and confidence in

me that I would be okay, there was a silver lining in all this. Because I had started working at such a young age—figuring out how to get from point A to point B—I learned valuable problem solving skills. I gained a sense of confidence and self-reliance. Plus, I found I enjoyed the thrill of new adventures and doing things on my own. These skills would set me up well for life in college and beyond.

As a sophomore at UCLA, when it came time to apply for a study abroad program for the following year, I chose Madrid—and my experience there was everything I hoped it would be. I spent my entire junior year in Madrid—from August of 1983 to August of 1984—and during that time, my Spanish friends all called me Margarita. I fulfilled my fantasy of living in a foreign country. I met interesting people, traveled to new places every weekend and became fluent in another language. The Spanish people were engaging and friendly. But most of all, they knew how to enjoy life! I loved the long meals, the quiet time during the daily *siestas*, the lively *fiestas*, and the late nights filled with crowds of people enjoying *tapas* and drinks at tiny outdoor tables.

I felt alive in a way I hadn't experienced before.

Ever since that 12-month stay in Madrid, I've always felt like a part of my soul lives in Spain. Perhaps I should have seen the foreshadowing of things to come when I won a Halloween costume contest in third grade. I dressed as a Spanish *señorita* in an exquisite costume with fancy lace and a black *mantilla*, cooling myself all day with a brilliantly colored painted fan. I wore bright red lipstick, and my mom applied rouge to my young cheeks. I remember feeling beautiful that day, all made up and in my grown-up costume. And I looked the part with my dark hair and green eyes. When I gaze at my younger self in a photo from that day—with my pixie haircut and big eyes—I can see the look of pure joy and glee on my face. It's a happy memory for me.

Living in Spain reinforced my love of new adventures. From taking an art class at the famed Prado Museum, to enjoying a sunny day in a boat in Retiro Park, to eating dinner at 11:00 p.m.—followed by dancing at a club until 4:00 in the morning. I experienced the joy of being befriended by a pair of Spanish brothers, Vicente and Javier, from the nearby town of Miguel Esteben, who were also attending the University of Madrid. They took me under their wings like protective big brothers and showed me all around the city, instilling in me a deep appreciation for all things *Madrileño*.

At first, I had a hard time getting into the rhythm of the mid-day *siesta* break. Being a list-maker and a doer most of my life, it was difficult for me to find stores closed when I wanted to check off a task or complete an errand. But I eventually learned to appreciate this time to connect with friends, or rest and recharge for the remainder of the day. I recognized that I was living my life more in the present and not thinking so much about what I needed to accomplish in the future. I came to love this pace of life.

I find it interesting that I didn't know about the Camino when I lived in Madrid. Then again, it's surprising how few Spanish pilgrims I met while I was walking across Spain. Many of the local Spaniards I talked to said they didn't have any desire to walk the Camino—or they were hoping to do part of it at some point in their lives.

I first heard about the famed Camino de Santiago sometime in the early 2000's. My sister-in-law, Ninni, was planning to walk it, and her daughter, my niece, Mika, was going to join her for part of it. I immediately knew this was something I wanted to do—adventure in the beautiful outdoors, the chance to meet new people, the spiritual component. It all appealed to me. Plus...it was in Spain! I *had* to make this happen at some point in my life. But I was busy raising three children, volunteering in the classroom and in the community. Trying to balance life as a mom, wife, daughter, sister and friend.

Getting back to Spain seemed very far away.

Then things changed in 2015. My eldest son, Jackson, had a chance to study abroad in Madrid for the Spring semester of his junior year at the University of Colorado. I was elated that he'd get to experience his version of living in Madrid. Naturally, I encouraged him to stay in Spain after the semester so he could walk the Camino. If I couldn't do it, I thought, at least my son could.

Jackson has my adventurous spirit, so I knew he'd be game. With little to no knowledge about the Camino, he bought a backpack and a pair of hiking shoes before setting off for what turned out to be an overwhelmingly positive and rewarding solo experience.

As I listened to some of Jackson's stories after he returned, I again felt the pull of the Camino. I was happy that he was able to do something I'd dreamed about for years—but dammit, I wanted to do this myself! And yet, I still had a daughter in high school at home. The timing still wasn't right.

But in August of 2016, I officially became an empty nester after my husband, Tom, and I dropped Mia off at college. She was happy to join her big brother Charlie at USC and we were thrilled to have two children on one campus. It wasn't long before Tom and I settled happily and easily into our new life of spontaneity and mid-week dinner dates in our Northern California bedroom community. We now had time to do all the things we'd put aside during our child-rearing years.

Having stayed home with our children for the last 23 years, I suddenly found myself in a state of transition. I no longer had the day-to-day responsibilities of raising my kids. Now what? Did I want to go back to work? Continue working in the family counseling arena, as I had done eons ago after earning my masters in Marriage, Family and Child Counseling? Find work in an entirely new area? Go back to school? Volunteer? I was only 52 and was grappling with the age-old question of what my purpose was in this lifetime. How could I contribute something meaningful in a way I would find fulfilling?

After a year or so of working in sales and marketing for a dear friend, a talented jewelry designer, I decided I wanted to enjoy some free time without any long-term obligations. I applied for a volunteer job at our local hospital while I continued to figure out what I would do next. Then in early 2018, I took a bad fall on a wet floor and suffered a terrible break in my left wrist. Recovery was long and painful. Eventually, it became clear that I probably should have had surgery immediately after the break to avoid the complications I was experiencing. But I couldn't change that. All I could do was change doctors and move on to plan B.

I wasn't used to being in a constant state of pain or being prohibited from doing an array of my normal daily activities. Just getting bathed and dressed was a laborious task, not to mention simple household chores like laundry and washing dishes. And being an avid tennis player, I missed the physical, competitive and social outlet this provided me a few times a week.

Recovering from my wrist injury was a humbling and difficult time for me. I like to think of myself as a positive, optimistic person, and I prefer to be busy and active. I have a daily list of "to-dos" and love the feeling of accomplishment when I check them off. But I was in an altered emotional state. I was feeling negative, sad, angry and frustrated. Too exhausted to think about checking items off my list, let alone even making a list.

Being in constant pain saps your energy, your enthusiasm and your spirit. This experience gave me a whole new appreciation for people who live their lives in this state. It made me realize how fragile and fleeting life can be. In an instant, your whole existence can change. And I was experiencing this realization with just a broken wrist.

Still, the pain was real. And it was debilitating.

It was during this time of recovery in the Fall of 2018 that I awoke one morning and felt an overwhelming urge to walk the Camino. No more waiting. I didn't want to take a chance that I would have another setback and not have the opportunity to fulfill my dream. I talked it over with Tom, and he was fully supportive of my desire to leave the following Spring. I asked if he might like to join me for part of the trip, and he agreed he'd come for the last two weeks.

After talking it over with Jackson and a few other people I knew who had walked the Camino, I figured out how much time I would need to complete the 500-mile journey to Santiago, plus an additional 50 miles to Finisterre (also referred to as *Fisterra* in the Gallego dialect). I added one day of rest while waiting for Tom to arrive, and one extra night in Santiago before heading to Finisterre.

I immediately booked my flights, allowing for an extra night in the French beach town of Biarritz before I started my journey. Plus, three additional nights in Madrid after completing the Camino, so I could revisit the city I called home during my year abroad—and maybe even reconnect with Vicente and Javier, my two dear Spanish friends. I had seen Javier in 2015 when I visited Jackson in Madrid, my first visit back since I left in 1984. But I hadn't seen Vicente since 1988 when he visited me in San Francisco.

With my flights booked, I mulled over how I wanted to experience the Camino. Did I want to carry everything on my back as Jackson had done? Did I want to stay in hostels, sleeping with groups of strangers and sharing bathrooms as I had done during my travels as a student three decades ago? Having dealt with back issues for the past several years, I decided that I didn't want to carry a heavy pack each day. It was more important for me to focus on the journey and not risk injury to my back. I decided to use a day pack for my essentials and then hire a company to transfer my duffel bag each day. I also decided that, at my age and being a single woman, I really didn't want to share sleeping quarters or bathrooms. So I opted to book a private room and bathroom each night.

I called a travel agent I'd used in the past and asked if she'd ever helped anybody plan a trip on the Camino. She said she had used a company to set up bag transfers and pre-book accommodations, so I asked her to help me. I told her I wasn't looking for anything fancy—I simply wanted my own room and bathroom at every stop.

I knew that by making this decision to pre-book rooms, I was eliminating the opportunity for a certain level of spontaneity. If I came upon a town I really liked, I wouldn't have the option to linger there longer than a night, as I would lose my room reservations for the following nights in the towns ahead. I loved the idea of having the flexibility to stay wherever and however long I wanted each night. I craved the ability to be spontaneous, a quality I was hard-pressed to embrace when managing the schedules of three very active kids. But I was also willing to sacrifice these things in order to secure a private room and bathroom at each stop. And frankly, having a set walking goal each day worked well with my personality. I love the challenge of setting a goal—however large or small—then doing everything in my power to achieve that goal.

Within a few weeks, my trip had come together. I was set to leave for my solo journey on May 20, 2019. Now all I had to do was gather my essentials: find good hiking shoes, a comfortable day pack and decent walking sticks—then test them out before boarding my flight eight months later. Giddy with excitement and anticipation, I was finally making the dream of walking the Camino a reality.

A few days before leaving home, friends and family encouraged me to set up a blog in case I felt like documenting some of my experiences on the Camino. I knew I didn't want to do this via social media, since I was trying to disconnect from my devices as much as possible. I set up a phone plan with Wi-Fi capabilities only and planned to use my phone primarily to take photos. I didn't know how much I would feel like writing on the blog, as I had intended to spend my free time writing in my journal. As it turned out, I started writing daily in both places— but the journal entries eventually ceased as it became too time consuming. The blog postings would have to suffice.

This book, in a way, is an augmented version of my blog as it recounts my journey day by day. But it's different in that I have expanded on some of my experiences, thoughts and reflections. And I have delved deeper into the relationships I formed on the Camino as well as the lessons I learned about what you can discover when you take one step at a time and... slow your roll.

Part One

The Joy & Challenge
of Solitude

T-Minus One Day

I arrived into the quaint town of Saint-Jean-Pied-de-Port, France on a beautiful sunny afternoon on Wednesday, May 22, 2019. I had spent the morning walking all over Biarritz, an elegant seaside town on the southwest coast of France. I wanted to revisit the beachside city where I had tasted my first steaming hot latte, served in an enormous mug 35 years ago during one of my weekend trips away from the University of Madrid. Nearly four decades later, Biarritz did not disappoint.

The sun shone brilliantly above the azure sea and the streets were filled with people out enjoying the lovely weather after several days of pounding rain. It felt good to move my body after a long day of travel from California the day before. I could feel the jet lag disappear as I soaked up the warmth of the sun. The excitement was building as I rode in complete silence with my French cab driver, who didn't speak a lick of English or Spanish. In just a few hours, I would be in the town where the thousand-year-old Camino Francés route began.

Once I arrived in hilly Saint-Jean-Pied-de-Port, I also realized how grateful I was that my stay in France would be brief. I only know a few words of French, and my attempts at speaking English or Spanish were often met with stony silence. I looked forward to being in a country where I could speak the native language. I simply had to survive the first day of hiking over the daunting Pyrenees mountain range and I would soon be in Spain.

After settling into my room at the *Hotel Les Pyrenees,* a charming family-operated hotel run by the Famille Arrambide, I set out for the Pilgrim's Office on the narrow cobblestone Rue de la Citadelle, where I collected a few maps to help me along the way. One was specifically for the first day—markers along the path to tell you which way to go and, more importantly, where NOT to go. Through the years, many pilgrims have lost their lives along the Camino due to falls on slippery terrain or scrabbly rock on steep descents. It was vital to pay attention to areas deemed unsafe. Another map showed the elevation gain during each stage of the Camino, so pilgrims could prepare accordingly.

After getting my Pilgrim's Passport stamped—a must for any pilgrim wanting to secure a *compostela,* a certificate of completion in Santiago—the clerk encouraged me to pick out a scallop shell to take with me on my journey. The shell is an iconic symbol on the Camino and can be seen on Camino path markers, hanging from pilgrim backpacks, fashioned into necklaces, bracelets and earrings, and displayed in various art forms along *The Way of St. James.*

According to "The Road to Santiago" website, the shell represents "the many different spiritual/religious/humanist pathways that lead to the same place, to the universal centre of all life-forms, the spirit, the soul...it represents our personal journey, the sacred path that we must take within." The scallop shell also serves a practical purpose, often used to ladle water for thirsty pilgrims. Back home, my friend Beth had given me a beautiful shell emblazoned with a cross of St. James to hang on my backpack. But with my adventure hours away from beginning, I decided to take another shell to keep as a memento of my starting place.

As I left the office, I looked down the long cobblestone street to see the road I'd be walking the next morning as I began my arduous journey. The little town was bustling with pilgrims preparing to walk, gathering provisions and talking excitedly amongst themselves. I could feel the electricity in the air. It was intoxicating. Just then I happened to look up and noticed the address placard for the Pilgrim's Office. What I saw took my breath away—the number 39. My lucky number. I knew it was a sign that I was meant to be walking the Camino. Everything would be alright. I could feel it in my bones.

I immediately texted a picture of the address sign to my family, mostly for my daughter's sake, to let them know what I'd seen. Mia had been worried about me being on my own for such a long period of time. Not that she thought I couldn't take care of myself. She just didn't like the idea of me being so far away and out of touch, seeing as how we normally talk and text on a daily basis. So she was relieved to see my picture, as she, too, believes in life's little signs. And seeing the number 39 was surely a sign meant for me.

How did 39 become my lucky number? It's kind of silly, but when I was a kid I entered a contest where you had to guess the number of candy pieces in a jar. I'd never won anything before, so I was ecstatic when my guess of 39 made me the proud owner of that little jar of candy. Ever since then, I have considered 39 to be my special number. And wouldn't you know it, I fell in love with and married a man who grew up in a house on 139 Saltair Avenue. It was meant to be.

Several months after I'd booked my Camino trip, I was hiking with a friend who was asking about my plans. She wanted to know how many days I would be walking. As I added them up, I felt a chill throughout my body as the realization set in—39 days of walking. I hadn't put it together during my planning. But to me, this was just another sign that I had chosen the perfect time for me to walk the Camino.

With a huge smile on my face, I left the Pilgrim's Office and headed back to my hotel to eat dinner in their small, window-lined restaurant facing the street. The company booking all of my accommodations booked each place with half board—meaning breakfast and dinner were included. At the onset, I thought this seemed like a convenient way to do things. No worrying about where I was going to eat. And it would be easy for me to buy snacks or a *bocadillo* (sandwich) along the way for my lunches. As the trip progressed, though, I would come to realize that I wished I had done things differently. I didn't *always* want to eat dinner at the place where I was staying. I wanted to make my own choice.

But this was the first night, so I was eager to get into my new routine. As much as I'd been used to doing plenty of things on my own, eating dinner alone in a restaurant was not one of them. This, I thought to myself, was going to take some getting used to. To make matters worse, I had stupidly forgotten to bring my book and the Wi-Fi signal was weak. Since I didn't have a data plan, I couldn't distract myself by scrolling through my phone. So I sat there, trying to feel and look comfortable while the other diners around me chatted animatedly, laughing at each other's jokes while sipping their glasses of red wine, *vino tinto*.

The waiter brought me a fancy menu made of heavy cardstock, with an exquisite drawing of the hotel on the front cover. Inside, listed in French —with zero translations—was the outline of a multi-course *prix fixe* dinner. I had no idea what I'd be served. And I had no desire to eat a fancy meal, full of unknown ingredients that might not agree with me, the night before embarking on the longest, most difficult hike I'd ever attempted. Until that point, the longest I'd ever hiked was 12 miles. Once. The first day of the Camino was around 16 miles, with a daunting elevation gain. I'd be crossing the Pyrenees! There was no way I wanted to deal with a funky stomach to complicate what was already going to be a challenging day.

So I barely ate. The waiter looked personally offended that I was hardly touching my food. As if he had cooked it himself. I tried to communicate with hand signals and my limited French vocabulary that I wasn't hungry. It didn't help. I pushed the mystery meat with creamy sauce around my plate to make it look like I'd eaten part of it.

Meanwhile, I began to feel anxious about the way my trip had been set up. This was *not* the dinner setting I had imagined I'd be enjoying on the Camino. I remembered hearing Jackson's stories about communal dinners and pilgrims sharing meals together. The place where I was staying didn't seem like a spot frequented by many pilgrims. And I wanted to connect with other pilgrims. That was one of the things I was most looking forward to.

Oh shit. What have I done?

Are *all* my hotels going to be this way? With fancy dinners I don't care about eating? And will I be eating alone every night, listening to everyone else having a good time together? I liked the idea of walking alone and having that time to myself— but I enjoyed connecting with other people during mealtime and was excited about the potential for that kind of experience. But now my stomach was twisting in knots. A feeling of doubt and dread momentarily washed over me.

As the waiter brought me yet another course of something I wouldn't touch, a woman from a nearby table—who I had just noticed was also eating by herself—asked if she could join me. Ahhh, how nice. Turns out she, too, was a pilgrim. Only she'd been walking the previous six weeks through France, on the Le Puy Route, which eventually meets up with the Camino Francés, the route I was about to begin. (The Camino Francés is but one of the seven well-established Camino routes to Santiago.)

Charlotte, a native of France, also spoke perfect English, since her mom was from Houston, Texas. She had shoulder-length, auburn-colored wavy hair, with a fair face sprinkled with tiny freckles. When she smiled, as she often did when relaying some of her travel stories, her entire face lit up. She exuded energy and enthusiasm with every word.

Charlotte explained that the following day would be her last day of walking for a while. She had to get back home for jury duty, but planned to return in a few weeks to complete her journey to Santiago. We ended up talking for over an hour. And when we finally said goodnight, I felt an immense sense of peace and calm, grateful that my dinner experience ended on a much more positive note than it had begun.

I returned to my room, a pleasant, light-filled space with a balcony overlooking the courtyard below. With jitters in my stomach, I started organizing my 24-liter backpack for the next morning. I filled my two-liter bladder with water, packed a few snacks, a windbreaker and rain poncho, a long-sleeve shirt, a first aid kit, some bandages, a blister kit, Kleenex, my passport and wallet, sunscreen and chapstick. I tucked in my journal and Camino guide book, along with a pen and the map handouts I received from the Pilgrim's Office. I looked at my itinerary and took a picture of the map to the hotel where I would be staying the next night.

I then attached my InReach Garmin device to my pack so it could track my progress by satellite. I brought this so my family could see where I was each day by clicking on the map link I had provided them before I left, and it would comfort them knowing I had successfully reached my daily destination. I wanted to disconnect from my phone as much as possible and wasn't intending to send daily texts to my family, so the Garmin would suffice.

I then laid out my clothes: water resistant slate blue pants, a gray short-sleeve quick-dry shirt, a navy quarter-zip pullover, a periwinkle Patagonia down vest, a royal blue neck buff, socks, my Merrell Moab low-top hiking shoes and my beloved hunter green Echo Lake hat that my son, Charlie, had given me after spending a weekend backpacking trip there. I loved that hat and decided to bring it on the Camino because I felt like Charlie was right there with me every time I wore it. He had the exact same hat, and I loved picturing him wearing it with his dark wavy hair peeking out and his brilliant green eyes twinkling under the brim.

I'm kind of sentimental that way. Many of the things I brought with me were selected because they had a special meaning to me: heart-shaped silver earrings with the word "hope" engraved on them, bought in Boulder, Colorado with Jackson at one of his favorite stores; a delicate gold chain bracelet with a tiny, dangling gold heart that Mia had given me for Mother's Day right before I left on my trip; a necklace with three tiny gold hearts and one big heart at the clasp that represented my three kids and Tom, also given to me for Mother's Day; a delicate ring in the shape of a Camino-like arrow that I had found in a tiny boutique near my home; and a gold cross necklace that Tom had given me for my birthday a few months prior, engraved with the initials of the five members in our family and blessed by our priest. I'd also purchased a small pair of pyrite earrings to take with me. Pyrite is a stone symbolizing protection, good physical health and emotional well-being. I decided to wear these earrings on the first day of my Camino.

Once I was prepared, I climbed into bed and snuggled against the pillow I brought from home. Despite my intention to pack lightly, I'd made the decision to cram my beloved pillow and a few pillowcases into a stuff sack so that I could give myself the best chance of getting a good night's sleep. Too often, I had experienced sleepless nights and a stiff neck after laying my head on rock hard pillows. I knew that getting a good night's sleep would be paramount in making it through each day's walk, so I made the choice to add this extra weight to my bag. And as I would find out in the ensuing weeks, this was one of the best decisions I made.

I set my alarm for 6:00 the next morning. I wanted to get an early start for what was no doubt going to be a long day. Feelings of self-doubt started to creep in, and my stomach was lurching with nervous energy. Could I make it through the day? I felt mentally ready, but would my body cooperate? Even though I knew I was in good physical shape, I hadn't ever attempted a climb like I would be facing the next day.

As my mind raced, I decided to pull out a stack of notes and letters that several of my friends and family had given me before I left California. I was instructed to read them the night before starting my journey. Many of my girlfriends wrote notes of encouragement or shared inspirational poems and prayers. I cried as I read each note from Jackson, Charlie and Mia, all of whom expressed how excited they were for me to have this opportunity to fulfill my dream and take time for myself after spending years taking care of them. They each said how proud they were of me, and they admired my courage to do this trip alone. In Mia's letter she wrote:

I am so proud of your ambition and courage, and your ability to push yourself to your limits. You truly are my hero, my queen, my role model. I strive to be like you more and more with every day, and I feel so fortunate for our relationship...I hope you take advantage of all the opportunities and explorations that await you in the next 39 days. Know that I will always be thinking of you, praying for you, and missing you. I value and appreciate everything you are to me—a mom, a friend, a confidante, an adventure buddy and my music tastemaker. I can't wait for you to experience this amazing lifelong dream of yours.

On the next page is a prayer often said at the end of Pilgrim masses along the Camino. I hope you find in it strength and comfort and reassurance that along with all of us at home, God is watching over you during this journey and will guide you safely on your path...Buen Camino Margarita! I love you to the moon and back. My heart is with you while you're away. Love you tons!

Xoxo, Mia

Camino Prayer

O God,
Be for us our companion on the walk
Our guide at the crossroads,
Our breath in our weariness,
Our protection in danger,
Our albergue on the Camino,
Our shade in the heat,
Our light in the darkness,
Our consolation in our discouragements,
And our strength in our intentions.
So that with your guidance we may
Arrive safe and sound at the end of
The Road and enriched with grace
And virtue we return safely to our
Homes filled with joy.
Amen.

Mia always knew how to pull on my heartstrings. Somehow I was lucky enough to have a daughter who consistently showered me with love, thoughtfulness and unwavering support.

In a way, Mia is my rock. We get each other in a way that no one else does. We often say the exact same thing at the same time—and we are astonishingly compatible. Astonishing in that I can't remember ever fighting with her, even during her middle school years. Perhaps because she grew up as a tomboy with two older brothers and preferred playing with boys, she didn't care for drama. In any case, we share a love of music, adventure, travel, food, fashion (she grew out of her tomboy stage in middle school) and entertainment. With her intelligence and quick mind, Mia is extremely witty and fun, and we genuinely enjoy each other's company. I was going to miss our daily texts and phone chats, but I knew she was happy for me to experience this adventure.

Jackson wrote in his note:

Dear Mom,

For all the things along the Camino that you may find funny, serious, difficult, easy, joyous, sad, beautiful, ugly; for the good times and feelings that will occupy your heart and mind; the soreness and the strength that will come into your body, and the will and the challenges in your mind; and for all the things as you walk along, all the people and trees and weather and conversations that may find you.

Buen Camino!

I am so grateful for all you have given as my mother. May it come back to you one hundred fold.

All my love,
Jackson

Being my firstborn, Jackson will always have a special place in my heart. We have a deep connection. Maybe because he's such a good listener and asks thoughtful, probing questions, I find myself opening up to him in a way I don't do with other people. He is accepting, encouraging and loving—and he seems to get me. We certainly had our struggles during his high school years as he was trying to figure out his path in life, while I was trying to determine the best way of parenting him. Jackson and I often butted heads. But after some tumultuous years, we have settled into a loving, harmonious relationship.

We also share a love for the written word and music. I was the one who bought him his first Baby Taylor guitar when he was eight. I used to quiz him about song titles and bands on my playlist during car rides back and forth from his various after-school activities. I played everything from Motown, classic rock, pop and country to my favorite singer/songwriters. In no time, thanks to his musical ear, Jackson was quickly able to recognize all of the artists.

I used to take him into San Francisco—to small venues like the Warfield and the Masonic—so he could experience live music. Jackson's first concert was a rollicking show by the Counting Crows. From there, we saw a variety of shows including the iconic Rolling Stones and Van Morrison, to lesser known bands we both loved—Jack's Mannequin and The Fray. We both still enjoy concerts and it was during an evening out with him at the Red Rocks Amphitheater in Colorado, before a Little Big Town/Ashley McBryde show, that I talked with him about my plan to walk the Camino. His reaction was perfect. He was almost as excited as I was, and not just because he'd already done the Camino himself a few years earlier. He knew how much I had wanted to do this. It was after my weekend with Jackson that I went home and booked my airline ticket to Spain.

And Charlie wrote:

I am so lucky to call you my mom. You are the most amazing woman I know. I am so fortunate to always have you to lean on for support and advice. You always know what to say. I am so proud of you for wanting to go to Spain and walk the Camino...some

days are going to be tougher than others, but I prom-
ise you will look back fondly on the times that test
your will...I will be thinking about you every day. I love
you to the moon and back! Thank you for being the
wonderful person that you are. I'm sending you big
bear hugs (with me standing on your toes).

Love,
Charlieo

Charlieo was the nickname I'd used for him since he was in pre-school. As a kid, he always used to step on my toes whenever he hugged me. He'd wrap his little arms around me and give me a huge bear hug. (*Bear* is Tom's nickname for Charlie.) Now, as a young man, he still gives me huge bear hugs. Only now, he's hugging me with big, strong young man arms. He'll even step on my toes sometimes for a cheap laugh from his mom.

Charlie is strong in every sense of the word—physically, spiritually, intellectually and morally. I admire his work ethic and marvel at his insatiable curiosity about life and how things work. He can spend hours reading about topics that interest him. I remember one weekend afternoon when he was in high school and I walked into his room. He was intently focused on his computer screen.

"What are you doing, Charlieo?"

"I'm reading about the rotational energy of the Earth and how this can be used as an energy source."

Right. Of course you are, I thought. This is what you do when you have spare time between school and rugby practice.

Charlie and I are also very close. I often look to him for words of reason and problem solving. He can look at a conflict or problem and find a way to resolve it in a non-threatening, reasonable manner—maybe this peacemaker ability is the by-product of being a middle child. He is also dependable, loving and sensitive. Plus, he's got a brilliant, subtle and sly sense of humor and can always make me laugh.

Charlie is an avid backpacker, so he was my go-to guy to prepare for the Camino. He accompanied me to REI to help pick out my backpack, walking sticks and other necessities. I told him I hoped he would have the opportunity to do the Camino one day—I knew this would be the perfect adventure for him.

Tom's note was equally supportive and encouraging—"*I'm amazed by your courage to do this alone, and I know you've inspired me and many others by your trip...you are so strong and independent, and take great comfort that God is watching over you!*"—and he said he couldn't wait to join me for the last two weeks of the trip.

I felt lucky to be married to a man who I knew was genuinely happy for me and wanted to see me realize my dream. Tom and I are well-suited for one another—we're both independent, competitive (even though he's probably the most competitive person I've ever met) and strong-headed. Neither one of us likes to be told what to do or how to do it—so neither one of us is a shrinking violet. This, of course, has accounted for some rather colorful *discussions* over the years. And we share similar values and priorities, especially when it comes to family life. Tom has been a devoted father and husband, and I admire and respect his unyielding work ethic and his moral compass. But perhaps most of all, I love his ability to make me laugh—that deep, belly wrenching kind that makes it hurt sometimes.

After nearly 28 years of marriage, and two years of dating, this would be the longest we'd ever been apart. I wouldn't see him for a little over a month. And, of course, I would miss him. Yet I craved the experience of being on my own. I loved the idea of strolling in solitude, lost in thought while walking at my own pace, whenever and wherever I wanted. No need to worry if someone else needed to stop for food or rest. I only had to think about myself. And *that* was a delightfully welcoming thought.

As excited as I was to be on my own, I found it interesting to think back on some of the reactions of friends and acquaintances back home who asked about my trip. "So are you going with a tour?" many asked. "A group?" When I answered, "No, I'll be doing this alone," several people shook their heads in astonishment. Many remarked, "I could never do something like that by myself." Or, "I've never traveled anywhere alone." Or they simply nodded their heads politely. Without saying a word, I could tell that walking alone across Spain was about the last thing they'd choose to do.

Others reacted with excitement and offered their encouragement. Many told me that walking the Camino was on their bucket list. Then there were the people who commented on the fact that Tom and I would be apart for over a month. Many women said, "I'm not sure if my husband would let me leave for that long."

LET me leave?

That phrase certainly gave me a knee-jerk reaction. I felt thankful that Tom was completely supportive of my desire to leave, never once expressing any reservations about the length of time I'd be away. Then again, I'm not sure I could stay with a man who didn't give me the freedom to pursue my dreams.

Throughout our marriage, Tom has encouraged me to pursue my interests. When we were first married, just two years after we met at a Stanford/UCLA football game, he was working 12-14-hour days trying to establish himself in the commercial real estate business. I was working 10-hour days in sales for a telecommunications company and commuting to San Francisco from our home in the East Bay. We would both come home from work wiped out.

When we thought about starting a family, I wanted to find a career which would offer me more flexibility to be home with the kids. I quit my job and enrolled in a two-year masters program in Marriage, Family, Child Counseling at St. Mary's College, only a short distance from our home. I liked the idea of working in the counseling field since I was intrigued by people's life stories, enjoyed listening and found satisfaction in helping people feel better. Tom supported my decision.

It took me three years to complete my degree, since I took a lighter load of classes while navigating motherhood for the first time. Jackson arrived, then Charlie. Then, three years later, when I was pregnant with Mia, I decided I wanted to stay home full-time with the kids. I thought I would return to work one day. But as the years passed and I became fully immersed in all that being a mother to three active children required, I happily stayed home. Of course, there were days when I wanted to scream and tear my hair out—on those days I would've given my left kidney for a day in a quiet office, where I could wear something other than a spit-up-stained t-shirt and engage in stimulating adult conversation. But overall, I never regretted my decision to stay at home with our children. I look at them now as young adults, and I like who they've become. I'm proud of them, and I genuinely enjoy being in their company. How could I have any regrets?

Feeling grateful for the support of my friends and family, I turned off my bedside table lamp sometime after 11:00 p.m. and tried to get some much needed rest. But with my mind swirling with thoughts of the next day and my stomach tight with nerves, sleep wouldn't come for several more hours. And the longer it took to fall asleep, the more worried I became about feeling tired for my big first day. It was a long night.

Day 1

I was awake before my alarm sounded at 6:00 in the morning. I dressed and took my time preparing my feet before sliding my socks on. As any pilgrim could tell you, proper foot care was essential on the Camino, and this topic often came up in conversation. I first spread rosemary-infused rubbing alcohol all over my feet and between my toes. This is something Jackson recommended, and since he didn't get any blisters during his Camino, I was all in. Then I slathered on Foot Glide, a product I'd discovered at REI that promised to reduce the formation of blisters. My feet were ready. It was go time.

Around 7:00 it was still too early to eat breakfast in the hotel dining room, as they didn't start serving until an hour later. Instead, I ate a banana and some cheese in my room, drank a little water and headed down to the front desk. I dropped off my duffel bag for the company who'd come by later that morning to deliver it to the hotel where I'd be staying at the end of Day 1.

With my backpack securely strapped on and my walking sticks in hand, I set out for my grand adventure a little after 7:30 on a crisp, sunny Thursday morning. It had been pouring rain and cold earlier in the week, so I felt thankful that the sun was shining on my departure day.

As I walked down the same narrow street as the day before, the cobblestoned Rue de la Citadelle, I could feel the excitement in the air. Throngs of pilgrims, known in Spanish as *peregrinos*, marched along to the starting point of the Camino Francés, a route that became a UNESCO World Heritage site in 1993. We were all heading in the same direction. And we all shared the collective goal of reaching Santiago de Compostela —a mere 778.5 kilometers (approximately 500 miles) away.

The wind blew gently and I could hear birds chirping nearby and cows mooing in the adjacent hills. As much as I love music, I decided to hike without headphones so I could fully enjoy my surroundings. My senses seemed hyper alert. And I felt strong and motivated to make it through this day, despite my lack of sleep.

As I began my initial ascent up the Pyrenees mountains on the higher left Napoleon route through Orisson, I could hear people speaking Italian, French, Spanish, German, Portuguese, Korean and Japanese. Not to mention English—with Irish, British, American and Australian accents. The Camino was a true melting pot of people from all over the world, coming together with the same intention of reaching Santiago. And each one of us had our own reasons for walking. As I looked at different pilgrims, I wondered to myself what his or her story was. What was it about this walk that drew so many people? And why was walking in nature so therapeutic and healing? I hoped I would find the answers to these questions along my journey.

What I knew so far was that I was slogging up the surprisingly steep mountain range alongside fellow pilgrims, many of whom shared my same sense of elation, struggle and joy on this momentous first day.

Even though I walked by myself, I didn't feel alone. One of the lovely pilgrim traditions is to wish each other a *Buen Camino* when passing one another. So no matter what language each pilgrim spoke, everyone knew how to say this phrase. It was a bond between pilgrims, and I never tired of hearing it.

So despite beads of sweat dripping down my face and body, I simply continued to place one foot in front of the other. Stopping every so often to admire the landscape around me and catch my breath. I stood in awe as I looked back to the point where I had begun only a few hours earlier, thousands of feet below me. I reveled in the beauty of the brilliant blue sky dotted with puffy clouds, and the bright green fields peppered with tiny white flowers and rocky outcrops. I welcomed the sight and sound of the wild horses and mooing cows along the way. And I inhaled the crisp air that smelled clean and fresh from the rain earlier that week.

I felt overwhelmed at the thought of the thousands of terror-filled people who fled over these same mountains during World War II, bravely trying to escape the brutality of Hitler's regime. I felt small in my vast, historical surroundings. But I also felt exhilarated. I was finally on the Camino, able to take in all these experiences.

After a nearly 4,000-foot elevation gain, it was time to tackle the steep descent. The terrain, still wet from the pouring rain a few days prior, proved to be quite challenging to navigate. Several times my foot slipped on a wet rock and I nearly fell. Unnerved at the thought of falling and reinjuring my wrist, still healing from surgery three months earlier, I gingerly and slowly made my way down. I was grateful to have my walking sticks with me to test solid ground and aid my balance. Days later I would find out that a woman fell on these very same rocks the day before me and had to be airlifted out. Treacherous indeed.

Towards the end of my walk, I met Sue, a petite woman with short cropped light brown hair who moved briskly and assuredly. She appeared to be somewhere in her forties and hailed from Australia. I'd noticed her throughout the day as we kept hopscotching one another—she would take a rest and then I would pass her and vice versa. Walking behind her for several miles, I also took note of her well-defined and very muscular calves, which were striking since everything else about her was petite. Later when I shared my observation with Sue, she laughed heartily, explaining that her friends from home often teased her about her impressive calves.

A little after 2:00 in the afternoon, as I neared the end of my day's walk and spied my final destination in the distance, I felt a huge sense of accomplishment and relief. I'd made it through Day One. All 16 miles. The longest distance I'd ever hiked. And I was in Spain, a country I loved, and a place where I could speak the language. If I could survive this initial day, I thought to myself, I was going to be just fine for the remainder of the trek. With a smile on my face, I practically ran down the final descent of the trail, and jauntily entered the quaint town of Roncesvalles.

Actually, calling it a town is a stretch. They have a few pilgrim accommodations, a café, a church and not much else. I soon learned that the population of Roncesvalles is 25—meaning that the daily influx of pilgrims may double, even triple the number of people in this tiny enclave. But I was just happy to have arrived, and Sue and I found ourselves an outdoor table at the tiny café, settling down amongst our fellow pilgrims who were all celebrating the completion of the day's challenging hike. We ordered two enormous mugs of ice cold beer, and happily chatted with each other about our plans and hopes for the rest of our journey. When I got up to order another beer, I ran into Charlotte, the woman who joined me at dinner the night before. What a lovely surprise! So of course I invited her to sit at our table, and the three of us enjoyed another round before saying our goodbyes. Charlotte was taking a bus back to France that afternoon to be home in time for her upcoming jury duty.

As we waved goodbye to Charlotte, Sue and I went our separate ways to our accommodations for the evening. I walked the short distance from the café, past the church, to my hotel, *Casa Beneficiados.* Thankfully my bag had been transferred successfully, so after checking in I located my duffel bag amongst the rest of the luggage. With my pack still on my back, my walking sticks in hand, I lugged it up three flights to my room, cursing myself for not bringing a different type of bag as my duffel bag was cumbersome and unwieldy. It was supposed to be a rolling duffel, but the wheels rarely worked correctly, and the bag often tipped over if not balanced precisely. I wish I'd brought just a normal hard-sided suitcase with working wheels like the others I'd seen people bring. And this was only my second night of the Camino. Ugh. It was going to be a long road ahead.

My room was simple, but spacious and clean. It had a small desk by the entry and the adjacent room contained a double bed and a tiny bathroom. I took a hot shower and organized my pack for the next day before heading down to the dining room for dinner. The hostess led me to a tiny square wooden table, and as I seated myself I looked around at the 15 tables or so and noticed that they were filled with groups of people eating together. I seemed to be the only person dining alone. This was going to take some getting used to. And dammit, I forgot to bring my book again.

I was seated next to a young Asian couple, and I tried

to make eye contact to indicate a friendly hello. But they were immersed in their own conversation in a language I couldn't understand. They didn't seem to notice my presence.

I read over the menu about a hundred times, trying to keep occupied until finally the waitress took my order. Not in the mood for a heavy meal and deciding to try something out of the ordinary for me, I ordered the fish of the day and then waited for what seemed like an interminable amount of time before it arrived. Well, not being a huge fish lover in the first place, I was somewhat mortified when the waitress presented me with an entire fish on a platter, eyeballs included. Oh my. But this journey was all about trying new things and challenging myself to get out of my comfort zone, so I dug in. And to my surprise and delight, it was delicious!

I savored each bite while enjoying a glass of *vino tinto*. I took my time, studying the people and activity around me. I felt slightly more comfortable eating by myself. But again, I hoped this wasn't going to be an every night occurrence. I wanted to share a meal at the end of the day with fellow pilgrims. Connect. This was one of the things I was most looking forward to experiencing. Was this even going to be part of my journey?

It was clear that this wasn't going to happen in Roncesvalles. So I finished my dinner and headed to the church next door to attend the 8:00 evening pilgrims' mass. I'd read about this particular mass before arriving and learned that since Roncesvalles was the first town in Spain along the Camino Francés, it was a nightly tradition to bless the pilgrims as they began their long trek through this beautiful country. And I felt I could use whatever blessings were offered to help me along the way. So despite my weariness, I entered the old stone church and sat down amongst a number of fellow pilgrims and listened to the priest's lilting voice, trying to decipher a number of Spanish words I wasn't familiar with. Soon, my eyelids felt heavy, and I struggled fiercely to keep them open. It was a battle, and I finally submitted, allowing myself to drift into a peaceful state of relaxation, only to be jolted awake a few minutes later when the priest called all pilgrims to join him at the altar.

As I made my way to the front of the church, I looked around at the group of a hundred or so fellow pilgrims, many of whom looked weary and still wearing their hiking clothes from the day. There were men and women who looked as young as 20 and as old as 75, maybe even 80. And judging by the various languages I heard spoken around me, these pilgrims hailed from a multitude of different countries. I felt a thrill that we were all here, in this church together, all striving to reach the same goal of making it to Santiago. And hearing the priest bless us made that instant feel intensely momentous. I could feel the gravity of what I was about to do, what I had already started that day. It's a moment I'll never forget.

Exhilarated but exhausted, I walked back to my room for what I hoped would be a good night's sleep. However, my body seemed to have a mind of its own, and sleep didn't come easily despite my fatigue. After tossing and turning for what seemed like hours, I finally drifted off—until I was suddenly awakened by a loud pounding noise. Startled, I jolted out of bed to figure out where the racket was coming from. As my sleep fog began to clear, I slowly realized what I was hearing. Rain. Not a light sprinkling. A pounding, driving rain. Really? This was what I had to look forward to on my second day? Well, okay, I thought. Bring it on. I'm ready. And I went back to sleep.

Day 2

With my fitful sleep the night before, I was late getting my bag downstairs by the 8:00 morning deadline. I overslept. Luckily, the luggage transfer company was late and didn't show up until 8:30, just as I was dropping off my bag for pick up. Relieved, I headed to the dining room for a light breakfast before beginning my second day of walking, this time in a pouring rain.

As I stepped outside, clad in my waterproof jacket, pants and hiking shoes, I was struck by two things. One, I felt totally comfortable in the rain—my clothes were keeping me dry, and as a result, I could thoroughly enjoy the sounds, smells and vistas created by the rain. And two, at 9:00 a.m., I seemed to be the only pilgrim on the Camino. I would soon learn that most pilgrims started walking from 6:30-8:00 a.m., as many *albergues* had early mandatory checkout times. Plus, many hostels and *albergues* had strict closing times at night. So if pilgrims didn't return by curfew, they would be locked out for the night.

Starting out on Day Two, I felt at peace. Happy to have the Camino all to myself. The soothing sound of the rain falling and the picturesque view of the long, winding path ahead of me—with its canopy of verdant bushes and trees—made me enter into a complete state of zen. I felt as though I were floating. My sense of sight, smell and hearing became heightened. As I put one foot in front of the other, I felt connected to the earth in a way I hadn't experienced before. I realized I had a huge smile on my face. This is what joy feels like.

I kept thinking of Jackson's mantra during his Camino journey—walk like a turtle, slow and steady—but I seemed to get into a pace that moved quickly. Eventually I saw other pilgrims on my way, their black or brightly colored ponchos flapping in the wind and rain. I wasn't rushed. But my strides must have been long, as I kept passing pilgrims, one by one. I recognized a few faces from the day before and passed my fellow pilgrims with a friendly *Buen Camino!*

Feeling strong and not wanting to disrupt my rhythm, I walked straight through to my destination for the evening without stopping even once for a snack or bathroom break. I walked through the quaint little towns of Burguete, Espinal, Viskarret and Linzoain, all nearly empty since the rainy weather appeared to keep residents inside. I climbed over hills with muddy dirt paths and vistas of lush green, and I soaked in the sounds of a rushing river as I walked along its banks. And after 13.5 miles of non-stop, blissful walking, I arrived in the tiny town of Zubiri at 1:30 in the afternoon feeling surprisingly good.

I crossed over the medieval Rabies Bridge—*Puente de la Rabia*—purportedly named so because it was believed that any animal that passed under the arches of the bridge or around the central pillar would be protected or cured from rabies. I didn't see anyone walking their pets through the arches that particular afternoon, but I wondered if any of the local people carried on this legendary tradition.

My accommodation for the night, *Hostería Zubiri*, wasn't open yet. So I found a nearby café, where I peeled off my wet jacket, plopped myself down at a tiny table and I ordered what turned out to be an enormous mug of cold beer and a large *bocadillo* with *jamón serrano,* one of my favorite things to eat in Spain.

I wrapped up half of my sandwich to take on my walk the next day, and made my way back to see if the *hostería* was open yet. Thankfully I was able to check in, and I saw that my bag had arrived. Then I noticed the steep steps up to my room. Once again I cursed myself for bringing such an unwieldy duffel bag as I lugged it up the old, narrow stairway. But my frustration quickly changed to gratitude as I saw that my bathroom had a tub! This would come to be a great source of joy for me—any time I'd discover a tub in my bathroom. It was always a welcome relief to soak tired feet and legs after a long day of walking.

My room was small, spartan and simple. But it was clean. And, of course, the tub made up for the tiny quarters. After a long hot bath, I washed my clothes in a Scrubba bag, a clever contraption I found online that seemed to do a good job of getting the mud and dirt out of my clothes. I then strung them on the clothesline I'd packed and hoped they would dry in time for my early morning departure. But with the damp, cool weather, I was doubtful. Deciding I couldn't worry about this for several more hours, I worked on my blog for the next hour or so. But it was slow going thanks to a very weak Wi-Fi connection, with each picture taking forever to upload.

By 7:30, it was time to head downstairs to the dining room for dinner. Even though Spaniards typically eat much later in the evening, pilgrims often eat a few hours earlier so they can try to get a decent night's sleep. Also, for those pilgrims who stay in a place without a dining facility or in an *albergue* with a curfew, having dinner on the early side is a necessity in order to make it back before lock up, usually around 10:00 p.m.

As my journey continued, I would soon learn that many pilgrims who normally stayed in multi-bed rooms at *albergues* opted to stay in private rooms in pensións and hotels every now and then to treat themselves to a good night's sleep. They'd also be avoiding curfews and the cacophony of sounds created by fellow pilgrim roommates—snoring, sleep talking, even vomiting from "over-served" pilgrims enjoying a night out. After hearing many stories of interrupted and disruptive sleep, I always felt thankful that I'd decided to book a private room/ bath and didn't have to contend with a curfew. I realize that I may have missed out on some of the pilgrim bonding that inevitably formed in the communal sleeping arrangements. But my desire and need for a solid night's sleep outweighed any feelings of FOMO.

The dining room was tiny, only big enough for 5-6 tables. I was seated next to a French man and woman who I soon discovered were brother and sister, fellow pilgrims who looked to be in their late 50s, maybe early 60s. Dominique spoke halting English. Her brother, Olivier, spoke only French. He simply smiled and nodded his head while his sister and I tried to make conversation throughout dinner. Dominique would pause often to translate for Olivier, and it was sweet to see him trying to find a way to communicate with me and be part of the conversation. It made me wish I knew how to speak French. I wanted to hear more about him and find out about the person behind such kind eyes. But I was also just happy to have *any* dinner conversation at all and connect with fellow pilgrims. Feeling grateful, I soon bid them a good night and climbed the steep stairs to my awaiting bed.

After checking my clothes and realizing they would never dry by morning, I laid them out on the two radiators in my room and prayed that would suffice. With rain in the forecast the next day, hanging my clothes on my backpack to dry wasn't going to be an option. Exhausted, I climbed into bed. Too tired to write in my journal or finish my blog. That would have to wait until the next day in Pamplona.

Day 3

I finally got a good night's sleep! After the last few nights of fitful rest, I felt refreshed and re-energized. I collected my clothes off the radiator, and thankfully they were dry enough to wear or pack in my bag. It looked cold and rainy again, but I was not deterred. I managed to lug my duffel downstairs by 8:00, and then I took my time eating breakfast, remembering how I'd enjoyed walking the Camino the day before without throngs of other pilgrims. By 8:45, I was on my way for what would be a 13.5-mile walk to Pamplona, the city where people from all over the world come to watch the annual *Running of the Bulls* in July—and the Spanish muse where Hemingway spent much of his time writing. And with a population of almost 200,000 people, it was the biggest city on the Camino Francés.

I decided to use my headphones for the first time, but as I listened to the Arga river rushing beside me, the birds chirping happily and the animated conversations of pilgrims I passed by, I kept telling myself to wait just one more mile.

About an hour into my walk and still without headphones, I began walking stride for stride with a local Spaniard named Ygnacio. He was on his daily three-hour walk, explaining that he was trying to lose the weight he gained after recently giving up smoking. He walked at a crisp, jaunty pace, spoke animatedly in Spanish, and he smiled often, as evidenced by the large smile lines around his kind eyes. I found myself enjoying his company immensely, and I relished the opportunity to practice my Spanish. Whenever I couldn't remember a word, I did my best to act it out, and we both laughed often at our attempts to communicate with one another.

As we walked alongside the rushing river on muddy ground and through open fields, Ygnacio happily pointed out bushes and plants grown in his local area—such as the berry used to make *Pacharon*, a type of anise. He urged me to try this yummy drink while in the area. He eventually started asking me about myself and my family. When he learned I had a 25-year-old son, he stopped short and bluntly asked me, "How old are you?"

Somewhat shocked, I answered, "55."

Suddenly, shaking his head, he burst out in fits of laughter. "I can't believe it. I am the same age as you. I thought you were in your early 40's. I feel like I look so much older than you."

Laughing, I thanked him for making my day. Who, besides maybe a kid, doesn't like to be told they look younger than they are?

I was sad to have to say goodbye to Ygnacio when he reached the end of his daily walk. After walking by myself for the first two days—like I generally preferred to walk—it was a welcome experience to walk with someone who exuded so much joy and warmth.

Telling myself that I needed to take time to stop every now and then, I decided to order a *café con leche* and rest at a little restaurant already filled with pilgrims sitting at outdoor tables. Several chickens scuttled in between tables, bobbing their heads furtively as they moved. As I looked around, I saw a few familiar faces and smiled. Again I noticed that most pilgrims were in groups, talking and laughing. I felt alone. But I was okay with this. I felt energized by my time with Ygnacio, and I was looking forward to reaching Pamplona by day's end.

The rest of my walk that day was beautiful and not too strenuous. I felt surprisingly good. But then, about a mile and a half outside Pamplona, I noticed a sharp pain on the top of my right foot where the pad of my shoe was rubbing. And my left calf felt distressingly tight and painful every time I took a step forward. Where was this coming from? I'd been feeling so good. So strong. Why was my body letting me down now?

I *slowed my roll* and invoked Jackson's mantra of walking slow and steady at a turtle's pace. Finally, I arrived in Pamplona around 1:30 in the afternoon. And it was hopping! The city was in the midst of some sort of *fiesta* celebration. Large crowds of people were gathered together all over the city, many with large mugs of beer or wine glasses. They were spilling out of restaurants and bars. Loud music was playing from somewhere I couldn't see, but it sounded live. Soon I saw a band parading through the streets and people in assorted costumes were following along. Several groups of revelers were wearing pink cowboy hats and carrying wine glasses. When I offered to take a picture of one such group I discovered that you could pay a fee, don a pink cowboy hat and begin tasting wine in participating bars and restaurants.

Being thrust suddenly into a place with so many people, bright colors, live music and boisterous revelry was a welcome change from the relatively somber atmosphere of the last few nights. And I was so busy taking it all in, I forgot about the pain in my foot and calf.

I found the *Hotel Tres Reyes* and was surprised to see that it was a fancy looking high rise. What a difference from the places I'd stayed the last few nights. I wasn't sure how I felt about this. It certainly didn't scream *pilgrim*. Hmmm. But at this point, I was nearly hobbling. So I happily checked myself in and collapsed on the bed.

The room was elegantly decorated and very modern. Everything was black and white. Nice bathroom, but no tub. I decided I liked the quaint charm of my previous accommodations over this sleek, somewhat cold place. But the Wi-Fi was strong, so that was a plus. I could finally FaceTime with Tom. What a comfort it was to see his handsome face and share some of my experiences with him.

I washed my muddy pants, took a long hot shower and applied Biofreeze to my sore spots. Then, despite my fatigue, I dressed again in my "evening uniform"—a few pieces of clothing I brought to wear at night including a navy quick-dry skort, a quick-dry pair of navy pants and two plain tees, white and mint green—and headed out in the now rainy weather to explore Pamplona. With no rest days scheduled until Tom arrived in Sarria, my 30th day on the Camino, I had to take advantage of the one day I'd be in each place and explore what I could. With that in mind, I started walking down any street that looked interesting. The crowds of people were now nowhere to be found. At 5:00, people were most likely recovering from the earlier festivities, and the rain was surely a deterrent as well.

I made my way to the *Plaza de Castillo*, where Hemingway reportedly spent much of his time writing at the *Café Iruna*. The place wasn't crowded, and after ordering myself a glass of Rioja at the bar, I found a table by the window and proceeded to write in my journal. I loved the idea that I was writing in the very same place as the famed Hemingway once sat! I became lost in thought as I recounted in my journal all that I had experienced so far, and my pen couldn't keep up fast enough with my inner voice. I wanted to document everything I'd seen so far, the people I met along the way, my feelings of gratitude and joy, my ailments and discomforts, and anything else swirling in my stream of consciousness. The next time I looked up a few hours later, I noticed that the restaurant was buzzing with activity and filled with people. The energy was palpable. I could feel the excitement of Saturday night festivities building all around me.

I soon felt a pair of eyes on me. I looked up and saw that an elderly Spanish woman, sitting beside a man who I guessed was her husband at a table next to me, was staring at me. I smiled at her.

"How long are you planning on staying?" the woman asked me in Spanish. "My husband and I are waiting for friends and we need a bigger table."

"I'll be leaving shortly," I answered. "But in the meantime, you're welcome to share my table."

Smiling warmly, the woman joined me and we began to chat.

It turns out Maria and her husband, Javier, had been married for 56 years. Javier was born in Pamplona and had lived there his entire life. While showing me photos from their dating years, Maria said with a slight sadness in her voice, "My husband was once a very handsome man."

Apparently, she didn't think age had been too kind to him. Maria showed me photos of their children and grandchildren. Then, she asked me:

"Why are you in Pamplona?"

"I'm walking the Camino de Santiago."

"By yourself?" she asked in disbelief.

"Yes. But my husband will join me for the last part of it."

Looking somewhat relieved at hearing this, Maria reached into her purse and handed me a small laminated card. "Here, I want you to have this. It's a picture of St. Fermin, the Patron Saint of Pamplona. Please keep it as a memento of your time here in my hometown."

I took the card and put it in my pocket. "Thank you, Maria. I won't ever forget this night."

Maria's warmth and kindness warmed my heart. And once again, I was thrilled to be practicing my Spanish and connecting with a local. We hugged and said our goodbyes, and I left the now bustling *Café Iruna* with a smile on my face and a spring in my step.

It was still cold and rainy out, but I enjoyed the walk back to my hotel. I stopped in a nearby neighborhood church—somewhat nondescript from the outside, but stunningly exquisite on the inside with its rich multi-colored stained glass windows and ornate altar—and kneeled down to give thanks for this experience. I prayed that my body would stay strong throughout the journey and I said a prayer of thanks for my family for their unwavering support and encouragement. And finally, I prayed for strength for a family from my hometown who I had just learned lost a son to suicide. I felt completely shaken by this recent news and couldn't wrap my mind around what his family must be feeling. Unbelievably tragic.

Dinner was a quiet affair. Only one other table was occupied. A middle-aged man and woman sat across the room, and neither one of them looked like they were fellow pilgrims. Once again I questioned why the travel company had booked my room at this hotel. Where were all the rest of the pilgrims? This wasn't what I wanted. This place seemed too fancy and certainly didn't seem to be a spot where other pilgrims stayed. When I first spoke with my travel agent, all I'd requested was a room and bathroom of my own. I knew from my previous research about the Camino that there were pilgrim *albergues* that offered the choice of either multi-bed rooms or private rooms.

Why wasn't I at one of *those* places?

This is where I'd hoped to connect with other pilgrims. I didn't want to be at a fancy hotel where business people and wealthy tourists might stay. This isn't what I'd signed up for. Another dinner alone. I tried to stifle my frustration and enjoy the meal before me.

Thankfully, I'd remembered to bring my book this time. So I happily dove into *Where the Crawdads Sing* as I enjoyed a flakey piece of hake and roasted potatoes.

Back in my room, I posted another blog entry and turned out the light around midnight. Shoving the rock hard hotel pillow aside, I again felt thankful that I'd decided to bring my soft pillow to sleep on, convinced that I would have been a complete sleep-deprived mess without it.

Day 4

My alarm sounded at 7:00 the next morning. Feeling re-freshed after a solid night's sleep, I prepared for what would be the second longest daily walk so far—14.5 miles. After a few days of walking, I noticed that, according to the GPS satellite device hanging on my backpack, I walked slightly longer distanc-es each day than what the Camino guide book listed. This was probably because the device was tracking my every step, so if I took a detour or started from my hotel off the Camino, I end-ed up walking further. With Moleskin on my sore foot and Biof-reeze on my stiff calf, I was out of my hotel by 8:30 after eating a light breakfast in the dining room.

Almost immediately, my right foot started to throb in pain and my left calf hurt with every step. I thought of my nephew Matt, a young Navy SEAL, who has endured unimag-inable physical and mental challenges. I visualized his hand-some face, with his piercing blue eyes, and told myself to just tough it out and walk through the pain—channel Matt's mental toughness.

Soon thereafter, I met up with two older men from Kent, England. Peter was 80 years old and had just undergone a hip replacement six months earlier. Amazing! He didn't walk fast, but he was out there, determined to finish the trek to Santia-go. His friend, Allen, who looked to be a decade or so young-er, said he felt called to do the Camino by s ome spiritual be-ing, so they were happily walking together. Talking with these spritely men took my mind off my aches and pains, and for the next few miles we merrily chatted away about our hometowns, our families and the gratitude we all felt about experiencing the Camino.

But then the rain began to fall. And the wind picked up, whipping with an astonishing force. The forecast hadn't predicted rain, so stupidly I hadn't packed my rain gear. Rookie mistake. Thankfully, I always carried my windbreaker with me. So I had to stop, fish it out and put it on before putting my backpack rain cover on. I said goodbye to Peter and Allen, hoping I might see them again. Sadly, that would be the last time our paths crossed.

I'd begun my day walking through the city streets of Pamplona, and I now found myself on a path surrounded by vast expanses of fields and hills, with Pamplona a mere speck in the distance. The path began to climb and soon I was ascending a very steep incline towards a group of massive windmills. The temperature had cooled considerably. The rain had begun to fall harder and the wind whipped so fiercely that I covered my face with my neck buff to protect it from the elements.

This was not a day I was rejoicing being on the Camino.

Keeping my head down to shield my face from the driving wind, I continued my long haul up, up, up. When I finally reached the top of the hill—where a large cut-out metal sculpture of a group of pilgrims overlooked the valley leading to Pamplona— it dawned on me that the pain in my right foot and left calf had miraculously subsided. So there was that to be thankful for.

But with the ravaging wind, I didn't linger long to take in the views below. Instead I plodded along and prepared to attack the downhill climb ahead of me. The path consisted of stones of varying shapes and sizes. Wet from the rain, the rocks were slippery and difficult to navigate. Yet again, I felt nervous about the possibility of falling and re-injuring my wrist. So I forced myself to focus carefully on each step, first testing slippery-looking spots with my walking sticks.

I soon found myself walking at the same pace as Kent, a divorced dad of two teenagers from Vancouver. This was his first day walking, and he'd only decided to walk the Camino a week ago. Kent explained that he had been on medical leave for the last year and was trying to decide what to do with his life. Having been diagnosed with narcolepsy 30 years ago, he'd been struggling to get through each day. He took amphetamines during the day and only got two to three hours of sleep each night. I listened in disbelief, wondering how he was going to make it all the way to Santiago.

At the same time, I was fascinated to hear his story and learn about the life of this fellow pilgrim. There is such a strong pull towards this magical Camino that attracts people from all over the world, and we all have our own unique reason for wanting to walk it. Most of us, I'm guessing, are looking for answers to our own internal questions or searching for answers on a more existential, spiritual level. Then there are the people just looking for a good walk.

For me, now that I was finished with my job of raising our children, I questioned how I would spend my time going forward. In the American culture we put a lot of emphasis on what people *do.* It's often the first question a person asks when meeting someone. And on several occasions, when I responded that I was a "stay-at-home mom," my answer was greeted with awkward silence. The apparent feeling was that this didn't quite measure up to a *real* career. Well, of course, this line of work certainly didn't offer any financial rewards or promise of exciting promotions. So in that way, it wasn't a career. But sometimes I couldn't help but feel that because I wasn't earning money for what I did, my job wasn't deemed worthy. It wasn't *enough*. And now that my job was finished, there was that nagging question again: "What do you do?"

Can't I just *be?*

After a few miles, I noticed that Kent was slowing down considerably. He suddenly seemed overwhelmed with fatigue. I suggested he take it slow, especially on his first day. He urged me to walk ahead and we said our goodbyes. That was the last time I saw Kent. In the days ahead, I often wondered if he ever made it to Santiago.

A little further along, I ran into Dominique and Olivier, the French siblings I'd met in Zubiri. They were stopping to get a coffee, and I discovered they'd be staying in the same hotel as me that night. How wonderful to see some familiar faces! I continued walking, realizing later that afternoon that I'd once again never stopped for coffee or a bathroom break since I began my walk. I suppose I was trying to get to my destination—and out of the elements—as quickly as possible.

I arrived in the enchanting town of Puente la Reina around 2:00 in the afternoon. I was staying in the *Hotel Jakue*, which was connected to a hostel of the same name. The hostel provided rooms with bunk beds or private rooms, while the hotel—a floor above—offered private rooms with bathrooms. Both the hostel and hotel shared the same dining area and laundry facilities. This was *exactly* the kind of place that I had hoped to stay at throughout my trek—where I had my own space, but I was in an accommodation bustling with other pilgrims.

After retrieving my bag and finding my room, I changed out of my hiking shoes to relieve the painful rubbing on my right foot. And for the first time, I put on my hiking Tevas, a last minute addition to my duffel bag after a friend, a Camino veteran herself, suggested I bring them as an alternative to my hiking shoes. Despite feeling like a complete dork wearing socks with sandals, I was happy to be walking pain-free as I headed out to explore the quaint, tiny town of Puente la Reina. I wanted to find the bridge that the town was named after, since a picture of it was emblazoned on the front of my pilgrim passport.

I walked down the narrow main street, stopping into yet another awe-inspiring church to give thanks for helping me make it through another day. Within a few minutes, I was at the end of town, facing the picturesque "queen's bridge"—*Puente la Reina*. Tomorrow morning I would be walking over this stunning Romanesque bridge built in the 11th century on my way out of town.

With my exploration complete, I suddenly realized I was ravenously hungry. I stopped at a restaurant near my hotel to eat a little something and write in my journal before heading back to shower. I was thrilled that my hotel had coin-operated washers and dryers—a real luxury after doing laundry in my Scrubba bag—so I took advantage of this amenity and hung out on a nearby couch while waiting for my clothes.

I soon noticed a young woman who was clearly in pain. In broken English, she was telling another young woman how she was suffering from pain in her shoulder and both knees. I walked over and introduced myself and found out Satchi had come all the way from South Korea to walk the Camino. I offered her some Aleve, and even though she'd never heard of the medication, she happily accepted it. Her anguished face turned into a bright smile of appreciation. I prayed that she would find some relief since it didn't look like she'd be able to walk by the next morning.

I also met Eboya, a woman from Hungary who appeared to be close to my age with short dark curly hair, large expressive brown eyes and a congenial smile. She spoke very little English. But with hand signals, facial expressions and broken English we were able to piece enough together so that I discovered it was her birthday. She smiled brightly, saying it was her greatest wish to be on the Camino on her birthday.

Later that evening when I entered the dining room, I was pleased to see that it was quite large and filled with people from many different countries. Pilgrims from both the hotel and hostel gathered together to enjoy the buffet. I saw Dominique and Olivier, as well as a few other familiar faces I'd seen on the Camino during the last few days. It was comforting to see faces I recognized. I was starting to feel less alone.

Eboya and I sat together for dinner, after each going through the buffet line and choosing from a selection of medi-ocre offerings. I opted for the mystery meat over the pungent smelling fish, foraged for any veggies that looked fresh in the salad bar, then grabbed a hunk of bread to fill me up. Despite our halting conversation, I was happy to have a dinner compan-ion. I also found myself wishing I knew more languages so I could communicate with more people. I could see how exhausting it was for Eboya to try to find the words in English to communi-cate with me. It made me remember how I felt when I was living in Madrid, so many years ago, trying to communicate in Spanish. It can be an absolutely draining process.

I reflected on how different I felt being in Spain 35 years later. It seemed like a lifetime ago that I was a young college student basking in the glorious Spanish sun, studying history, art and literature during the day and going out to nightclubs and *fiestas* until the wee hours of the morning with my new friends. And almost every weekend we would travel by train to visit nearby cities or explore nearby countries. Life was carefree and spontaneous, and I didn't think much about future plans.

Now I was married with three adult children, and my life for the past three decades or so was far from spontaneous. It was full of plans and schedules and to-do lists. I felt very far away from that Margarita from so many years ago. But I hoped that might change before too long.

Feeling tired myself, I said goodnight to Eboya and returned to my room to read and get a good night's sleep.

Day 5

I awoke around 6:00 a.m. and laid in bed for the next hour reading texts and emails from family and friends. I found their words of encouragement immensely comforting. Buoyed by their support, I dressed for the day and packed up.

By now, I was feeling confident about my daily routine and transitioned smoothly from one *albergue* to the next. When I arrived at my new accommodation for the night, I asked what time breakfast and dinner were available and if the dining facility was on or off the property. I made sure I received the Wi-Fi info and I never failed to get my pilgrim passport stamped. I'd then find my bag in the luggage room, haul it to my room, often up several flights of stairs. Once in my room, I'd wash my dirty clothes, remove my pillow from the stuff sack and replace the hard rock *albergue* pillow. I'd then jot down some notes from my day and jump in the shower before heading out to explore the town.

After dinner, I laid my clothes out for the next morning, posted a blog entry if I had decent Wi-Fi and took a picture of the map to my hotel for the next day. At around 11:00, sometimes midnight, I turned my light out and quickly fell asleep.

In the morning, I swiftly packed up and had no problem getting my bag down in time for the drivers of the transfer company. The routine became a no-brainer. Every day I did this like clockwork. But when I reflect upon it now, it's amazing to think about sleeping in a different bed for nearly six weeks. But somehow it all just felt normal. And only a few times did I become confused in the middle of the night, thinking I was in the room from the night before. (On Day 5 in Estella, after sleeping in eight different beds since I'd left home, I walked into the closet mistaking it for the bathroom.)

At breakfast I reviewed my upcoming route for the day, referring to both John Brierley's Camino "bible" (*A Pilgrim's Guide to the Camino de Santiago*) and the Camino app on my phone, which gave the distances to each town I would pass through. The app noted if there was a café, pharmacy or supermarket in the upcoming towns. The app also listed the number of empty beds, if any, on the road ahead. This was essential information for planning how far you needed to walk before finding something to eat, going to the bathroom or securing lodging for the night.

Of course, some pilgrims stopped between towns to relieve themselves. I wasn't opposed to the idea, behind the privacy of a large tree or bush. But some days were spent walking through vast open fields with no place to hide. Planning out liquid intake became crucial.

On my fifth day of the Camino, I left my hotel at 8:30 after a mediocre breakfast of yogurt and a piece of crusty old-looking cheese. But today I finally used headphones. Music! What a brilliant way to start the day. Listening to my playlist—heavy with tracks by country artists Chris Stapleton, Maren Morris, Kacey Musgraves, Keith Urban and Eric Church—took my mind off the fact that the weather was still cool, cloudy and windy. When I initially prepared for the Camino, I had imagined I'd be walking under the brilliant Spanish sun. But so far I still hadn't had an opportunity to wear my sunglasses since Day 1, let alone a t-shirt and shorts. But at least on this day, I had beautiful music. And music always makes everything better.

I thought about Mia and our shared love of music. She enjoyed going to concerts as much as I did, and we loved seeing shows together. We've seen a number of country stars together, including several of the artists I was currently listening to. The weekend before I left on the Camino we went to a lively Eric Church concert in Los Angeles, and I felt insanely lucky to have a daughter who didn't seem to mind going to concerts with her mom—I hoped that would never change. I wasn't planning on curbing my appetite for live music, and Mia always made our outings entertaining and amusing with her quick wit.

For the next 30 minutes, I slogged up a dauntingly steep incline. I was thankful I had my music to push me forward as it was hard work! My right foot was protected by a few layers of Moleskin and an Ace bandage, and I had packed my Tevas in case the pain became unbearable.

As the day progressed, I saw enormous fields on either side of the path, all dotted with flaming red poppy-like flowers. It was breathtakingly beautiful. Despite the cool, cloudy weather, I was mesmerized by the dazzling landscape.

I soon found myself walking at the same pace as a woman who looked to be about my age. Colleen was from Vancouver. She was on her own as well, and she, too, was getting her bag transferred ahead. Despite these similarities, I didn't feel a real connection with her, and eventually we parted ways. Time to put the headphones back in.

That's one of the beauties of the Camino—there's never any pressure to walk with someone. The process is fluid. Pilgrims may walk together for a while and then move on from one another. Or they find a strong connection and decide to walk together every day. Or they connect with someone, but walk separately during the day and arrange to meet up at night. Anything goes. I never found any judgment or pressure if I didn't want to continue walking with someone. In fact, I preferred to walk on my own, getting lost in thought and reflection. And many times I found myself simply putting one foot in front of the other, naturally falling into a meditative zen zone without any thoughts—instead I was hyper-alert to the sounds and vistas around me.

After eight or nine miles, I stopped for a snack and coffee in Lorca, a tiny town with a whopping population of 150. As I emerged from the café, I saw a group of three pilgrims who I'd seen sporadically over the last few days. One of them was a young guy, perhaps in his late twenties, who I'd noticed on my very first day when I stopped for a rest in Orisson. He looked fit and athletic, clean cut, with sandy blonde hair and a handsome face. He was walking with a man who looked several years older than him, with an extremely long, unruly beard. They were joined by a young girl who looked to be in her early 20s, with long dark hair and beautiful, nutty brown skin. We said hello to one another, but then went our separate ways. I had a feeling I was going to meet each one of them in the near future.

The rest of my walk that day was fairly uneventful, with the exception of running into Satchi. She was hobbling and walking at a snail's pace. When I asked how she was doing, she smiled and insisted she was "great," attributing her condition to the medicine I had given her. From what I could see, it didn't look like the Aleve had helped one bit. But Satchi was trying her best to put on a brave face. My heart ached for her. She seemed so young and vulnerable. But she insisted she was fine and urged me to walk ahead. Begrudgingly, I continued on, trying to respect her wishes.

I finished my 14.5-mile walk a little after 1:00 in the afternoon and arrived in the town of Estella, a major wine producing center in the wine region of Southern Navarra known as *Tierra Estella*. I checked into the charming *Hospedería Chapitel*, and after a hot shower, it was time to explore.

I found the main square, but none of the outdoor tables were occupied since it was still cool, breezy and rainy. I ate a small snack of *jamón serrano and*...bread. Yes, bread *again*. For the gluten-challenged, a Camino diet can be as daunting as crossing the Pyrenees with a full backpack on a hot summer day. I shudder at how much bread I consumed. I ate bread every day. At every meal. Carbo loading, Camino-style. But one of the many beauties of the Camino is that I *never* worried about my calorie intake. I ate and drank whatever I pleased. With all the exercise I was getting, I was burning off whatever I ate. This was a refreshing change from life at home, where I use more discretion about how much I eat to maintain my weight. After my daily dalliance with bread, I was feeling cold and tired. So I returned to my room to take a much needed *siesta*.

Dinner was downstairs in the small dining room. Yet again, I ate by myself, book in hand. As much as I was getting used to the routine, I yearned for lively conversation during my evening meal. I didn't mind being on my own for breakfast or while I was walking. I was even okay eating lunch alone. But dinner was a different story. This was the time I'd hoped to connect with other pilgrims. I wanted to laugh and enjoy a glass of *vino tinto*, sharing stories about our respective days. Just like the group of pilgrims behind me, who were laughing, cracking jokes and enjoying each other's company. I tried to stifle my pilgrim envy and focus on finishing *Where the Crawdads Sing*. I needed to appreciate the simple fact that I was able to have this opportunity to fulfill my dream of walking the Camino.

Energized after my *siesta*, I didn't feel like returning to my room after dinner. Instead, I thought I'd return to the *Plaza Mayor* to see if there was anything interesting going on. No such luck. The town was completely dead—which surprised me, since I always think of Spaniards spilling out of bars and restaurants until the wee hours of the morning. But Estella is a small town. It was a Monday night. And it was cold and rainy. Apparently, even the Spaniards need a night off.

Feeling defeated, I returned to my hotel bar to see if they had *Pacharon*, the drink that Ygnacio, the local Spaniard, had told me about when we walked together a few days ago. Luckily they did—and it was delicious!

The same group of pilgrims who were sitting behind me at dinner were now also in the bar—and they invited me to join them. Finally! I soon learned that one couple was from Germany, another was from Australia and a third was from New Zealand. The three couples were only walking a segment of the Camino and they'd soon be returning to their faraway homes. I was so happy to be sitting at a table with other pilgrims, enjoying the evening together.

After an hour or two of sharing laughter, funny stories and warm wishes for a *Buen Camino*—not to mention ample amounts of alcohol—we said goodnight and headed upstairs for a well-earned rest. Knowing we'd likely see one another on the road in the days to come.

Day 6

Are you there, sun? It's me, *Margarita*.

That was my first thought of the day—and a nod to the young adult novel by Judy Blume that many of my girlfriends and I read when we were reaching puberty. Yes, it was another cold, cloudy day. And the wind was not my friend.

For 14 long miles.

Huge gusts pummeled me all day long. I resorted to pulling my neck buff up under my nose to shield my face while bundled up in several layers of clothing. Where on Earth was the Spanish sun?

This was a challenging day for me. The constant sound of my walking sticks hitting the ground—*click, click, click*—and the realization that I had nowhere to relieve myself (we only passed through one town at the beginning of the walk) made it difficult for me to get into a peaceful and relaxed mindset. The rest of the Camino that day meandered through vast, open fields with not a single tree in sight to hide behind. *Click, click, click.* I just couldn't bring myself to squat in an open field as other pilgrims passed by. I hoped I would never become that desperate.

Once again, music saved the day. I listened to everything from the *Les Misérables* and *Hamilton* soundtracks, to classical, pop, rock and country. I reflected on the fact that I could feel myself growing stronger each day. I kept a steady pace, managing to climb up hills without too much extra effort. And the sore spot on my right foot and the pain in my left calf had subsided.

But the wind had not.

One person who *wasn't* getting stronger was poor Satchi. She was literally limping along. I asked if I could help and stopped to give her another Aleve. She said she couldn't go on anymore and decided to take a bus to the next town. She'd developed blisters and her knees and shoulders were still in a lot of pain. It was heartbreaking to see her suffering so much. But I was glad to see Satchi taking care of herself, taking a bus and getting some much-needed rest.

If I hadn't stopped to check in with Satchi, I have no doubt that another pilgrim would have done the very same thing. One of the remarkable things about the Camino is that the majority of pilgrims tend to be very outwardly focused on the welfare of their fellow *peregrinos.* Time and time again I witnessed pilgrims assisting others with their heavy packs, their blisters or other various ailments. We helped each other find our accommodations, shared food and drink, and translated languages when we could to ease communication. We listened to people's stories, allowing them to share their joy or heartbreak in a safe and accepting atmosphere. We cared about one another's well-being. There is something magical about the Camino that seems to bring out the best in people. I often thought about this phenomenon, convinced that our world would be a better place if it were run by pilgrims with this mindset.

When I arrived in Los Arcos a little after 1:00 in the afternoon, I immediately found the nearest church—yet again, another work of beauty—and gave thanks for helping me make it through this particularly challenging day. I also remembered to give thanks again for this opportunity to walk the Camino, which I was determined not to take for granted. I realized how lucky I was to have the physical, mental and financial ability to do this. And to have the time to reflect on so many things—my life's journey so far and my hopes for my future—was a true gift. Despite the various challenges I'd encountered so far, I was still enjoying the entire experience. It was gratifying to know I could still persevere through whatever difficulties I faced, and this gave me a sense of confidence and inner peace.

One of the things I often reflected on during my long walks was how lucky I was to have such a loving and supportive family and group of friends. Their encouragement and kind words gave me fuel—during the times I was feeling frustrated by the weather or when I was feeling lonely while eating by myself at the end of the day. But after this particularly challenging day, my heart ached. I missed my family and friends.

I had always intended on walking the Camino alone. I yearned for the time by myself and the chance for enlightening self-discovery. I looked forward to the opportunity to gain some clarity about what I wanted as I navigated through the next phase of my life.

But then there were times when I would see couples, groups of friends, a mother/daughter, a father/son or whole families walking together. They would laugh and joke and there was an ease and lightness about their togetherness. At times, I would miss that part. I'd miss sharing an inside joke, just walking side by side with someone I cared about who knows me well.

As interesting as it could be to meet new people, it could also be exhausting. The conversation so often consisted of small talk and could end up being somewhat superficial. Then there were the people who could literally end up telling you their life story. I often found myself reverting back to the person I was during the days when I worked in the counseling field—listening to people's stories and giving them space to vent their thoughts and fears. It became clear that many people sought refuge on the Camino, looking for answers to help them sort out very complicated lives back home. Luckily, I have always been interested in people's stories, their backgrounds and how their life experiences shaped them. So I enjoyed being a sounding board. I never tired when fellow pilgrims shared intimate details of their lives. I always felt honored that they felt comfortable enough to tell me about themselves.

But even though the Camino can feel like a fast track to connection, I have found that for true friendship to flourish, it takes time to build trust and intimacy. Time is required to build up shared experiences. So as much as I wanted to connect with my fellow pilgrims, I realized that this may not be a driving force of *my* Camino. And I had to be okay with that. I told myself that I needed to appreciate all the benefits of being on my own— going at my own pace, having my own space and time to think and reflect. Doing whatever I wanted, whenever I wanted—and feeling the strength that comes with independence and competence. #Girlpower at its finest.

Feeling tired from the day, I decided I didn't have the energy to explore Los Arcos, today's new town. Instead I found a nice restaurant for lunch, sat myself at a table by the window, book in hand, and treated myself to a delicious meal with not one, but two glasses of *vino tinto*. It was the highlight of my day.

The plan for today's accommodation was a little different. My itinerary showed that I was supposed to meet at a particular spot in Los Arcos and a car was going to take me to my hotel for the evening.

When booking my initial trip, Helen, my travel agent back in California, had explained that some nights I would be staying in hotels that were a bit outside of town—hence the need for a car transfer. The itinerary showed car transfers on six different days. Sounded reasonable enough. I knew some of the towns I was passing through were very small, so it made sense that I might need to find a room somewhere close by.

But Helen—not having walked the Camino herself and not entirely familiar with the logistics—had decided to use a travel company in Southern California to do all of the Camino hotel bookings. Helen assured me that this travel company booked Camino trips "all the time," so I was in good hands. I had no reason to doubt her—until I realized, almost a week into my trek, how the car transfers were going to adversely affect my Camino. I immediately sent an email to my travel agent.

May 28, 2019

Hi Helen,

I just walked to Los Arcos today, and my transfer took me about six miles west to the next town, Viana, to spend the night. I don't see a transfer to take me back to Los Arcos tomorrow, so it looks like I will be skipping that part of the Camino. I don't understand this. I wanted to walk the whole path and not skip parts. I'm hoping this isn't going to happen again. Can you find out for me? Thank you.

To my utter disbelief, the car had taken me ahead to the next town. *What?!* I was furious. This was NOT what I had signed up for. Now that I had a better understanding of the Camino logistics, I immediately looked ahead at my itinerary and saw that the rest of the car transfers intended to take me to towns several miles ahead of my stopping points. In some cases, I would be missing an entire stage of the Camino.

What the hell?!

This was ridiculous. I had been waiting for over a decade to walk the Camino and I was here to WALK it—not get transferred to some hotel that might be a little nicer than what I might find in a smaller town. I was absolutely livid. I was not going to let this happen and needed to figure out a plan B.

Feeling exhausted by the physical and emotional toll of the day, I checked into the *Hotel Palacio de Pujadas* in Viana, a beautiful hilltop fortress town founded in the year 1219. I noticed a sign on the counter advertising massage services and asked the receptionist if I could make an appointment. To my great relief, she confirmed that, yes, I could have an appointment at 8:30 that evening. With Javier. In my room. Would that be okay?

Hmmm. It seemed legit. But in my room? With a strange man? Would I be stupid to agree to this? Wanting to trust that I was in a decent hotel, and feeling tired and sore, I confirmed the booking.

In the meantime, I settled in my room, showered and headed downstairs to eat something light while I was waiting for my appointment. I happened to sit by a young man and woman in their late 20s, maybe early 30s, who looked like they might be pilgrims. They both spoke English, the man with an Irish accent and the woman with some kind of Scandinavian accent. Wanting to connect, but also not wanting to impose since they seemed to be deep in conversation, I eavesdropped for a bit while pretending to read my book. Turns out, they were pilgrims, and I was eager to meet them.

I soon mustered the courage to say hello and introduce myself. I met John, a man with a jolly face covered with a close-cropped mustache and beard. Smile lines creased John's bright, kind eyes and friendly, warm grin. He was sitting with Laerke, an attractive woman from Denmark with bright blonde hair and an inviting smile. We chatted for a while and I asked if they were going to Logroño the next day, the town where I'd be spending the following night. To my dismay, John said they'd be walking farther down the road, as Logroño was only about 10 kilometers away. I fully understood that strategy. Again, I felt confused as to why the travel company booked my trip the way they did. Why did they feel the need to transfer me ahead—then have me only walk six miles the next day? And now I wasn't going to see these friendly pilgrims again since we'd be on different schedules.

Before long, I was ready to put my frustrations aside and enjoy a relaxing massage. I said goodnight (and goodbye) to John and Laerke and walked upstairs to my room.

Javier arrived on time. Thankfully, after talking with him for a few minutes, my intuition told me I'd be okay. My room was small, but after moving the two twin beds together, Javier was able to set up his massage table. Feeling relieved that I seemed to be in a safe environment, I climbed onto the table and immediately sank into a total state of relaxation. Javier had magic hands. My body screamed in appreciation as he worked on my strained muscles. After he finished, Javier told me that my body clearly needed this treatment! Rejuvenated and beyond grateful, I thanked him, tipped him well and said goodbye. When I finally crawled into my twin bed, sleep came quickly and soundly. It had been a long day.

Day 7

The next morning, I could see the sun trying to peek through the clouds. I was feeling optimistic and wanted to make this a good day. I knew it was going to be a short day of walking. But I'd also read that Logroño was a city with a lot of charm and activity—plus a winery offering tastings from the local vineyards.

About an hour into my walk, I noticed a pilgrim walking ahead of me with a small guitar attached to his pack. Curious, I quickened my pace to get a glimpse of his face. As I approached, I was pleasantly surprised to see John, the Irishman I met in the restaurant last night. How wonderful to see a familiar face! After talking for a few minutes, I wished him a *Buen Camino* and we said our goodbyes, feeling a bit disappointed that our paths wouldn't cross again. I would eventually learn that you never knew when or if you'd see the same pilgrim again. Everyone had their own rhythm. And the pilgrim who you thought was moving at a much brisker pace than you might be temporarily sidelined a few days down the road due to blisters or opt to take a few rest days. I would soon discover that goodbyes never felt quite final.

It was 10:30 that morning by the time I reached Logroño, a bustling city of about 155,000 and the capital of the famous wine-growing region of La Rioja. Despite the early hour, I was able to check into my room at the *Hotel Calle Mayor*. And unlike previous days, I had nearly the entire day to explore. But before heading out, I needed to email my travel agent again.

May 29, 2019

Hi Helen,

I walked from Viana to Logroño today—it was only six miles so I'm considering this a rest day. But I feel cheated that I missed that chunk of the Camino from Los Arcos to Viana. I had no idea this company was going to bring me ahead to places and skip parts of the Camino. I simply thought they were going to take me to a hotel perhaps off the way a little and then drop me back to where they picked me up. Can we figure out a way to fix this?

I see my next transfer day is June 4th. It looks like they are picking me up in Burgos and then driving me to Hornillos—that would be missing an entire stage of the Camino! But I don't think I can do two stages in one day. How did this happen? I'm feeling pretty upset right now.

The next transfer after that is June 12th and it looks like, again, I would be missing an entire stage and a half. Can you talk with the company and find out what we can do about this? I understand that will make some of the days longer. I never said I was willing to miss walking parts of the Camino—that's the whole purpose of my trip!

Please let me know what you find out. Thank you.

With that email out of the way, I freshened up and spent the next several hours walking through the city streets. Despite the cool, drizzly weather, I was thrilled that I had a chunk of time to enjoy this bustling and lively town. I was well-rested and my muscles felt rejuvenated after my massage. I loved wandering around aimlessly, taking in the sights, sounds and vibrant energy generated by all the people walking around me. Eventually I stopped in a brightly lit, cozy looking restaurant to warm myself with a *café con leche* and work on my blog. I stayed for a few hours, ordering a second cup of coffee and basking in the luxury of having the time to sit in a peaceful place and let my thoughts flow freely on the page. This was not something I practiced at home. I was more likely too busy, trying to check things off my to-do list. This pattern was something I wanted to change when I returned to America.

On my blog that day, I wrote:

> *One thing I've noticed about being in Spain is that whenever you order anything at a bar, they don't insist you pay right away. They give you your wine or coffee or whatever and you almost have to track them down to pay your bill when you finish. There is something so civilized and nice about this. There is no sense of urgency and a level of trust that you won't leave without paying. It's more about the feeling—it's just very* tranquilo *here, not rush, rush, rush as it is at home. I can get used to this.*

Yes, there is something about the Spanish way of life that is good for my soul. I definitely felt happy that day. As I was leaving, I recognized a few pilgrims I had seen on the Camino eating at a table nearby. We chatted briefly and I could see that they, too, looked like they were enjoying a blissfully relaxing afternoon as well!

With my spirits elevated, I decided to walk to the Visitor's Center to see what sort of events might be happening that evening. I thought it could be fun to see live dancing or music or any other entertainment. But being a Wednesday night, not much was going on. The woman in the Visitor's Center suggested I walk over to the *bodega* (winery) and check out the tasting room. What a fabulous idea! I love all kinds of wines and was especially looking forward to trying the *Albariños* when I reached Galicia.

As I made my way over the bridge from the center of town to the winery on the other side, I noticed a large patch of velvet blue sky surrounded by huge puffy white clouds. It was a stunning evening.

The tasting room inside the winery was packed with people, many of whom looked like fellow pilgrims. As I tasted a few of the Riojas, I met two couples. Fernando owned a bakery in Madrid and was engaged to Haley, a Stanford-educated engineer from San Diego. Misa, also from San Diego, was a professional cellist who lived in London with her British husband, Chris, a paralegal. They were all walking the Camino together for about a week—except Haley, who was going to continue on to Santiago by herself. They welcomed me into their group and we sat outside on the winery lawn, laughing and trading stories.

They asked if I ever felt scared being on my own. I said I'd felt safe the entire time—but there *was* one weird thing that happened to me a few days earlier. I'd been walking by myself and couldn't see anyone behind or in front of me. All of a sudden, a Spanish guy who looked to be in his forties or so suddenly appeared on his bike. He stopped and asked (in Spanish) if I could take a picture of him.

"Of course," I said in Spanish, taking his phone from him.

He grinned and said, "You take a picture of me naked."

I laughed, thinking there was a translation problem going on here. "I don't think you realize what you just said. You just asked me to take a picture of you naked!"

"YES!" he said nodding his head vigorously, a huge smile plastered on his face.

"NO!" I cried as I gave him back his phone. I immediately walked away and never saw him again.

Despite the weird interaction, I never felt I was in danger. I just chalked it up to meeting a harmless crazy guy.

After telling my story, Haley said the exact same thing happened to her! *What?!* This guy must sit on his little perch, waiting until he finds a woman walking by herself to go though his creepy routine with. I suppose we should have reported him. Instead we both laughed hysterically about it, empowered by our ability to move on.

Before long, a large group of pilgrims was sitting on the grass next to us. When one of them started playing a ukulele, I looked over and noticed that it was John, the Irishman I'd said goodbye to earlier that morning. I was so happy to see him! When I asked what he was doing here—since I assumed he was walking ahead—he told me he heard Logroño was a fun place to stay, so he changed his mind. Ah, the beauty of not planning ahead. I loved the idea of being spontaneous and just stopping where I wanted or staying longer in places I liked. But I accepted my fate and tried to make peace with the fact that I'd chosen to book my rooms in advance. Oh, well.

Hearing John's sweet voice and his beautiful music— while sitting in a gorgeous setting with fellow pilgrims, drinking delicious wine as the sun peeked in and out of the clouds—I felt truly happy. *This* is how I imagined the Camino might be. And true to the relaxed Spanish vibe, when the winery workers locked up for the evening, they told us to take our time out on the lawn.

"Just leave your wine glasses before you take off," the workers said as they waved goodbye.

It's almost like the Spaniards expect you to act civilized, so you want to reward their trust in you. What a concept.

It was still light out at 9:00 p.m.—sunsets would often be close to 10:00 during my time in Spain—when I said goodbye to the group before returning to town for dinner. Since my lodgings were booked with half board, breakfasts and dinners were included in my room rate. Sometimes the accommodations didn't have kitchens on site, so I would receive a voucher for a nearby restaurant. At the beginning of the Camino, I enjoyed the convenience of this system. But as my journey progressed, I preferred to choose where I wanted to eat dinner.

During my stay at the *Hotel Calle Mayor* in Logroño, my dinner was at a nearby restaurant. When I walked in, I soon realized I was the only person in the place. After such a lively evening, I was disappointed to be in a setting without any atmosphere or fellow patrons. But I was hungry. So I settled into my spot and looked at the offerings on the pilgrims' menu.

Just as I was scanning the choices, I heard some people enter the restaurant. To my great surprise, I saw Haley, Fernando, Misa and Chris walking in! Of all the restaurants in this busy city, they happened to choose this place. Hallelujah! But, of course, they invited me to join them. Naturally, we picked right up where we had left off, laughing, drinking more wine and staying out far too late for those of us with hopes of

an early morning departure.
    It was a brilliant day.

Day 8

Despite my late evening, I was on the Camino at my usual departure time of 8:30 a.m. Even though I had a slight hangover, I was overjoyed to see the bright, crystalline blue sky. It was my first day in shorts, t-shirt and sunglasses, and I gladly soaked up the warmth washing over my body. I felt ready to attack what would be my longest walk yet—19.5 miles.

As I marched along, I marveled at how well the Camino was marked. Regardless of whether you were in a city or out in the middle of nowhere, yellow arrows *(flechas)* and/or Camino shells pointed you in the right direction—often marked with the distance to either the next town or the ultimate destination of Santiago. I viewed them as happy reminders that I wasn't alone on this journey. The signs were there to assure me that I wouldn't get lost and to encourage me to keep pushing forward to my goal.

I also reflected on the unique aspect of this particular walk. Everyone was walking in the same direction. It was rare to see anyone walking the other way, unless, of course, you were in a big city. There is something quite powerful and moving about this—everyone is pushing forward to the same collective goal of reaching Santiago. Every pilgrim is united by this objective. Having this common goal creates a sense of connection and camaraderie, which feels like a minor miracle considering you've got a wide spectrum of pilgrims from across an increasingly contentious planet coming together. And it's an odd sensation to walk mile after mile with no one passing you from the other direction.

The scenery on my walk today was absolutely gorgeous —vineyards everywhere, with rolling hills in the distance and bright red wildflowers lining the pathways. Absolutely stunning. And I loved how the sun made everything glitter and shine.

After about 11 miles, I could feel my body getting tired. As happy as I was to see the sun, the heat was taking a toll on me. I wasn't used to the sudden increase in temperature. Just as I began to feel aware of my growing fatigue, I happened to pass by a doorway with a huge "39" above it. I smiled. To me, that was a sign encouraging me to keep going. My lucky number popped up just in time to remind me that I could do this. Another example of the magic of the Camino.

With a renewed sense of purpose and energy, I continued on my journey. A few minutes later, I heard a great clunking noise. It was growing louder and louder, and it seemed to be coming from behind me. I soon spotted the source of the noise. It was a pilgrim with a bright orange pack on his back, walking at a tremendously brisk pace. He looked to be in his mid-30s or so, and he carried a huge wooden stick that he forcefully shoved into the ground with each step. *Clank, clank, clank.* The noise was alarming. Within no time, he was ahead of me. I watched with growing curiosity as he often stopped suddenly, darted off the path to quickly snap a photo, then just as suddenly resumed his quick pace. He moved like a jackrabbit, with a frenetic energy about him.

Around mile 13, I stopped to get something to eat and take a break. As I was ordering my food, I saw the man with the bright orange pack next to me at the bar. This is the day I met Dan from Vancouver. He was about 5'8" and wiry, with brown hair and a close cropped mustache and beard. His smile was warm and friendly. I liked him immediately. We chatted for a while, and I teased him about his loud walking stick and fast pace. He confessed that other pilgrims had told him he was rushing along and not taking the proper time to enjoy the Camino. But that was the way he wanted to experience it. So who were other pilgrims to make that judgment?

After lunch, I stood up and suddenly my left calf started hurting. Then my left knee felt a painful twinge. I'd never experienced knee issues in my life, but the downhill sections of the Camino were definitely wreaking havoc. And stopping for a rest hadn't done me any favors—I'd have been better off if I had just kept walking. But I had an Ace bandage in my pack, so I wrapped my knee and continued on. Only 6.5 miles to go. *No problema!*

Just as I was approaching my final destination of Nájera, I saw Dan again. It was just after 3:00 p.m. and I wasn't sure how I caught up. He must've stopped along the way somewhere. I asked Dan to take a picture of me in front of a beautiful hedge of bright pink roses, and then I did the same for him. We then walked into Nájera together. He was looking for a bed in a hostel and asked if I was doing the same. I told him I had pre-booked a room already, so we said goodbye at the first hostel he found. I wished him good luck finding a bed and continued on to my hotel.

I meandered through the narrow streets of Nájera, a charming town on the Najerilla river with a population of about 8,000 in the La Rioja region. I walked over a small stone bridge that overlooked the winding river, taking in the beauty of the sun glistening on the water. Outdoor tables filled with people eating and drinking dotted the river banks, and the buildings nearby looked old and charming. What a welcome sight to see after my longest walk yet!

My hotel, the *Duques de Nájera*, was just a stone's throw from the river. After lugging my pack upstairs, I literally collapsed on my bed. I felt exhausted! But after a hot bath—I did a little celebratory dance when I peeked in the bathroom and saw that it had a tub—a rest and a trip to the pharmacy to get some athletic tape, a knee brace and pain cream, I felt tremendously improved.

Before dinner, I decided to sit at one of the lovely outdoor tables by the river and enjoy a glass of wine. I went inside to the bar, where I ordered a glass. Only, the bartender gave me the entire bottle, saying it was cheaper to order it this way. Well, okay then. If you insist.

So with my full bottle of wine and empty glass in hand, I found a table outside and happily sat down. Ready to relax after my long, exhausting day. I immediately struck up a conversation with an American woman who seemed to be about my age. She was sitting by herself at the table next to me, and I soon learned her name was Debbie and she was from New York City. She had short-cropped dark blonde hair, similar to Dorothy Hamill, with brownish hazel eyes and fair skin.

I could see Debbie eyeing my full bottle of wine.

"I don't normally order an entire bottle for myself," I said laughing. "The bartender said it was cheaper to order it this way. Would you like a glass?"

"Sure. Wanna join me?"

I soon discovered that Debbie was walking the Camino on her own, too. She was single, divorced twice, and had one grown son. She had lost her other son two years ago to a drug overdose. Eventually, she would tell me that she was carrying his remains and was looking for the right spot to spread her son's ashes. She pointed to her fanny pack laying on the table in front of her.

"They are in there. That's Philip."

Her story was heartbreaking. But she had an engaging way of infusing comedic commentary into her Camino stories. I cracked up as she told me about her adventures staying in various hostels with groups of strangers. One time she stayed in a room with all men, one of whom stood directly in front of her in nothing but his tighty whities as she lay in her bottom bunk. Her view at eye level made her cringe, and she later quipped, "I've never spent the night with so many men without having any fun." Soon after that experience, she started booking private rooms for herself.

As we talked, I noticed Dan sitting at a nearby table with a group of other pilgrims, many of whom I recognized. Debbie saw me looking over at Dan and said she had befriended him a few days earlier on the Camino. He reminded her of the son she lost and she felt a special connection with him. Something about his intense, frenzied—yet sweet and vulnerable—manner triggered thoughts about her son. Debbie confessed she worried about Dan. She believed she was meant to meet him. I could see that she felt a strong, protective, motherly bond with him.

I suggested we go over and say hello to Dan and the other pilgrims. Dan happily welcomed us, and I finally met the three pilgrims I'd seen a few days earlier. The fit, handsome young guy was Sean. He was from Florida. The older man with the unruly beard, a former Green Beret from San Diego, was Michael. And the young woman with the beautiful hair and skin was Rachel, who'd soon be moving to Northern California to get her masters degree in ministry.

I also met another pilgrim named Michael, who I had seen from time to time during the past week. The last time I'd seen him was when he was singing with Irish John out on the winery grass in Logroño. Michael was from Denmark, blonde and burly with a huge smile, large dimples and an infectious laugh. When he spoke, he sounded exactly like Arnold Schwarzenegger. It was uncanny. He'd soon come to be known affectionately as "Big Michael." And Green Beret Michael was referred to as "Bearded Michael."

Back at our table, Debbie said she was waiting for Laura, a woman from Bath, England, who she'd met earlier that day. They had made plans to have dinner together at a restaurant nearby. Turns out, it was the same restaurant where I was supposed to use my dinner voucher, so Debbie invited me to join them.

Laura soon arrived, and I offered her a glass of wine from our bottle, but she said she preferred sparkling water instead. She had short, wild hair framing her attractive face and bright blue intelligent looking eyes. Laura laughed with a joy and gusto that made me instantly like her. We immediately hit it off. Like Debbie, she was also single, divorced, with two grown sons—and walking the Camino on her own. Laura explained that she would be joined during the last part of her journey by friends and family so they could all walk into Santiago together on her 60th birthday. She carried herself with a confidence and strength that I admired, and I was interested to know more about her.

At dinner, I discovered that Laura was walking the Camino utilizing the same arrangements as me—she had used a company to pre-book all of her rooms and her bag was being transferred ahead each day. I found out she'd also brought a pillow from home. Soul sisters! She laughed heartily when I told her it was the best decision I'd made. Laura said she couldn't imagine how she would have made it through sleeping on the rock hard pillows found in every room so far.

I was curious about how Laura's trip was arranged. I asked if she was being transferred ahead at any point of the Camino, thereby possibly missing various stages. She assured me that she was walking the entire Camino. Again, I became frustrated that my trip wasn't booked the same way. I didn't want to miss walking any part of the Camino. I needed to figure out a way to solve this problem.

Debbie's approach was similar to that of most pilgrims —with everything on her back, she needed to find a bed in each town as she went along. She had recently started to book a private room a day ahead of time so she could be assured of getting her own sleeping quarters. But Debbie was still carrying her backpack. She confessed this was a real struggle, as her pack was quite heavy and she was having trouble. Especially when the terrain became more challenging.

Debbie was also embarrassed when she confided to us that she was dealing with a physical ailment that made it difficult for her to walk. Apparently, she had a medical condition that made her constantly feel like she needed to go to the bathroom. This made it hard for her to go long distances when there wasn't a restroom to relieve herself.

Both Laura and I suggested she use a company to transfer her bag ahead, a practice used by many pilgrims. In fact, I noticed that as the journey progressed, more and more pilgrims resorted to using this transfer service to make their daily walks more enjoyable. But Debbie said she wouldn't feel like a *real* pilgrim if she didn't carry everything on her back. This wasn't the way the original pilgrims walked, she insisted. She'd feel like she was cheating if she did it any other way.

Laura and I, obviously doing things differently, said we felt the Camino was more about the experience of walking. Neither of us felt like we had to carry a heavy pack on our backs to feel like we were getting an extraordinary experience. But to each his own. There are so many ways to experience the Camino, and each pilgrim needs to figure out what works for them.

After a dinner filled with laughter and storytelling, I said goodbye to Debbie and Laura and hoped I would see them again. However, they both revealed that they planned to take rest days along the way. So I was doubtful that I might see them again, since I didn't have any rest days planned until Day 30, when I reached Sarria—the day Tom was supposed to arrive in Spain. I questioned whether I had allowed enough time to complete this journey and I prayed that my body would hold up. It seemed that most pilgrims I met had planned several rest days throughout their trek. Yet, I only had one. I hoped this wouldn't end up being a stupid decision.

Back at my hotel, I received a response from my travel agent regarding the email I'd sent the day before:

May 30, 2019

Dear Meg,

...There was really no way to do the entire trek in the

time you have and also it would have been a very dif-
ficult walk. The company tries to minimize discomfort
by having you stay in accommodations that are better
than basic and the trek is based on that...

What? I was so confused. I had based my walking time on the stages set out in John Brierley's Camino book. Using Brierley's calculations, I could most certainly walk the entire Camino in the time I had allotted. Of course, it would be difficult. If it was easy, it wouldn't have the same impact. And I never said I needed anything other than basic—I just wanted my own room and bathroom. There were plenty of places along the Camino that offered these options. I wondered what kind of clientele this company was targeting. Were they working with people who wanted to experience just bits and pieces of the Camino, pilgrims who weren't intent on walking the entire distance? And was comfort more important than anything else? All signs pointed to this conclusion.

But this is not what I wanted. Nor had I requested "minimized discomforts." I needed to make some changes. I was not going to miss the experience of walking the full Camino, no matter how difficult a challenge this would be.

Exhausted, I fell into a dreamless sleep.

Day 9

On the ninth day of my Camino, I posted the following entry on my blog:

The body is a remarkable thing. The restorative power of a good night's sleep is amazing. I awoke feeling pretty good—my knee was still sore, but I was able to walk without any problems today. It was another gorgeous sunny day and the temperature each day is rapidly rising.

I left my hotel around 8:30, and in no time I removed my outer layer so I was just in a tank top. The 14-mile walk today led me through more rolling hills with vistas of vineyards all around. I only passed through a few small towns, so the majority of the time I was out in the open space with time to think.

I thought about the fact that I've slept in a different bed for the last 10 days, 11 if you count the airplane. And I have 35 more nights to go (counting my time in Madrid after the Camino). For someone like me who is a "nester" and likes to create a cozy space, this has been a transition. The days have started to run together and sometimes I wake up in the middle of the night and can't remember where I am.

I'm also only nine days into my Camino and already I'm sick of looking at my clothes. Yes, it's easy to have so little to choose from, but I like options, depending on my mood for the day! But that is not going to happen for the next five weeks, so I'm just going to have to embrace the simplicity of my wardrobe.

I also thought about some deeper issues. What's my life going to look like in the next five years? The next 30? How do I want to make an impact in this world, and how can I achieve that? What is my path now that I have finished raising my children? These are some of the questions that I hope I can find some answers to on my Camino.

It was definitely a good day for contemplation, and it seemed like a quick walk by the time I arrived in the tiny town of Santo Domingo de la Calzada at 1:30 in the afternoon.

I was staying in the *Parador Santo Domingo*. A *Parador* is a type of hotel in Spain that has been converted from a former castle or some type of historic building, and the furnishings inside were magnificent. My room was filled with antiques, elegant chandeliers and tastefully framed paintings giving it a feeling of old world Spain.

I splurged and took advantage of the hotel's laundry service, thinking how nice it would be to have my clothes washed and dried in machines rather than in my Scrubba bag and clothesline. After showering and freshening up, I headed outside to explore the tiny town famous for its tall tale of the miracle of the hen and the rooster. According to the tale:

Legend tells of a German Pilgrim called Hugonell who was walking to Santiago with his parents, when they decided to rest at an inn in Santo Domingo de la

Calzada. The owner of the inn's daughter immediately fell in love with him; however her feelings were not reciprocated, so the girl, angered, placed a silver cup into his luggage and accused the boy of theft. Thieves at that time were punished by hanging, and this was the fate of Hugonell. His parents, saddened by his death, continued the pilgrimage, and upon arriving in Santiago de Compostela, began their return journey to visit the grave of their dead son. When they arrived in Santo Domingo however, they found their son still hanging in the gallows—but, miraculously, alive. Hugonell, excited, said to them: "Santo Domingo brought me back to life. Please go to the Mayor's house and ask him to take me down." Quickly, the parents arrived at the Mayor's house and told him of the miracle. The incredulous Mayor, who was preparing to have dinner with friends, responded: "That boy is alive as these two roast chickens we are about to eat." Suddenly, the chickens came to life, sprouted feathers and beaks and began to crow. And so, to this day there is a saying about town which goes: "Santo Domingo of the Way, where the roosters crow after being roasted."

In front of the mausoleum there is a stone, polychrome and gothic henhouse, which was built in the middle of the 15th century to keep alive a hen and a rooster in memory of the most famous of Santo Domingo's miracles. There are documents from Pope Clemente VI dated 1350 allowing these live animals inside the cathedral. Below the cage is a representation of the pilgrim being hanged, painted by Alonso Gallego. Above *the cage there is a piece of wood from the gallows.*

Whether or not the tale is true, the rooster and the hen are alive and well inside the Cathedral of Santo Domingo de la Calzada. Fun fact!

After walking around town for a bit, I returned to the outdoor patio of my hotel to get a glass of wine and write in my journal. My knee was hurting, and I told myself that I needed to find a better brace the next day. I was tired and didn't feel like searching for one that afternoon. And besides, Laura and Debbie had both texted me saying they were staying in the same town that night and wanted to meet up for a drink. How fun! I was so happy I would get to see them again.

When Debbie arrived, she sent a text to tell me how incredible her room was. She was staying at the other *Parador* hotel in this tiny town, and it, too, was elegantly furnished and quite lavish.

"Wow! This is the nicest room I've been in so far. My room is huge! And it even has its own confessional in it," Debbie wrote in her message.

Confused, I texted back, "What?" Send me a pic. I want to see this."

A few seconds later, the picture came through. I immediately started laughing to myself. I saw a small square wood shutter with a handle. "I don't think that's a confessional. It looks like a tiny window is behind that," I wrote.

"Oh, you're right," she texted back. "Well what do I know? I'm Jewish!"

When we met later that evening, it was like being together with old friends. Debbie ordered her apparent go-to drink of vodka (Absolut if they had it) and soda, while Laura ordered her usual sparkling water, *agua con gas*. I felt so comfortable and relaxed. Conversation was effortless, and we laughed easily. I learned that Debbie was a trained court reporter but was now working at NYU and Columbia transcribing lectures for hearing impaired students. Not knowing her well, but observing that she had several ADD tendencies and could sometimes find it hard to stay focused, I jokingly asked how she stayed still long enough to accurately record what the professor was saying.

"I know, right?" she answered. "I've been doing it so long that it's just automatic. But I knew I needed to get out of court reporting when I started daydreaming too much."

"What do you mean?" I asked.

"Well one time, the testimony was just really dragging on. I got bored. I started thinking about all the things I needed to get at the grocery store later that night. I was making a list in my head when all of a sudden one of the attorneys asked me to read back the transcript. I panicked."

"Oh no! What happened?" Laura and I both exclaimed.

"I don't know how I did it. I hadn't missed a single word. Kinda crazy. But I knew it was time to move on."

Laura and I both laughed out loud at this. Debbie's self-deprecating humor and ability to tell stories in an entertaining way made her exceedingly likeable.

Laura had a background in the book publishing business. But then, like me, she became a *stay-at-home mom* to her two sons. She had a passion for Ashtanga yoga and said it changed her life. She worked on her practice daily, even on the Camino.

We shared some of the challenges we each faced that

day. Laura and I both were dealing with knee pain. And Debbie had found it extremely difficult to walk with her heavy pack, especially in the heat. Once again we encouraged her to at least try sending her pack ahead one time, just to see how she liked it. Debbie finally decided to make the five Euro investment and filled out the paperwork in my hotel lobby so that the bag transfer company knew where to pick up her pack and where to take it the next day. I could tell she felt somewhat relieved—and a little disappointed in herself that she wasn't being a *real* pilgrim.

Debbie also lamented that she didn't know where she would be spreading Philip's ashes. She hoped this would become clear to her at some point on the Camino. She described how holding his ashes, securely inside the fanny pack that never left her side, felt like a huge emotional weight. Laura and I assured Debbie that she would know when it was the right time to part with her son's ashes.

We walked around town together for a little while afterwards, trying to find a hat for Debbie. Her face was getting scorched by the sun. Laura and I, in full mama bear mode, convinced her she needed some protection. Debbie ended up getting a navy floppy hat, with a bright yellow shell and *Camino de Santiago* emblazoned on it. Feeling satisfied, we all said goodnight, wanting to get an early dinner and a good night's sleep. We were all going to the same town the next night, so I was thrilled I would get to see my new Camino friends again.

Back at my hotel, I found my way to the dining room for an early dinner. As soon as I sat down, I started feeling nauseous. My head began to throb. It dawned on me that I hadn't drunk enough water throughout the day. With the increasing heat I endured today, I was probably severely dehydrated. So I ordered a large bottle of water and left the dining room without eating anything. It was time to head to bed and get some well-earned sleep.

Day 10

I awoke feeling much better. My headache was gone, and I felt well-rested and ready to face the challenge of my 15-mile walk today. It was a HOT day, the hottest so far, and I made sure to hydrate well as I walked along. But my knee was hurting. Not finding my knee brace effective, I wrapped it with an Ace bandage and challenged myself to take slow, small steps each time I faced a downhill climb.

About four miles into my hike, I got a text from Debbie. She wasn't sure she could make it through the day. Her medical condition was making it difficult for her to walk, so she had stopped in a town I was just about to enter. When I arrived, I saw Debbie sitting at an outdoor table. The minute she saw me, she started crying, her anguish and despair palpable. She was convinced that she wouldn't be able to finish the Camino—the constant feeling of needing to go to the bathroom was stressful, uncomfortable and unfathomable for the long journey ahead. Not to mention embarrassing. She doubted she could go on this way.

Just then, Laura appeared and joined us. Over coffee, Laura and I consoled Debbie and encouraged her to continue, trying to convince her that she was stronger than she gave herself credit for. This was simply a blip that she would overcome. We all had our struggles, manifested in different ways, and this was just part of the Camino experience.

Feeling better, Debbie said she would see us at the end of the day in Belorado. Since we all walked at different paces, we said goodbye and continued on our way.

For the next 11 miles I enjoyed feeling the sunshine wash over my body as I walked through the picturesque countryside. I was awed by the wildflowers dotting the grasses and the adorable cottages with brilliant flowers growing in their well-tended gardens. And I was amazed by the abundance of different shades of green in nature—leaves in hues of brilliant emerald and chartreuse, grasses in pear and lime, and scrub brush in olive and sage—a dizzying display of beauty.

I arrived in Belorado, a tiny town with just under 2,000 residents, around 2:00 in the afternoon, and later I wrote the following in my blog:

> ...the Plaza Mayor *was abuzz with activity. A Medieval fiesta was in full swing—people dressed in costumes, hay bales everywhere, music blaring, food and trinket stands set up all over, kids running around with toy swords and people performing various dances. What a welcome!*

Spanish people know how to have fun, and they find all sorts of reasons to throw a party. Arriving into a town on a Saturday meant there was a high likelihood that some sort of *fiesta* was being celebrated, and I was thrilled to be a part of the festivities.

Debbie and I were booked at the same place, *Hotel Jacobeo*. After finding our bags and lugging them upstairs, we both showered and made a plan to meet at a bar in the *Plaza Mayor* later. First I wanted to find a brace, since my knee was in a lot of pain. But being such a small town, I was out of luck. And with it being Sunday the following day, a real day of rest in Spain, none of the pharmacies would be open. I would have to tough it out for a few more days until I reached the large city of Burgos 32 miles down the road.

I was also dealing with a few hot spots on my feet. With the increased temperature of the last two days, my feet were certainly sweating more than they had been in previous days, hence causing added friction. When researching what to pack on the Camino, I read that Compeed would be good for fighting blisters, the arch enemy of many a *peregrino*. Even though I didn't have a blister at this point, I decided to be proactive and apply a Compeed bandage to my hot spots, hoping this would prevent the onset of a blister. With my ailments attended to, I set off for the *Plaza Mayor*.

I arrived at the bar before Debbie. As I went inside to order an ice cold beer to cool me off on this sweltering hot day, I realized that I recognized almost everyone in the bar—an odd sensation when you're halfway around the world from home. As I ambled to the bar for my beer, I stopped to chat with several people: I saw Bearded Michael from San Diego, Sean from Florida, a few women from Colorado who I'd met a few days before and Big Michael from Denmark—all pilgrims who I traded smiles and a friendly *Buen Camino* with each day as we walked at our own paces. I suddenly felt part of a community, no longer alone. This was my Camino family. The faces I would see after completing our daily stages. Some pilgrims might walk faster or slower. But it always amazed me how every few days, a pilgrim who I thought was either behind or ahead of me would pop up in the same place as me. What a delightful surprise to see the friendly face of someone who I thought I would never see again!

And this was another reason why I didn't want to be transferred ahead—I wanted to be on the same general schedule as all these pilgrims I began walking with in Saint-Jean-Pied-

de-Port. And I wanted the satisfaction of knowing I could persevere through any physical, emotional and mental challenges
and walk the entire Camino. The next transfer date was coming up—only two days away—and the travel company hadn't
made any changes to my itinerary yet. I needed to solve this
problem. Quickly.

Laura and Debbie joined me at my table, and I confided
in them about what was going on with my travel arrangements.
They were both in shock that the trip was planned this way, and
they could understand why I was so upset. We discussed the
idea of biking instead of being transferred by car, since biking
was certainly a way that some pilgrims experienced the Camino.
But this wasn't a practical solution for me. Besides, I wanted to
walk, not bike.

Laura shared that her knee was also in a lot of pain. She
had a mishap on her very first day of the Camino as she navigated the dangerously wet and muddy terrain. She aggravated an
old knee injury and it seemed to be getting worse each day.

Debbie admitted that not carrying her pack was a huge
relief, and she enjoyed her walk much more today. She still
struggled with the concept of sending her bag ahead. But she
was going to continue to do it anyway. She had enough to worry
about with her physical challenge.

All three of us were dealing with various issues. But it
felt good to share with one another. I could feel our bond growing. My sisters on the Camino.

Even though Laura was staying at a different place,
our dinner vouchers were at the same restaurant on the other
side of the *Plaza Mayor*. So the three of us soon made our way
there. By now, we'd all grown accustomed to our nightly pil-

grim's meal—starter of soup, salad or some local specialty... main course of meat, chicken or fish...dessert...and a bottle of water. Plus a glass of *vino tinto*. And bread again. Always lots of bread. I continued to eat it at almost every meal. Bread and cheese in the morning. *Bocadillo* at lunch. And more bread at dinner. No wonder I wasn't losing any weight on this walk!

The restaurant was small—only about ten to twelve tables—so it filled up quickly. A fellow pilgrim, a man from Brazil, asked to join us. Of course, we welcomed him—but it turned out to be an awkward meal. He didn't speak English or Spanish and made no attempt to communicate with us, despite our efforts. It seemed he just didn't want to sit at a table by himself. I could relate.

It was still light out, even though it was almost 10:00, as we walked through the *Plaza Mayor* after dinner. We marveled at all the *fiesta* activity. The crowd had grown substantially, the music was at full blare and it didn't look like the party was going to end anytime soon. As much as I might have liked to stay and enjoy the celebrations, my body was tired and feeling enervated by the heat. And I needed to prepare for a 16-mile hike the next day—without a new knee brace.

As I was undressing, to my horror, I saw that underneath one of my Compeed bandages a huge blister had formed. How had this happened? Compeed was supposed to *prevent* blisters, not create them. Ugh. I would deal with this in the morning.

Time for bed.

Day 11

The next day I posted, in part, the following on my blog:

Having done laundry in my room the evening be-fore, I left my window open all night so my clothes would dry. Spaniards know how to have fun and like to stay up late. Very late. Or should I say—early. I heard loud singing around 4:00 in the morning and shouting and laughing sporadically throughout the night. But I guess I was tired enough that I had no problem going back to sleep and felt pretty good when I awoke.

I had discovered an enormous blister on my heel the night before (my first in 10 days, so not bad!), so I de-cided that today was the day to break out my Tevas (with socks!) and try hiking in them. So putting my vanity aside (not an easy task for someone who ap-preciates fashion), I put on my "crusty" shoes, rubbed some pain cream on my knee and set out for what ended up being a 16-mile walk. Amazingly, my shoes worked great. And despite how ugly I looked today, I heeded Charlie's advice to "embrace the dork" and remember that "comfort is king." And my knee felt a little better—still sore, but not quite as painful.

It was a real revelation knowing I could hike such long distances in Tevas without experiencing any pain or further blisters. I said a prayer of thanks for my friend who suggested I take them on my trip. I was able to thoroughly enjoy the long stretches of dirt paths, often beautifully canopied by lush, green foliage. Much of the day, I walked the Camino without seeing any pilgrims ahead of me—I could enjoy the magical vistas all on my own. And being completely on my own, surrounded by the beauty of nature all around me, provided me with a deep and powerful sense of inner peace and joy. Again, I said a prayer of gratitude for this opportunity, realizing how lucky I was to have the time and ability to experience the magic of the Camino.

I could feel myself transition into a more reflective state of mind, now that my mind was less clogged with figuring out the day-to-day routines and logistics of the Camino. I had more space to think about some of the deeper issues I had hoped to explore on my journey—figuring out what I wanted in the next phase of my life, exploring my spirituality, my hopes and desires, and reacquainting myself with the person I was before I became a wife and mother.

I asked myself why I put so much pressure on myself to figure out what I wanted to *do* next. Being a planner, I have always liked having a goal to reach or a project to work on. But I was enjoying this pace of life on the Camino, and I started thinking that perhaps I didn't need to make any plans for my future. Perhaps I could just take things one day at a time and let things unfold. Learn to slow down and live my life more in the present rather than continually looking forward without everything mapped out. What a concept.

I made a concerted effort to walk a little more slowly (at Jackson's self-described *turtle pace*)—not only to take care of my knee and blister, but also to savor the journey itself. Coincidentally, one of my favorite songs to listen to while walking was "Slow Your Roll" by Brothers Osborne. Mia and I had seen them perform at Stagecoach, an annual three-day country music festival in Indio, California, and I was obsessed with their music. Indeed, I was learning to slow my roll, taking my time each day to appreciate my surroundings, my inner reflections and my connections with other pilgrims. It was not in my nature to do things slowly. But the Camino was teaching me the benefits of doing things differently. My new mantra became *Slow Your Roll*.

At one point, I came upon something hanging on a wood post near the Camino trail. As I walked closer, I saw that it was a navy, floppy sun hat with a yellow shell and *Camino de Santiago* emblazoned on the front. I immediately started laughing to myself. Debbie! She didn't even last a day wearing a hat. So much for our motherly advice.

I eventually ran into Laura, and we walked for a while together. She, too, was walking carefully so as not to further aggravate her knee. The more I spent time with her, the more I liked her. She was warm, intelligent, funny and interesting. She loved to laugh, and did so often in an infectious, hearty manner. She exuded strength without coming off as harsh, and I respected her direct, no nonsense approach to life. I could see spending time with her outside of the Camino, and I hoped I would one day have the chance to meet her two grown sons with whom she seemed to have a very close relationship.

Since Laura was walking to the next town beyond me that day, about four kilometers further, she wanted to stop and rest before continuing on. So we said goodbye and promised to see each other in Burgos the following day.

I soon came upon a charming *donativo*, the word used to describe a rest stop, found sporadically throughout the Camino. The typical *donativo* offered beverages and/or food, sometimes even Camino trinkets for a donation. Some were simply laid out with a basket nearby for donations, while others were operated by one or two people.

This particular *donativo* had several wooden benches offering a place for weary pilgrims to rest. A large totem pole with brightly colored arrows pointed to different destinations around the world, with the distance listed in kilometers. Meanwhile, loud, joyful music played from a nearby boombox, brightening our spirits. The young woman standing behind the table of goodies greeted me with a huge smile and offered me a piece of juicy watermelon. I could see that she also had coffee, water, sodas, fresh juices, beer and wine. A map was displayed on her table so pilgrims could see where they were and how much farther they needed to walk. I took another piece of watermelon, gave the woman a bunch of loose coins from my pack, then sat down to enjoy this peaceful, unexpected setting.

Feeling refreshed, I finished my walk for the day and arrived at my destination of San Juan de Ortega shortly after 2:00 in the afternoon. Had I walked for another two minutes, I would have been on the outskirts of this tiny town, teeming with a whopping population of 20. The town consisted of a church (of course), two bars/restaurants, a tiny hotel and an *albergue*. That was it. I was told by some other pilgrims that this little town was in Emilio Estevez's movie *The Way*, but not having seen the film myself, I couldn't confirm that one way or another. In any case, I found better Wi-Fi there than I had the night before in Belorado. Amazing.

Dinner was at the same bar where I'd checked in, across

from my hotel and next to the church. I sat at a table with two German women, Birgit and Erna, who were walking the Camino in stages. Every year they would complete a section, and this year they were walking from Pamplona to Burgos. I had met other pilgrims, mostly Europeans, who walked the Camino this way. I supposed because it's so close, it's easy for them to use their vacation like this. Birgit and Erna were warm and friendly, so I was sorry that I wouldn't be seeing them again beyond Burgos. We enjoyed a drink outside after dinner, joined by two couples from Australia who were also leaving once they reached Burgos.

It was a beautiful, warm night, and I loved sitting in this quaint old town. Feeling a million miles away from the hustle and bustle of normal everyday life at home. I felt completely engaged and present as I enjoyed the companionship of my fellow pilgrims. I loved meeting people from all over the world and seeing that in so many ways, we are all alike. And unlike the United States, which is insulated from the rest of the world, the Camino offers *peregrinos* the opportunity to experience a global community in a safe, accepting atmosphere. Differences can be appreciated rather than feared. Our world would be a better place if we had more Camino-like settings. I was grateful for the opportunity to get out of the *American bubble* that I was safely wrapped in back home. And I was inspired by my interactions with new people from across the globe, who gifted me with their world views and opinions. It was a good night.

Back at my hotel, the *Centro de Turismo Rural La Henera*—a long "L"-shaped building with a bunch of simple little rooms, with only a small sitting area at its entry—I attempted once again to make some headway with my travel agent. I only had one more day to figure out how to make changes to my itinerary. I would be in Burgos the next day, but a car was scheduled to pick me up the following morning and drive me ahead to Hornillos, thereby bypassing an entire section of the Camino. I did *not* want to get in that car. Somehow, some way, I was going to figure out how I could walk the whole distance—just as I had originally hoped to do from the start.

June 2, 2019

Dear Helen,

> *...Is there a way to reconfigure my walk until I meet Tom in Sarria so I do just a little bit longer each day? I'm willing to give up my rest day in Sarria. I really want to walk this whole thing. I didn't realize how much until I've been walking every day. And going through this experience with so many people, I would feel cheated of this bucket list experience that I have been looking forward to for the last decade or so...*

Helen responded:

June 2, 2019

Dear Meg,

> *Would an option be to stay with your accommodations as they are now and redo the stages so you get picked up and dropped off whenever there is a need, which may be a lot of the days since the accommodations aren't going to match the stages?*

Reading this response, I felt deflated, frustrated and angry. This was not how the Camino was supposed to go for me. I didn't want to be in and out of a car every day. This seemed like a horrible idea. And anyone who has walked the Camino would understand why this wouldn't be an ideal solution. The experience is about walking. (Or, for some pilgrims, biking.) Getting in a car on a daily basis was not something I wanted to contend with. I felt like I was pounding my head on a brick wall and not making any progress at all. Exhausted, I fell into a fitful sleep.

Day 12

I tossed and turned all night long, feeling upset about my predicament. I awoke in the middle of the night and wrote Helen another email trying to come up with a more plausible solution. I then tried falling back to sleep, knowing I needed rest before the long day ahead. I had an 18-mile walk ahead of me.

My alarm sounded at 6:15 a.m. and I readied myself for the day, wanting to leave a little after 7:00 to beat the heat. My blister was feeling better, so I wore my hiking shoes. I brought my Tevas too—just in case. My plan was to walk for an hour or so, then stop for a coffee. Instead I ended up walking eight miles before I finally found a place to stop. And the stony path was proving difficult to navigate. I treaded carefully, still nursing my sore knee and blister. It was going to be one of those days. But no one ever said the Camino was easy.

After a relaxing coffee break and a photo with Birgit and Erna, who had also stopped for a rest, I was on my way again. The day seemed to stretch on forever. The heat was taking its toll on me. I noticed my blister starting to become painful again, so I stopped and swapped my hiking shoes for my Tevas.

Ahhh. My feet instantly felt better. But now my hiking shoes felt leaden and heavy in my pack. The lack of sleep, combined with my worry and frustration about my travel arrangements, were clearly getting to me. And to make matters worse, the last eight miles of my long walk today were on busy roadways through the industrial outskirts of Burgos.

No pretty scenery to take my mind off my troubles. Instead, I focused on not inhaling deeply to avoid the noxious fumes of the heavy trucks rumbling past me. The blaring noise only heightened my already frayed nerves. The atmosphere was far from peaceful.

At last I reached Burgos, the second largest city on the Camino Francés, a little after 2:00 p.m. But being a large city, with a population over 350,000, it took a while to reach the city center. After walking for what seemed like another several miles, I was thrilled to finally find the street listed on my hotel's address. And then, once again, I experienced the magic of the Camino, as I later wrote on my blog that day:

> *The highlight of my walk was right at the very end. I had just found the street where my hotel was located. I happened to turn and see a young girl, obviously a pilgrim, who looked lost and tired. So I asked if I could help her and she said she couldn't find the place where she was staying. So I asked a local in Spanish and he directed us to her place. We then started talking and I asked her where she was from. It turns out she just moved to Boulder and recently met my son Jackson! How crazy is that??!!!! I ended up walking her to her lodging to make sure she got there okay and we both couldn't believe what just happened. Kismet!*

I firmly believe that I was meant to meet Leah that day. Our paths were intended to cross, and meeting her gave me a much-needed lift at the end of an arduous 18-mile slog. We chatted animatedly about Boulder, her studies and how she happened to meet Jackson recently at a mutual friend's birthday party. We exchanged contact info and vowed to meet again one day.

Once I found my accommodation—the *Hotel Silken Gran Teatro*—I was thrilled to find it had a tub. I took a long soak, followed by a hot shower, before walking to the old part of town where the famous Cathedral of Saint Mary of Burgos attracted tourists from all over the world. I found a small plaza nearby and decided to sit at a table outside while waiting to meet up with Laura and Debbie. We were going to celebrate our last night together, since we each had different schedules going forward. I felt terribly sad that I would soon have to say goodbye.

I noticed a pilgrim ordering a gin and tonic, and it was served in a large goblet with a few slices of lemon. (Limes were rare to find anywhere.) It looked astonishingly refreshing and I had to have one. As I sat and sipped my drink, I admired the beauty of the surrounding plaza, with its brightly colored buildings in hues of brilliant gold, salmon and pale yellow. Colorful flowers hung from pots on the balconies above and lush trees provided shade outside the many storefronts lining the square. The plaza was abuzz with activity with young lovers strolling hand-in-hand, mothers pushing strollers, pilgrims walking with their packs still on, looking like they had just arrived into the city, and bikers whizzing by, trying to avoid hitting the pedestrians. I felt happy and relaxed taking in the scenery, and relieved to have the brutal day's walk behind me.

Debbie arrived a few minutes later, telling me we were supposed to meet Laura by the cathedral. When we finally met up with Laura, I was shocked to see her with her leg propped up on a chair, walking sticks by her side. She soon filled us in on her horrible day. Laura was in so much pain at the start of the day, she could only walk a short distance before deciding to take a taxi to Burgos. It was heartbreaking to see her in so much misery. But she had luckily scheduled a few days of rest in Burgos, so she was hopeful that she'd be ready to walk again after that.

We enjoyed our last meal together, laughing and trading more stories about our Camino adventures. Debbie was still sending her bag ahead and seemed to be feeling better on her walks, despite the constant worry that she wouldn't be able to complete the Camino. I updated them on my hotel/transfer saga, and they commiserated with me and encouraged me to keep trying to make it work.

"Hey, by the way," I said to Debbie. "I saw your hat on my walk today. Hanging on a wood post."

Laura started laughing loudly. "I saw that, too!"

Debbie looked sheepishly at both of us. "It just wasn't me." We all burst into giggles.

Both Laura and I chided Debbie for not wearing a hat in this intense heat, and Debbie promised to find another hat, one more suitable to her liking, after dinner.

Once we finished our meal, we wanted to see the inside of the stunning old cathedral. Laura literally hopped on one leg, using her walking sticks for balance. It was painful to watch. And when we finally arrived, we were told it had just closed. It was one of those days.

Instead, we helped Laura hobble along to a pharmacy, where she and I both bought decent knee braces. Then we helped Debbie pick out an all-weather floppy hat that she convinced us she would wear and could use again at home in New York. We walked by a sign with an arrow saying only

461 kilometers (about 286 miles) to go to reach Santiago. We were making progress.

Debbie and I helped Laura walk back to her hotel. We shared a sad goodbye and said we hoped to meet again one day. Even though it was only a little before 8:00, I was ready to head back to my hotel and try to get a good night's sleep.

Once back in my room, I checked my email and saw Helen had responded:

June 3, 2019

Dear Meg,

I just called the travel company and they suggested you talk to someone in the office in Santiago to figure out how to proceed.

Feeling tired and frustrated, I told myself to get some sleep and deal with this in the morning.

Day 13

I awoke early, my mind racing. I knew the transfer car would be here in a few hours, and I wasn't intending on getting in it. But I still needed my bag transferred. So I packed up and brought it down before the 8:00 deadline. My bag was scheduled to be transferred to Castrojeriz, a town a full stage ahead of Hornillos, where I would be walking today. But I figured I would deal with that problem later.

I returned to my room, too anxious to eat anything and worried that I would now be getting a very late start for today's 15-mile walk. But I was determined to get this issue resolved. So I waited until the appointed time to call the travel company in Santiago.

June 4, 2019

Dear Helen,

It's 10:00 in the morning, and I just tried calling Nuria in the Santiago office at the time you said to call and no one answered. Most pilgrims leave in the morning as early as 6 or as late as 9 to beat the heat. Now I'm going to be very behind. And it makes for a long day.

After firing off that email, feeling overwhelmingly frustrated, I tried calling the Santiago office one last time before leaving. Thankfully someone answered. I was told Nuria wouldn't be in until later that morning. As I tried to hold back my tears, the woman in Santiago asked if she could help me.

That was all I needed to hear.

A flood of emotions suddenly burst, and I began to sob uncontrollably. The poor woman did her best to calm me down, and eventually I was able to explain the entire situation to her. She said she would forward all my emails and info to Nuria and they would take care of everything. She assured me that they would help me achieve the Camino experience I desired. Unlike the travel company Helen had been working with in Southern California, they seemed to understand how important it was that I didn't miss walking any parts of the Camino.

Feeling mollified and embarrassed by my crying outburst, I thanked the woman profusely and hung up. I prayed Nuria would come through and help me resolve this fiasco. By now it was already 10:30. Oh, boy. I only had a long 15-mile walk ahead of me.

Since I was already so late in starting my day, I figured I would take advantage of the situation and finally visit the famed Gothic cathedral now that it was open again. Indeed it was an exquisite visual feast with its magnificent stained glass windows, its many chapels adorned with all types of religious art and its several tombs scattered throughout. The cathedral was absolutely massive and another masterpiece of beauty and architecture. It was also the burial site of the Spanish national hero, El Cid. After meandering through this place of beauty, I understood why UNESCO recognized it as a World Heritage Site in 1984. Before leaving, I took the opportunity to say my prayers of gratitude and ask for strength to help me make it through my journey.

Outside the cathedral, I saw a WhatsApp message to Debbie and me from Laura:

Hey Camino buddies. Hope your morning has started well— Margarita, that your travel plans are working out and you are walking. Debbie—hope that hat is on your head!!! Xxx My knee is MUCH better—it is so unbelievable—I am walking without poles—but slowly. We are such resilient species!! Keep safe.

It was so comforting to hear from Laura. For one thing, I was happy that she seemed to be feeling so much better. Plus, it was such a relief to be able to share my travel problem with someone. I had been feeling a tremendous amount of angst about not being able to walk the entire Camino. That is *not* what I paid a travel agent for. But it wasn't something I was sharing with other pilgrims until I met Debbie and Laura. And feeling their support and encouragement really lifted my spirits and gave me strength.

I was ready to get on with my walk.

For the first time yet, I had trouble locating the yellow— *flechas*—Camino arrows. Being in a big city like Burgos made it challenging to find the usually-ubiquitous Camino scallops and the yellow arrows that were always, once spotted, met with a small sigh of relief. But since I was leaving so late, I couldn't see any pilgrims ahead of me to follow. So I stopped several locals along the way, and thankfully none of them seemed to point me in the wrong direction.

Just as I was nearly out of the city, I spotted another lone pilgrim also searching for a yellow arrow. As I approached her to figure it out together, I recognized her as a woman I had met about a week earlier in Puente la Reina. Sonia was from Fort Collins, Colorado, probably slightly older than me and ridiculously fit. She was walking the Camino solo. Carrying everything on her back and staying at hostels along the way. I felt like a softie next to her. But I didn't feel any judgment from Sonia.

She turned out to be an interesting and pleasant companion for the next seven miles. And she confirmed the misleading info about the benefits of Compeed. She said she knew of several other pilgrims who had developed blisters while using Compeed. Then Sonia showed me the Spanish brand she used to prevent blisters—*Cinfa Farmalastic Sport Protectores de Ampollas*—and said she hadn't had any blisters so far. She was remarkable. I loved how the Camino inspired this desire to help one another, to pay it forward. There was this sense that we were all in it together. There was an understanding, respect and compassion that often seemed to be missing back home. Plus, where else could you get invited to walk alongside a near stranger for miles and miles?

We parted ways when she said she needed to relieve herself in the bushes. I wanted to give her privacy, so I said I hoped to see her at some point later. Even though I, too, had to relieve myself. I told myself I could make it to the next town, only a few kilometers down the road.

About 10 miles into my walk I entered the little town of Rabé de Las Calzadas, with a population of around 200. I was happy to find a nice clean bathroom and a cozy café to drink coffee and eat a small snack. And I was thrilled when I connected to the Wi-Fi and saw an email from Nuria at the Santiago travel office. She had arranged for a taxi to pick me up in Hornillos and take me to Castrojeriz for the night. Then a taxi would pick me up in the morning and take me back to Hornillos to start my walk where I had left off. She was working on changing all the rest of my accommodations so I wouldn't have to miss walking any of the Camino or get in a car again after that. Hallelujah! Nuria was making it happen! I was so happy and feeling exceptionally grateful that she was helping me. What a huge relief. The last several days of dealing with this had been such an ordeal and took a heavy emotional toll on me. Suddenly, I felt optimistic, cheerful and energized.

With a huge smile on my face, I looked up from my phone. What I saw hit me with a wave of Camino bliss: an entire wall covered with handwritten notes, bills of currencies from a myriad of different countries and all sorts of trinkets—mini stuffed koala bears from Australia, keychains, religious medallions and Camino shells. Pilgrims from all over the world had stopped in this very café and left these mementos with their name and hometown scribbled on them. It was a sight to see. And, of course, I wanted to leave my mark as well, hoping that one day I might return and see it still tacked up on that impressive wall of pilgrim postings. I searched through my pack and found a dollar bill, scribbled "Margarita" along with the date, my hometown and *"Buen Camino!"* on it before securing it to the wall with a push pin.

Feeling refreshed, I ventured outside again into the whipping wind. The clouds were swirling above, and it was like watching an art show in the sky as they reconfigured themselves every few minutes into new and interesting shapes. I found myself transfixed by nature's power and beauty. And then, suddenly, I stopped. Out in the distance—beyond the lush and vast green fields of grass sprinkled with fiery red flowers, beneath the cerulean sky and cotton ball white clouds—stood a lone tree, its full green branches swaying majestically in the wind. I was awestruck by the beauty of the scene. To me, this looked like the tree of life. A symbol of eternal life bearing fruits of strength, hope and positivity. This was a magical Camino moment to savor. And seeing this after receiving the good news from Nuria made me feel like everything was going to be alright.

I finally arrived in Hornillos del Camino, a village of no more than 60 people, at around 3:30. I immediately found the church to say my prayers of thanks and gratitude. I could feel a higher power watching over me, and I wanted to acknowledge this.

I've always considered myself spiritual in the sense that I believe in a power greater than ourselves. But I have questioned how religious I truly am. By that I mean, I often struggle and disagree with much of the strict doctrine of the Catholic church, the religion that Tom and I raised our children in.

Tom's parents, devout Catholics, sent Tom to a K-12 parochial school and they both attended mass on a regular basis. When Tom and I married, I went through the RCIA program to convert from Episcopalian to Catholicism. I didn't want to be the odd man out when raising our children in the Catholic church. It wasn't a far leap from the Episcopalian faith, and I was drawn to the many virtues offered by a Catholic education that we intended to provide for our children—focusing outward on others, learning to be of service to the community, conducting yourself with integrity, respect for others and using a strong moral compass to guide decisions, to name a few.

Still, I had many doubts and questions throughout my time attending mass in the ensuing years. For instance, I struggled with the church's intolerance of homosexuality, their belief that priests shouldn't marry or be female, their stance on abortion and a myriad of other issues. I loved the community of people throughout my children's school, and I loved the care and concern for other people fostered by the Catholic educational system. But these other issues weighed on me. At times, I felt like I didn't belong. But I also knew that I had a strong faith in a higher being. So I prayed every day—despite my resistance to attending weekly mass.

Walking the Camino helped me understand myself better in this arena. I was starting to accept that it was okay to not feel a true belonging in the Catholic church. I could still feel confident in my spiritual beliefs without having to follow a strict doctrine. And I still enjoyed entering a church and finding my own way to connect with God.

As I walked outside the church and made my way further into town, I saw Debbie sitting on a bench, happily chatting with a fellow pilgrim. What a nice surprise! I started to think that perhaps we might reach Santiago together after all. She seemed to be managing her physical challenge just fine. In every other way, she was the Energizer Bunny again. She moved quickly—in fact, other pilgrims referred to her as *the fast walker* since she often whizzed by them, her arms swingly wildly by her side as she bid a hurried *Buen Camino*. Little did they know, she was spurred on by her need to reach the next bathroom, thanks to her everlooming medical issue. She also spoke rapidly and made decisions quickly—often to her detriment when she changed her mind about where she wanted to stay, which led to double-booking accommodations multiple times in the days I was with her. Debbie entertained everyone she met with her quick wit and hilarious energy.

There was also something about Debbie, a vulnerability, that made people feel like they wanted and needed to take care of her. She told us the story of how a fellow pilgrim carried her heavy pack on the very first day from Saint-Jean-Pied-de-Port to Roncesvalles. She'd been crying and didn't think she could make it with the weight of her pack, so some kind pilgrim offered to help by lugging her heavy backpack. She had numerous stories of pilgrims helping her find her way, figuring out how to do something or consoling her when she was upset. She was almost childlike at times and I often felt like I wanted to protect and take care of her. It was easy to do. She had such a kind and huge heart. Not to mention an uncanny ability to make other people laugh with her zingers.

I greeted Debbie with a hug and told her the good news about my hotel problem getting sorted out. We sat together at an outdoor table while I waited for the taxi to pick me up and take me to Castrojeriz for the night. We made plans to walk together the next day.

"What time are you coming back to Hornyville?" asked Debbie, clearly a non-Spanish speaker.

I laughed and told her I was getting dropped off at 7:30 in the morning. The plan was to meet at this very same table tomorrow morning.

Once at my hotel in Castrojeriz, *La Posada de Castrojeriz*, I breathed a sigh of relief that I could unpack and actually stay in the same hotel for two consecutive nights. I could do laundry and not worry about my clothes being dry the next morning. They would have an entire day to hang on my clothesline.

Before dinner I made my way to the pharmacy. Yet again, I needed to deal with my nagging blister. It wasn't going away and I needed to find something other than Compeed to protect it. The pharmacists were extremely kind and helpful, and despite my limited knowledge of Spanish medical terms, I was able to figure out how they proposed I take care of my blister using a sterile pin to drain it, antibacterial cream and bandages.

I then walked to the restaurant just down the street from my hotel, where my dinner voucher was to be redeemed. The place was humming with activity, and the ambiance was warm and inviting. I was greeted by the hotel innkeeper, Carlos, who also ran the restaurant. He took good care of me, seating me right away and attending to my every need as he served me a delicious meal of fresh gazpacho, garlic chicken and *vino tinto*. When he discovered that I was going to be picked up at 7:00 the next morning, he even packed a breakfast for me so I wouldn't be hungry on my walk. Such a sweet and kind man. I felt happy that I'd be staying in Castrojeriz for two nights.

As I reflect back on that night, I remember feeling completely comfortable as I enjoyed dinner by myself. I didn't feel awkward or fidgety. I didn't feel the need to have a book to distract me. I savored the delicious food and took my time eating, sometimes looking around at the other diners—but not feeling uncomfortable being alone. This was a big change from my very first night in Saint-Jean-Pied-de-Port.

And I had my routines down. I knew the drill: walk for several hours, find my new place to sleep, unpack for the night, wash clothes, figure out my route for the next day, explore the town, eat dinner, post on my blog, pack up in the morning and do it all over again. I was a third of the way to Finisterre and 22 days away from reaching Santiago. I could feel a shift in my thoughts. I had more space to reflect on some deeper issues now that I was more comfortable with the logistics. And best of all, thanks to Nuria, I didn't have to expend any more energy worrying about not walking the whole Camino. I knew I had some long walking days ahead of me.

But I was excited and ready for the challenge.

Part Two

Amigos

Day 14

I awoke much earlier than usual so I would be ready in time for the taxi to take me from Castrojeriz back to "Hornyville," where I planned to meet Debbie. I got dressed and felt relieved that I didn't have to pack up my bag, since I would be returning to my room later that day.

The taxi arrived at 7:00, and we got to Hornillos about 25 minutes later, driving on a road different than the Camino path. It was amazing to me how little time it took to drive there, knowing that I'd be walking for several hours to make the 14-mile trek back to Castrojeriz.

When the taxi dropped me off, I noticed that the tiny main street of Hornillos looked deserted and wet with rain. The bar where Debbie and I sat the night before was boarded up. The outdoor tables were dripping wet. No sign of Debbie yet, but I was early.

Then I heard a friendly "hello" and turned to see Dan, the Canadian pilgrim who walked with a noisy clang each time he thumped his walking stick into the ground. He was strolling slowly down the street, heading in the opposite direction of the Camino route. He looked disheveled and a bit disoriented. Even slightly embarrassed. He explained that he had such a fun time in the bar the night before that he missed his hostel's curfew and was locked out for the night. He had to spend the night in the bar curled up on a bench—but it was an epic night and totally worth it, according to Dan. I laughed and said

I hoped he had a good walk today, teasing that I had no doubt I'd hear him as he approached with his loud, clanging walking stick before leaving me in the dust as he sped by.

A few minutes later Debbie appeared, a smile on her face and full of energy. She was ready to start the day and we forged ahead in the now pouring rain. But it wasn't easy. Luckily I was prepared, as the wind was kicking up sporadically. I spent the first few hours flipping my hood and zipper up and down.

Not long into our walk, Debbie started to panic. She felt the sinking sensation that she wasn't going to make it to the next town without having an accident. She needed to relieve herself. Walking at a brisk clip, she swung her arms quickly, like pistons propelling even faster. Since she was no longer carrying her heavy backpack—she had downsized to a light daypack—she was able to move at a breakneck pace. I hurried to keep up, trying to calm her down. But since I still had a fairly heavy pack on my back, it was a challenge. She was close to tears, dreading the embarrassment of having an accident in front of other pilgrims.

We eventually saw a small, abandoned-looking building down a road just off the Camino and made a beeline for it. In no time, we were there—only there were no bathrooms. At least we were off the Camino route, in an area that provided some privacy. Thankfully, Debbie avoided an accident. Crisis averted! Feeling relieved, she thanked me profusely for walking with her and helping out.

Back on the road again, the terrain became increasingly muddy—thick and heavy as it stuck to our shoes. Each time we raised our foot, it felt like we were carrying an extra

10-pound weight. Every few minutes I would stop to scrape the mud off the bottom of my shoes with my walking sticks. I had discovered a new kind of workout. It was comical.

When we came to the next town, Debbie decided to stay and rest for a while. I told her I would see her at dinner in Castrojeriz. I noted in my blog later:

...I arrived into Castrojeriz around 12:30 after walking 14 miles. I am amazed that walking that distance doesn't seem as daunting as it did when I began. To me, that was an easy day. I know that I have much longer days ahead of me so it's comforting to see how my body is adjusting to this practice of walking. Yes I have my challenges with my knee and some blisters, but so far so good...

The sun had finally appeared. I found my way to the *Plaza Mayor,* where I made my first purchase on the Camino. (Besides pharmaceutical supplies for my various ailments). I bought a simple wooden Tau cross to hang from my backpack, as I had read it symbolized the power of love and offered divine protection against evil and sickness. It would be a special memento of my journey and I felt it was a perfect symbol of the loving spirit of *peregrinos* on the Camino.

Feeling happy and at peace, I enjoyed another delightful dinner in Carlos' restaurant with Debbie. She had unknowingly booked herself that night in a trailer park. I had noticed this unusual place as I walked into town today, wondering to myself who would opt to stay here. Turns out, my friend Debbie would. Somehow this didn't surprise me. She often seemed to have booking issues—either double booking hotels, resulting in non-refundable charges, or ending up in unusual places. I could always count on her for a funny story.

Debbie was feeling much better after her incident earlier. It looked like we were going to be on the same walking schedule for the next few days. We missed Laura, who was still back in Burgos resting her knee. She messaged us, saying she was hoping to start walking the next day. Debbie and I said goodnight, and knowing that she liked to leave much earlier than me, I wished her a *Buen Camino* for the following day. We planned to meet for dinner again since we would be staying in the same town.

Day 15

I was now walking the approximately 220 kilometer (about 137 miles) stretch of the Camino called the *Meseta*, expansive flat plains stretching from just outside Burgos all the way to Astorga. Many pilgrims find this stretch monotonous and uninteresting. Some even opt to bypass this part of the Camino altogether, taking buses ahead or starting their Camino to Santiago somewhere beyond the *Meseta*. In hot weather, this stretch of the Camino can be brutal, as the path offers very few trees for shade. And in windy weather, as I would soon discover, the lack of trees allows the wind to swirl and pummel anything else in its path.

My day leaving Castrojeriz started a little rough. I was on my way by 8:30 in the morning, and later I wrote on my blog:

...I had developed a massive blister on my right heel and a small one was developing on my left heel. My knee hurt enough that I used my knee brace for the first time. I walked out of my hotel feeling like a 90-year-old woman walking at a snail's pace. I wondered how I was going to make it through the 16.5-mile day. Small steps. I tried to ignore the pain and decided to listen to a podcast to take my mind off of it. And then about a kilometer into my walk, I saw a massive hill in front of me. No problem. But then, what goes up must come down. My knee was screaming with pain. My internal mantra on

repeat: Small steps. Breathe. Focus on the podcast...

This was definitely a test of my mental fortitude. I willed myself to keep moving forward.

The scenery was beautiful—brilliant ocean blue skies with large puffy clouds swirling in the wind, creating endless interesting cloud art. Despite what I had read about the *Meseta*, I didn't find it boring or monotonous.

When I reached Itero de la Vega later that morning, I stopped for a coffee and rest break. I was happily surprised to see Dan in line behind me. Knowing how fast he walked, I figured he would have been far ahead of me. We ended up sitting at a table together and talking for the next hour or so. He told me he was a flight attendant for WestJet in Vancouver, where he lived. He was hoping to finish the Camino, but wasn't sure he'd be able to because he had to return to work by a certain date. I urged him to appeal to his boss and ask for extra time to finish. I could see how much he wanted to walk the entire way.

Dan opened up to me about his previous struggles with addiction and his stint in rehab. He was feeling strong and healthy on the Camino, and seemed to have a renewed sense of purpose and vigor for life. We also shared how we both loved the community of pilgrims. Most of the pilgrims we'd met were loving, kind, outward focused, willing to spend the time to listen and connect with others. We agreed that our world would be a much better place if it were run by pilgrims.

Dan observed that in the *real world*, there was an immediate sizing up process. When meeting someone, people often tried to figure out where the other person stacked up, determining where he or she would fit in the hierarchy of life. Often this might be dependent on education level, appearance, profession and perception of financial wealth. Dan railed against this sizing up and appreciated the fact that, on the Camino anyway, we were all essentially the same. We were all wearing the same kinds of clothes, staying in similar accommodations—and we all had the same collective goal of reaching Santiago. Materialism had no place on the Camino. What we did as a profession or how much money we made back home wasn't nearly as important as actually connecting with one another. I found this to be one of the most beautiful things about the Camino, too.

I also liked that, in some ways, I was similar to a blank canvas. No one knew anything about me. When other pilgrims met me, they seemed to see me as *me*—and we either connected or we didn't. They didn't base their impression of me on what I did, where I was from, what school I attended, how much money I did or didn't have, etc. They didn't know any of that. And there was something really refreshing about that.

I found Dan to be a kind and thoughtful young man. He shared that, at 36, he still hoped to marry and have a family one day, now that he was getting his life back on track. In the hour or so that we talked, I felt that we were able to delve into some fairly deep issues, and he told me how much he appreciated me listening to him. I felt like it was meant to be that we ran into each other at that café. A picture of us taken that morning shows us smiling brightly, arm in arm like old friends.

Dan and I said our goodbyes, and he sped off so all I could see was his bright orange pack ahead of me. I continued on for a few more hours, then stopped for lunch in Boadilla del Camino. I found an amazing *albergue* with a beautiful big lawn filled with all kinds of artwork—sculptures, paintings and a mural covered wall. Bright potted flowers lined the pathway from the entrance of the *albergue* to the dining area, and the outdoor tables were filled with other pilgrims.

I recognized a few of my fellow travelers and sat beside them as I ate my lunch. One guy was from Germany and another was an American walking the Camino for his second time. When I first started the Camino, I didn't really understand why someone would want to do this more than once. I figured that if I had this amount of time again, I'd want to try something different. But as I progressed along the way, it eventually became crystal clear to me why a person might want to experience the magic of the Camino again. I would understand this more fully when I returned home.

With a few more hours to go before reaching my destination, it was time to leave my cozy haven and brave the wind that had suddenly kicked up. As I walked next to the Canal de Castilla, I felt like I was walking in a wind tunnel all the way until I reached Frómista. The powerful gusts slapped my ponytail back and forth, and my face felt dry and chapped. I finally had to stop to tighten my baseball cap so it wouldn't blow away. Brutal.

Thanks to my two longer stops today, I didn't arrive until close to 3:30. By then, I was practically limping along feeling shattered and spent, willing myself to just make it to my hotel so I could attend to my sore knee and excruciatingly painful blisters. I felt battered. Thankfully the hotel desk clerk at the *Doña Mayor* was exceedingly kind and helpful. She assisted me with my laundry, providing me with a drying rack so I had another way to dry my clothes besides my clothesline. Then she directed me to the *farmacia* so I could get reinforcements for my blisters.

Even though I was exhausted, I agreed to meet Debbie for a drink before we went our separate ways for dinner. Since it was cold and windy, we were looking for any place inside where we could get warm. We found a lovely respite in the *Hostería las Palmeros*. The sitting area/bar was filled with comfy dark red tufted leather couches, antique wooden tables, beamed ceilings and an overall warm and inviting ambiance. They even had Absolut vodka for Debbie and Hendrick's gin for me. We plopped ourselves down on the cozy couches, thrilled with our fabulous find.

Back at my hotel, all I wanted to do was enjoy a quiet dinner and then go to bed early. I found a table in the dining room adjacent to the lobby, and as I smelled the amazing aroma, I realized how hungry I was. Walking 16.5 miles had definitely worked up my appetite. As I perused the menu, suddenly I heard, *"Ay ay ay ay, canta y no llores, porque cantando se alregran, cielito lindo los corazones."* An old woman sitting at the bar was singing this. Over and over. Again and again. And not in a pretty, melodic way. I tried not to stare while trying to discern if she was drunk. Or just crazy. Or both. Whatever the case, she was disrupting my peace and calm, not to mention the peace and calm of all the other diners. I picked up my wine glass and the rest of my belongings and moved to a table as far away from her as possible. If I hadn't been so tired, I might have found it a bit more entertaining. But I just wanted to eat in peace and go to bed.

I'm not sure if the wait staff asked the woman to leave or if she simply grew tired of singing, but thankfully I didn't have to wait too much longer for the restaurant to become blissfully silent again. The food was as delicious as it had smelled, and I ate almost every bite of my meal. With a full belly, tired body and hopes of healing for my knee and blisters, I walked upstairs to my room and fell asleep the second I laid my head on my soft pillow.

Day 16

This was supposed to be an easy day of walking. Only 13.5 miles, with no elevation gain. Nice and flat. Sounded simple enough. I was ready to have a less strenuous day.

But things turned out a little differently than I had expected. The Camino had a way of wreaking havoc with even the best laid plans. And learning to adjust to the change in circumstances with equanimity was one of its greatest lessons. I wrote on my blog:

...it felt like 40 miles. I've never been in such gale force winds in my entire life. I felt like I was on the top of a high mountain at Squaw Valley in Tahoe during a massive winter storm. I constantly felt like I was going to blow over, and it took all my strength to walk forward as the wind continued to push against me. One pilgrim, with her hood tied tightly around her head and her face completely covered with a scarf, tried to walk backwards to avoid the frontal battering. That looked very slow going. I, on the other hand, walked as quickly as I could—head down, windbreaker hood tied tightly over my baseball cap with my poles clicking double time. No time to think about my blisters or my knee. My only focus was to get to my destination as rapidly as my body would allow. No time for scenic pictures...

Psychologically, it was also difficult to walk today since it looked like I was heading down an endless path leading to nowhere. During the previous days, I could usually see the town or city where I was heading in the far off distance. I had a visual of where I was heading. But today I only saw open fields in every direction. I didn't even get a glimpse of the town I'd be staying in until the last half-mile or so. When I finally arrived in Carrión de Los Condes at around 1:00 in the afternoon, I felt cranky and battered.

My hotel was on the far end of town, so I had to walk through the shop-lined streets to find it. I could see that the town looked charming. But for the first time, I didn't feel like I would have the energy to explore it.

On the way to my hotel, I ran into Debbie as she was going into one of the adorable shops adorning the narrow street through the center of town. She had a smile on her face and seemed to be in good spirits. She'd arrived earlier, loved the room where she was staying and said she had a good walk—despite the wind. She asked if I might want to meet up and check out the town, since it looked so appealing. But I told her I needed to get out of my cranky funk, and I was going to just stay put for the night.

I am generally pretty even-keeled and don't often feel irritable. But I was definitely in a downward spiral, and I didn't want to subject anyone to my negative energy today. How was it that I had such a different walking experience than Debbie? She had to deal with the wind also. Why was *I* in such a bad mood? I knew going into this that I was going to have difficult days ahead of me. But I felt mentally tough and ready to face these challenges. Yes, I was dealing with ongoing pain from my knee and blisters, but some kind of pain was to be expected after walking long distances for multiple consecutive days. I needed to buck up and get over it. I needed to do a little attitude adjustment.

My mood certainly elevated when I arrived at the *Hotel Real Monasterio San Zoilo*, an old monastery that had been converted into a marvelous hotel full of old world charm. I could feel my heart rate lower and my agitation melt away as I entered the beautiful old building, filled with antique furniture and gorgeous artwork adorning the walls. And my room had a tub!

The day was turning around. I needed to shake myself out of my bad mood and I couldn't think of a better place to reset my mental outlook.

In the meantime, Debbie was dealing with something entirely different. She messaged Laura and me on WhatsApp:

I just spent some time by the river and sent Philip with the waves and birds to find some peace...peace is what I'm feeling in my heart at the moment...

I felt happy that Debbie finally found a place that called to her where she could spread Philip's ashes. I wondered what it was about this particular town that spoke to her. Somehow she knew this is where he would be at peace.

I spent the afternoon in the glass-encased dining area adjacent to my hotel, overlooking the surrounding tree-lined grounds. The space was bright and cheerful, with views of the outdoors in every direction. I ordered a glass of *vino tinto* and took advantage of the strong Wi-Fi, updating my blog with news from my last few days on the road. It was *siesta* time and I enjoyed having virtually the whole place to myself.

I savored the peace and quiet, the rich and melodious sounds of the acoustic Spanish guitar music playing and the beauty of the manicured lawns just outside my window. I no longer felt cranky.

In closing, I wrote on my blog that day:

...I know that not all my days are going to be easy. If they were, then reaching Santiago wouldn't be as rewarding as I suspect it will be. And tomorrow is going to be a very long hike beginning with about an 11-mile, completely flat stretch without anyplace to stop. I will be careful not to drink too much water during that time. But as Scarlett O'Hara says, "I'll think about that tomorrow." For now, I'm planning to enjoy this gorgeous setting and enjoy the old-world charm of this fabulous hotel.

Day 17

Here's how I described the start of today on my blog:

I awoke determined to have a better day. I needed to stop my whining, strap on my Tevas and make it a great day. The sun was shining, and the dreadful wind had turned into a delightful, gentle breeze...

The only challenge that I knew of beforehand was that there'd be a nearly 11-mile stretch without passing through a town to eat, drink or use a restroom. I needed to think very carefully about what I was going to ingest before I took off. I didn't want to deal with the discomfort of having to relieve myself on this long stretch of open plains with no trees to hide behind.

Amazingly, my positive attitude matched the kind of day I experienced. My 16-mile walk went smoothly, and I was able to make it through the long open stretch without feeling the urge to relieve myself. Crisis averted.

When I finally had the chance to stop for a coffee break, I saw several pilgrims I recognized inside the café, including Sean and Bearded Michael. Knowing that they walk fast and often did 30-40 kilometer days, I figured they'd be way ahead of me. But they had taken some rest days, so we were on the same path again. This is one of the things I loved about the Camino—running into people you never thought you were going to see again. And I am a firm believer that there is a reason why each one of us continues to cross paths with certain pilgrims—it is the destiny of our own, unique Camino.

While enjoying my coffee, I saw a young man talking with Sean and Bearded Michael. He had shoulder-length curly hair, parted down the middle, with fair skin and soulful eyes. And I noticed that he, too, was wearing sandals similar to my Tevas. He introduced himself as Alfie, and I soon learned that he was from London. We chatted for a bit, but then it was time to finish my walk for the day. So we said our goodbyes and I wondered if our paths would cross again.

Since I'd left early that morning at around 7:00, I arrived in the little town of Terradillos, pop. 70, a little after 1:00. This place wasn't on my original itinerary, but since I had changed things, I was now staying in what my travel company had termed a *basic* accommodation. In other words, they wouldn't normally book a place like this for their clients. But the *Albergue Los Templarios* was lovely! It had a large lawn in front dotted with a few tables surrounded by red plastic chairs, a place to do laundry with a long clothesline to hang clothes in the sunshine, and a nice dining area and bar adjacent to the check-in desk. I had my own room and bathroom. Other pilgrims either had the same or they shared a room with multiple beds. It was just the kind of place I thought I would be staying in all along the Camino. And even better, for the first time, I was staying in a place with familiar faces.

After showering, I walked out on the lawn to enjoy the beautiful sunshine. To my surprise, I spotted Bearded Michael, Sean and Alfie—along with several other pilgrims who I'd seen throughout the Camino. It was a completely different feeling to be amongst so many familiar faces, compared to my other hotels where I rarely knew any other pilgrims.

I joined Michael, Sean and Alfie at their table, and for the next few hours we sat lazily in the bright sunlight enjoying each other's company. I learned more about Michael's background as a Green Beret, and it was obvious that he thrived on adventure. His large, intense eyes brightened as he regaled us with some of his war stories. He shared some photos of himself when he was serving in the Army, and I was shocked to see his handsome, clean-cut face staring back at me. This was hard to reconcile with today's long beard, obscuring the square jaw of his Army years. He looked like an entirely different person.

But Michael seemed proud of his beard, explaining that he hadn't cut it for several years. That much seemed evident, as it was at least six inches below the bottom of his chin. I couldn't help but think that his beard made him look much older than he probably was. I guessed he was somewhere in his 40s, but it was hard to tell. I also discovered that this was the second time Michael was walking the Camino, and he seemed to be thoroughly enjoying the experience, despite the redundancy of walking the same path twice. At home in San Diego, California, he lived in his van, equipped with a bed and kitchenette, and he enjoyed taking road trips seeking exploration and adventure.

I learned that Sean had only recently decided to walk the Camino after a sudden broken engagement left him searching for answers. He looked to be in his late 20s/early 30s and was clean-cut, strong and athletic—a picture of health. So I remember feeling surprised when I saw him light up a cigarette—somehow seeing him smoke didn't jive with his image of health and fitness.

Sean and Bearded Michael met one another only a

few days after they started the Camino, and they became fast friends. I always saw them together, and Michael said walking with Sean, a passionate history buff, was like watching the History Channel. Sean would talk animatedly for hours, sharing stories and discussing past events with an energy and enthusiasm that made the day fly by.

In recent days, he'd begun walking with Jenny, an attractive young French woman around Sean's age, with dark wavy hair, brown eyes and fair skin. Jenny soon joined our table, and it was obvious that she and Sean were attracted to one another. After hearing a little about Sean's previous heartbreak, it made me happy to see the two of them together.

And then there was Alfie. He looked to be in his mid-20s. He was facing the sun, and I noticed his fair skin burning slightly under the blaze. His brown curly ringlets fell just above his shoulders, and his blue eyes flickered in delight every time he found something funny. He was wearing *his* evening clothes—a red and navy plaid t-shirt worn open, with the sleeves rolled up, and a gray t-shirt underneath, dark jeans with the hem rolled up a few times and open-toed Teva-like sandals. He'd been quietly listening to the conversation as he smoked his e-cigarette, smiling now and then, but not saying much. I wanted to find out more about him.

Trying to draw him out, I asked where he was from. In his beautifully clipped English accent—an accent which he later unsuccessfully tried to convince me wasn't a *pure* British accent—Alfie explained that he was raised in London by an English father and an American mother. He often spent time in New York City and had lived in various parts of the world, including other regions of the United States.

"Where else in the U.S. have you lived?" I asked.

"I lived in Los Angeles for a while," he answered.

"Really? Where?"

"I actually went to school there for a bit."

Now my curiosity was really piqued. "Where did you go to school?"

"USC."

I couldn't believe it. "Any chance you were in the Greek system there?" I asked, fully expecting him to laugh in my face. He did not look like a typical frat boy from USC.

Chuckling slightly, Alfie replied, "Yeah, I was Phi Psi."

My mind was blown. "Do you know Charlie Maloney?"

I couldn't believe Alfie's answer. "Yeah, he was in the pledge class ahead of me!"

No way. This was crazy. Here we were, in a miniscule town in the middle of Spain, and I had just met my son's fraternity brother. What were the chances of that?

There are a couple sayings I learned on my journey: *The Camino provides* and *It's a Camino thing*. The first one proved over and over to be true. For example, if a pilgrim lost their hiking poles one day, miraculously they might encounter a pilgrim the next day who offered to give theirs away. Or a pilgrim might show up to a busy town with no reservations and somehow find a decent place to sleep. No matter how grim the prospects, things always seem to have a way of working out.

The second saying—*It's a Camino thing*—alludes to the magic of the Camino. That's my interpretation, anyway. So many times a sign would present itself to me just as I was feeling tired or discouraged. Like a few days ago, when I saw that number 39 in the doorway, and it inspired me to forge ahead. Or the day I met Leah, the young girl in Burgos who knew my son Jackson. And now Alfie, who knew my other son Charlie. What are the odds?! I couldn't help but feel like this was kismet in the highest form. Definitely a Camino thing.

I felt an immediate connection to Alfie. He explained he only stayed at USC for a short time and didn't finish school there. Apparently, it wasn't a great fit for him. I laughed, observing that his bohemian look certainly didn't fit the often-mistaken stereotype of a typical USC student. The university had come a long way in diversifying its student body. We talked about people we knew in common. I told him that a guy in his pledge class, Matt, was one of Charlie's best friends. Laughing harder, Alfie pointed to his plaid shirt and told me that he was, in fact, wearing Matt's shirt. Unbelievable.

I learned that Alfie enjoyed writing poetry and had been working on a novel based on his experiences living in Florence one summer. We talked about my son Jackson's love of poetry, and I shared one of his poems with Alfie, recognizing that I had connected with someone who could appreciate the beauty of this form of expression. He also loved music, often spontaneously breaking out into a freestyle rap. Sean and Bearded Michael showed me a video capturing one of his recent displays, and it was quite impressive. Alfie certainly seemed to be a creative soul, and I was intrigued.

As we continued talking, I noticed a few more familiar faces had joined our gathering. Dan, the fast walker with the noisy walking stick, arrived with Summer, a young South Korean girl who he'd become extremely smitten with and who seemed to reciprocate those feelings. She was part of a large organized group of South Korean pilgrims walking together. I often saw many of them throughout the day, rarely ever walking solo. I noticed that they tended to stick together in their groups, preferring to seek the company of each other rather than other pilgrims. I guessed this was, in large part, due to the language constraints. Not many of them appeared to speak English or Spanish, so it made sense that they were more comfortable in each other's company.

I also saw Rachel, the young woman who I'd seen walking from time to time with Bearded Michael and Sean. And I met Almandine, another young attractive woman from France who I'd seen at various times during the last several days. Both women looked like they were somewhere in their 20's. Almandine had brown eyes, a sweet smile and long wavy brown hair, tousled in a way that looked like she had just rolled out of bed. She wore an oversized pink sweatshirt over her small frame, with black and white patterned leggings. She had the air of a winsome waif and something about her screamed of fragility and vulnerability. I found her exceedingly charming.

I soon learned that I wasn't the only one who recognized her appeal. I heard stories of other pilgrims helping Almandine escape the unwanted attention of some admirers. Nothing sordid or dangerous, but more of an annoyance that she apparently had to contend with on a regular basis. Her friends also teased Almandine that she was the perfect example of *The Camino provides*. They explained to me that she had a habit of getting a late start in the mornings, a risk for pilgrims without room reservations. And yet she always managed to somehow get a bed at night, dispelling the notion that only early risers secured lodging.

Several hours passed in what seemed like minutes, and soon it was time for dinner. Alfie, Bearded Michael, Sean, Jenny, a few other pilgrims whose names I don't remember and I found a large round table in the back of the small dining room. I don't remember what we ate that night. But I do remember playing a lively and highly entertaining game of *Two Truths and a Lie* and laughing non-stop throughout my meal.

We continued our festivities out on the lawn after dinner, until the cold night air forced us inside and reminded me to get to bed at a decent hour. My early morning alarm would be going off before I knew it.

It had been a perfect day. And it wouldn't have happened with my original itinerary. I felt grateful for this Camino experience.

And I wasn't the only one who had an outstanding day. Debbie sent Laura and me a message on WhatsApp:

> I had a really good day. Honestly, I don't get it but I feel lighter today. I didn't realize how heavy that little bag of Philip was on my heart. It was a good day for me...

But then she added:

> I think I may have screwed up again on my reservation for tomorrow night...I can't cancel my other reservation. I can't keep doing it like this. Ugh.

Oh, Debbie. Not again! This was wreaking havoc on her Camino budget...

Day 18

After a solid night's sleep, I was elated to see the sun shining brilliantly outside my window. My blisters were still healing, so I strapped on my Tevas and prepared for the 15-mile walk ahead of me. The weather was crisp, cool and clear. But as the day progressed and the temperature increased, I was able to shed my layers and walk comfortably in a short-sleeve shirt.

Soon into my walk I met a pair of older Europeans: Jane, a friendly and talkative English woman who lived in Germany, and Paul, a mild-mannered and reserved Irishman. They appeared to be about the same age, probably in their 50s. The pair met on the Camino and had been walking together the last few days. Both explained how they'd been walking the Camino for several years, bit by bit. Jane had begun walking several years ago, starting in Germany, and hoped to finally reach Santiago the following year during her vacation time.

Meeting these two got me thinking about how different this experience would be—walking the Camino in sections, spaced out over the course of years. Perhaps blisters wouldn't be an issue if pilgrims only walked a few days or weeks at a time? Or maybe carrying a heavy pack wouldn't be such a burden if you knew it was only for a week or two? And what would it feel like to reach Santiago after a number of *years* as opposed to a few weeks? These questions simply reminded me that there are several ways to do the Camino—there is no *right* or *wrong* way.

The three of us happily chatted for the next several

miles until we reached Sahagún, the halfway point of the Camino Francés route to Santiago. I felt immensely joyful and somewhat incredulous that I was already at the halfway mark. I didn't want this experience to be over too soon.

The three of us wanted to get our *Carta Peregrina*, an official certificate hallmarking this achievement. After asking several locals where we could find the *Santuario de La Peregrina*, a museum atop a hill where the certificate is issued, we finally arrived. Once inside, we waited in a short line. After giving the clerk my name and a few Euros, I was given a thick sheet of paper with beautiful black calligraphy with my name at the top. Beginnings of some words were capitalized in bright red, and the certificate was embellished with the colorful coat of arms of Sahagún. It was a stunning certificate, and I was glad we made the effort to track it down.

Both Paul and Jane decided to stay and look around the museum, so we said our goodbyes since I felt ready to move along. It was a little past 1:00 p.m. when I arrived at the *Albergue La Perala,* my lodging for the evening in the tiny town of Bercianos del Real Camino. It was a brown and tan u-shaped building, with tiny windows on the bottom half that gave it the appearance of an industrial shed. The place was plopped in the middle of a field of tall grass, with absolutely nothing else around it but for a few outdoor tables with blue and white umbrellas and red plastic chairs. It certainly didn't have the charm of my place the night before. But it was clean and my room was comfortable. And to my happy surprise, Debbie and Alfie were staying there as well. I introduced Alfie to Debbie and they seemed to hit it off immediately. Then Dan showed up, too. *Mis amigos.*

After enjoying dinner with the three of them, Alfie, Debbie and I decided to check out the only other *albergue* in town. Dan opted to stay behind, so the three of us—undaunted by the sudden downpour—bundled up in our rain jackets and headed outside. In a matter of minutes, we'd arrived at the other *albergue*, and despite our wet clothes, we were happy to have made the excursion. The bar was filled with *peregrinos*, some of whom I recognized, and the atmosphere was warm and lively.

At the back of the bar, we spied a dart board. So after ordering some *vino tinto*, we proceeded to play some darts—with the game quickly evolving into a fierce competition. In reality, it was more like a competition between Debbie and me—Alfie seemed to be too entertained by our banter with one another to actually focus on hitting the bullseye. In the end, both Debbie and I declared ourselves the winner. And Alfie wouldn't side with either one of us. We had a good laugh, fueled by *vino tinto* and competition, before deciding to head back to our *albergue*.

As the rain poured down, Debbie peered up at the sky and exclaimed, "I wish I could see a rainbow. Just one. Is that too much to ask?"

A few steps further, she lamented, "Please. I'm not asking for much. I really want to see a rainbow. For Philip. It would make me so happy."

And literally, just like that, a magnificent rainbow appeared. We stopped in our tracks, stunned at the miraculous sight before us. Debbie squealed with delight, her face radiating joy.

"Can you believe what just happened?" she asked incredulously.

She immediately pulled out her iPhone to capture

the rainbow's beauty. She started jumping up and down, unable to contain her excitement over what she had just witnessed. Chills rushed up and down my body. It truly was a moment I'll never forget. The three of us huddled together to take a selfie to commemorate the experience, and I still get goosebumps when I look at that picture today. It was a spectacular way to end a memorable day on the Camino. I was halfway to Santiago and thoroughly enjoying this journey with my new friends.

Day 19

I decided to get an early start, around 7:30, since I had a 17-mile walk ahead of me. I was still trudging through the *Meseta*, so I wasn't expecting varied scenery to buoy me throughout the day. Thankfully I didn't have to contend with hot weather. So after a quick breakfast of eggs and bread, I mentally geared up for a long, monotonous trek through lengthy stretches of open fields. I knew Debbie preferred to leave very early in the morning, around 6:30 or 7:00, so I didn't see her on my way out. Nor did I see Alfie or Dan. But I suspected they preferred to leave on the later side, since they both seemed to be night owls.

I don't remember much about this day, which is surprising since it was a long walk. What I do remember is that I put on my headphones and listened to what turned out to be my very favorite album on the Camino—*Port Saint Joe* by Brothers Osborne. Every song put me into a great mood and motivated me to walk with purpose. I fell into a rhythm, almost trance-like, and the hours just seemed to slip away. I couldn't tell you what I was thinking about or whether my blisters were hurting or my knee was throbbing. I just let the music overtake my body and leaned into the moment. All I know is that I arrived in Mansilla de las Mulas, a sleepy town surrounded by a 12th century medieval wall, a little after 2:00 in the afternoon.

I located my hotel, the *Albergería del Camino*, and to my great delight, it seemed more like a cozy cottage with a home-like atmosphere. It oozed with charm and comfort, and the innkeeper was warm and friendly. I settled happily into my room, up one flight of stairs and admired the wide plank wood floors, the pale yellow walls, the sun shining through the large window overlooking the courtyard below, the antique furnishings and the crisp white comforter on the double bed. The room was perfect. Except, of course, for the rock hard pillows. Those never seemed to change, no matter where I stayed. I once again felt a surge of gratitude for my soft pillow.

Just outside my room was a sitting area with large, overstuffed couches and book-lined shelves for guests to peruse. Downstairs, next to the reception area, was an inviting outdoor courtyard filled with tables and chairs, surrounded by colorful flowers and greenery.

I decided this would be a perfect place to work on my blog and enjoy a little rest after my long walk. But first I needed to deal with my laundry. Not wanting to deal with handwashing in my bathroom sink, I asked the innkeeper if there was a place in town where I could do laundry. She directed me to a place just down the street, so I collected my clothes, including some of my bigger items that were hard to wash in my room, stuffed them in my extra pillowcase and set off for the laundromat.

When I arrived I was thrilled to discover that it wasn't a do-it-yourself kind of place. Instead I was able to simply drop off my clothes and they'd be laundered and ready to pick up 90 minutes later. What a treat! This meant that I could enjoy the next hour-and-a-half writing on my blog, while sipping a glass of *vino tinto* at a table in the lovely courtyard at my hotel. Excellent.

A few hours later, I heard from Debbie and we made a plan to meet at my hotel and eat dinner together. Alfie was also staying in the same town, so we invited him to join us as well. He introduced us to Fabienne, an Austrian girl in her 20s with long brown wavy hair and a lovely, infectious laugh. The four of us enjoyed a delicious dinner in the wood-paneled, cozy dining room of my hotel. It felt like I was in a home rather than in a restaurant. And I felt like I was eating with friends I had known for years rather than what was, in reality, only a few days. Every so often, Alfie would excuse himself from the table to go outside and smoke his e-cigarette.

"You know that's not good for you," Debbie chided Aflie with a motherly tone when he returned. "You should really think about quitting."

"She's right, you know," I chimed in lightheartedly. "We just want you to be around for a long time."

With a smile on his face, Alfie just nodded his head and didn't reply. Debbie and I got the message. Subject closed. No use in bringing this up again.

In addition to putting bread on the table, the waiter brought us a dish of olives. Excited to try something other than bread, I helped myself and remarked how delicious they were. Debbie looked dubious and admitted that she'd never tasted an olive before. What? Was she serious? We all laughed and insisted she try one. Now. She made a face and tentatively picked one up, sniffed it gingerly and popped it begrudgingly into her mouth.

"It's not bad," she confessed. "I might have another."

Alfie and I laughed and announced we had a mission for the next day when we reached León. Knowing that Debbie loved vodka, we were going to find her a killer martini with *three olives*. We insisted she was going to love it. I'm not so sure she was convinced. But we were game to find out.

At the end of another laugh-filled meal, we said good-night and promised to see each other the next evening.

Day 20

My day started pretty rough. I awoke at 2:30 in the morning, my left heel throbbing in pain from my blister. It took me over 20 minutes to gingerly remove my bandages just so I could soak it in hot water. I'd worn my hiking shoes the day before, but clearly I wasn't ready to make the transition from my Tevas. Time to pack away the hiking shoes and pray my Tevas would carry me through the day during my 12-mile hike into León.

After soaking my throbbing foot in hot water for another 20 minutes, I finally got back into bed for a few more hours of sleep.

I left my hotel a little before 7:30 a.m., hoping to have enough time to explore León—and to accommodate my slower pace. Fairly soon into my walk, I met Gunnar, a young man from Kiel, Germany. He had a neat, short haircut, huge dimples and an easy smile. Gunnar looked fit, strong and athletic, and we ended up walking together for a few miles. He was interesting and engaging, but our conversation was interrupted when we caught up with a few pilgrims ahead of us and Gunnar realized he knew them. While he stopped to chat, I struck up a conversation with another pilgrim who had also stopped. Seeing that Gunnar was going to be waylaid for a while, the other pilgrim—a man looking to be somewhere in his 30s—and I said our goodbyes and proceeded to walk ahead.

The man had jet black hair and intense brown eyes, introducing himself as Takashi. I soon learned he was from Japan but lived in Murcia, Spain. He was wearing a turquoise Native American blanket wrapped around his shoulders as he stepped with an unhurried purpose. He exuded a profound sense of calm, peace and wisdom. I was immediately drawn to him.

As he spoke in his kind and gentle manner, I discovered that Takashi was walking the Camino Francés for the eighth time. *What?* That was a first for me. I'd met a few people walking it for their second time—but *eight?* I was intrigued. He was clearly drawn to the Camino's power and mystical ability to inspire human connection. And he never tired of the journey, since each time Takashi made his way across Spain he experienced new things, met different people and walked during different seasons of the year. On his third Camino he met a beautiful Spanish woman, fell in love and got married. Magic struck on the Camino once again.

As we continued to walk, I became completely engrossed in our conversation. We covered a myriad of topics—our various experiences on the Camino, our families, Native American culture, books we liked (*Siddhartha* was one of his favorites), our views about reincarnation and the power of positivity.

Both Takashi and I shared similar beliefs in the existence of reincarnation and the idea that we may have lived past lives. He shared his conviction that people in the world today are reaching a higher level of consciousness and more open to the possibility of connecting with our past lives. He talked about his experiences on the Camino and witnessing pilgrims' generosity of spirit, concern for others, and immense displays of love and compassion. These were the things that kept drawing him back to the Camino year after year.

Takashi was adept at asking questions and drawing out answers. He was an excellent listener and when he smiled, his eyes twinkled. Takashi asked me all about Tom, how we met and how I felt about walking without him. He asked about Jackson, Charlie and Mia and wanted to know what they were like and what interested them. He was interested to hear about Jackson's Camino and seemed happy that I could share my own experience with Jackson when I returned. I could feel his warmth and genuine caring spirit. The hours passed swiftly, and I felt like the Camino had gifted me the honor of walking with this kind sage. It was the first time I'd walked with another pilgrim for more than an hour.

When we arrived in León around noon, Takashi insisted on walking me to my hotel, since it can often be more challenging to find the Camino arrows in a big city. Plus, unlike me, he had a data plan on his phone, so he could plug the location into his maps. I was touched by this gesture, and when we found the *Hotel Silken Luís de Leon,* I was sad to say goodbye. I told Takashi that I hoped we would soon meet again.

My hotel was apparently in the midst of construction. The noise was unbearable. This was certainly not the relaxing atmosphere I'd hoped for after a long day of walking. Talking with Takashi had taken my mind off the pain of my blisters, as well as the ache in my knee. But now that I was settled into my room, the din of construction still aggravatingly loud, my knee throbbed and my blisters felt hot and irritated. If I was going to make it through the following day, I needed to tend to my ailments.

After showering, I decided to return to the front desk

and ask where I could find a pharmacy with a pharmacist available. (Not all pharmacies offered this.) I also wanted to know where I could get a good massage. I now understood why I saw so many advertisements for massage services along the Camino—a good massage could prove to be an essential offering for many *peregrinos* in desperate need of relief from their aches and pains.

The pharmacy was closed until 5:00 p.m., but the clerk was able to make a massage appointment for me at a place just a short walk from the hotel. I was ecstatic to think I might get some relief for my knee. And thrilled to be leaving the clamor of construction.

The clerk jotted down the address of the massage place for me, and I immediately went on my way. Within a few minutes I reached the appointed location—only it looked like a tiny herb store. Confused, I entered the store and explained to the shopkeeper that I was looking for a massage service. He smiled and asked me to wait a moment while he called for his daughter, motioning with his hands that the massage room was in the back of the store. Okay, I thought. A little unorthodox, but I was desperate for some relief.

A young woman, looking to be in her early 20s, appeared and asked me to follow her to the back of the store. She led me into a small room brightly lit with fluorescent lights. It looked more like an exam room at a doctor's office than a healing zone of relaxation and rejuvenation. But again, I was desperate.

The young woman signaled that I should take my clothes off so she could begin the treatment. But she made no attempt to leave the room or turn around while I undressed. This was new to me. But maybe modesty wasn't a big deal to her. So shoving my discomfort aside, I quickly undressed and hopped onto the table under the sheet. For the next hour, while soft classical music streamed out from the speakers overhead, I sank into a deep meditative state and my body soaked up the masseuse's healing touch. Despite the unconventional setting, the massage was excellent.

With my knee feeling better, I focused my attention on my blisters. I was worried that they might be infected and wanted a pharmacist to take a look. I found the *farmacia* recommended by the hotel clerk, and to my great relief the pharmacist said she didn't think my blisters were infected. Armed with a new and improved medication/bandage routine, I set off to meet up with Debbie, Alfie and Fabienne to begin our search for the perfect martini.

We met just outside the *Catedral de León*, a stunning example of Gothic architecture and beauty. After exploring inside the cathedral for a short time, we began our search. The first bar we tried made a horrendous concoction of something that tasted nothing like a martini. We tried another bar, and the same thing occurred. And then another. It became evident that martinis aren't a popular drink in Spain. At least not in the bars we tried in León. As a last attempt, we found an American-themed bar in the *Plaza Mayor,* and the bartender assured us he knew how to make a proper martini. It didn't exactly turn out like a martini you might see Don Draper drinking on *Mad Men*, but it was passable. At last. And the bartender made it with three olives. Excellent. Debbie assured us that she enjoyed her very first martini, even eating all three of the olives.

Next we decided to partake in one of the more delightful

Spanish customs—barhopping, accompanied by *tapas* tastings. In many Spanish bars, depending on the geographical location, the custom is if you order a drink, you will then get a *tapa* (also called *pincho* or *pintxo* depending on where you are) for free. So if you're in a group, it's fun to try the various offerings, since you can each get a different kind of *tapa*. And it's a great way to fill up on food without breaking the bank. Perfect for hungry *peregrinos*.

Fabienne had plans to meet up with some other friends for dinner, so Debbie, Alfie and I began our bar crawl. As we headed out of the *Plaza Mayor*, I was thrilled to see Takashi and a few other pilgrims walking towards me on their way to dinner. We embraced like old friends, and I told him I hoped we would see each other again soon.

The night was still young. And since the Spaniards don't typically get going until later in the evenings, the bars weren't overly crowded. So we were easily able to find tables where we could sit and enjoy our food and beverages.

I found the conversation effortless and entertaining between the three of us. And I found it curious that Alfie, being a few decades younger than Debbie and me, chose to spend his time with us rather than with other pilgrims closer in age to him. Of course, I knew he'd met several pilgrims his own age whom he liked and enjoyed being with. But both Debbie and I felt happy that he wanted to spend the evening with us.

Debbie talked about her feelings of relief over finding a place to spread Philip's ashes.

"I am so much happier. I really didn't realize how much those little ashes were weighing me down. I loved that little town of Carrión de los Condes. It was the perfect place for Philip."

"I'm so glad you finally found the right place for him. It's funny how we had such different experiences that day. I hated the entire walk. I was in the worst mood and so cranky," I said. "The wind was absolutely brutal."

"I can't imagine a cranky Margarita," Alfie chimed in.

"It doesn't happen often," I assured him. "But believe me, you wouldn't have wanted to be around me that day."

Alfie just shook his head. "I find that hard to believe."

Alfie seemed to feel comfortable with us, and I noticed that as we spent more time together, he allowed himself to open up and reveal bits and pieces of his background. From what I could gather, he seemed to have a complicated relationship with his parents, and he struggled with finding his place in the world. Alfie was highly perceptive and seemed wise beyond his years. I found him to be an old soul. Perhaps that's why I didn't notice the age difference between us. Age became irrelevant. We just connected, so that's all that was important.

I loved watching Debbie and Alfie banter back and forth. She could always make him laugh at something she said—like when she butchered the pronunciation of a Spanish word with her New York accent. They'd get in silly little arguments about meaningless things. Watching Alfie, who was usually somewhat reserved, laugh whole-heartedly was quite entertaining for me, and I found myself grinning from ear to ear as I took in the scene. Something about Alfie tugged at my heartstrings. He seemed to feel things quite deeply, and I detected an inner sadness. Seeing him break out into a smile or hearing him chuckle softly made me happy.

One other thing that Debbie and I discovered about Alfie is that he hated having his picture taken. He had a hard time smiling for the camera. Of course, Debbie and I wanted to capture some of these momentous adventures on the Camino, so we insisted that he just *try* not looking miserable in our photos. We often resorted to saying something outrageous or tickling him just as the camera snapped the photo, and happily we succeeded in making him smile more than once.

After visiting a few bars and enjoying many laughs, I realized I felt incredibly tired. Even though the streets were filling up with people and the revelry was becoming louder and livelier, I needed to get to bed for some much needed rest if I wanted to make it through the next day.

Just as I was about to leave, we ran into Dan. He was with some other pilgrims, some of whom I recognized and others who I had never seen before. With a big smile on his face, Dan introduced us to Emi, a young woman from Japan who he'd met recently on the Camino. She was smiling broadly and seemed to be completely enamored with Dan. He had his arm draped loosley around her shoulders and looked at her adoringly. He seemed smitten. I later learned that Summer was no longer in the picture. Dan now had his sights set on Emi. I hoped, for his sake, this time he found somebody he could be happy with.

We decided to have one last drink together before I headed back to my hotel. Dan seemed so happy to see Debbie and me that I couldn't refuse. We took a picture together that night, Dan in the middle with his arms draped around the two of us, and a smile on his face emanating pure joy. It's a happy memory for me. I'm glad I decided to stay for that last drink. And months later, I would reflect on that night in a new light, thankful for my decision. I said goodnight to my new friends. And with my blisters and knee aching anew, I hobbled back to my hotel.

Day 21

The next morning I woke up and saw I had a WhatsApp message from Dan.

Margarita! So glad to have seen you last night. You've become such a special part of my Camino. Grateful 🙏

He seemed so happy with Emi. I hoped he'd soon hear good news from his boss letting him know he could take a few more days off work to make it to Santiago. And I wanted to be there with him to celebrate our achievement.

Alfie had decided to take a few rest days in León, so I wasn't sure if we'd reach Santiago at the same time or not. I certainly hoped so. I wanted to be there with as many of my Camino friends as possible. It would be amazing to celebrate our arrival together.

Debbie seemed to be walking just fine—she sped from one destination to the next without developing a single blister or any other new ailments. Amazing. Her embarrassing medical issue was still aggravating her at times. But she seemed to keep it at bay well enough to get through each day. I was feeling hopeful that we would reach Santiago together.

I left my hotel around 8:00, determined to *slow my roll* today in deference to my bum knee and painful blisters. Later I wrote on my blog:

I felt happy to leave the big city of León behind. As

much as I enjoyed it, I felt somewhat overwhelmed being in such a busy city after spending so many days in small, quiet and quaint villages. Normally I love a bustling city teeming with people and activity, but not on the Camino. Here I seem to crave peace and quiet and connection.

I walked nearly three miles before I was finally out of the city after having passed dozens of kids of all ages either walking to school or being dropped off by their parents. The city was electric with all the activity. I noticed a lot of pilgrims walking whom I had never seen before and subsequently found out that a lot of people started their Camino from León. And as we get even closer to Santiago (pilgrims have to walk a minimum of 100 kilometers in order to get their certificate of completion, a compostela), the Camino gets busier and busier.

As I finally left the noise, I happened to notice a pilgrim stopped at a bench getting something out of his bag. It was Takashi! What a wonderful surprise to see him again. We ended up walking the whole day together. This was a first for me, as I usually walk alone and at times walk with others only for a short while. Takashi said this was a first for him too on this particular Camino (having already walked it seven times). What a blessing it was to have his company all day. First of all, there wasn't anything scenic about the walk—it ran alongside the highway and we didn't walk through any cute towns. And again it was flat, dusty and rocky. Takashi asks deep questions, and we were engrossed

in philosophical conversation for most of the day, mak-
ing what could have been a lackluster 14-mile walk to-
tally engaging. And my Tevas held up well. My blisters
are healing, but I'm still not ready to put my hiking
shoes back on.

When I arrived in my town for the night, Villadan-
gos del Paramo, I was surprised to see how vacant it
seemed. No people milling about and the Plaza Mayor
consisted of a smoky restaurant without Wi-Fi and only
two tables outside. And no pilgrims anywhere in sight.

I found my lodging for the night, the Hostel Libertad, *definitely* not *a hotel and a step down from an*
albergue. *The check-in was at the bar next door, and*
it was filled with old men smoking and chatting. Not
one woman in sight except for the one who checked
me in. And she couldn't have been less friendly. I would
bet that a smile hadn't crossed that woman's face in a
very long time.

Once I got my bag, I got to the top of the stairs,
and it was pitch dark. I had to search for the hall
light switch so I could find my room. Upon opening
the door I think I actually groaned out loud. First of
all, the room was as frigid as a meat locker with no
apparent way to control the temperature. It was a
dingy green color with a similar shade of bedspread
that looked like it hadn't been washed in decades.
Mia would call it "crusty." When I sent Debbie a
picture of my room, this was her reply:

"You have a lovely bedspread. Don't touch it."

This was my introduction to the town of Villadangos del

174

Paramo. It was the first time I couldn't find one charming thing about where I was staying. The town seemed deserted and ghost-like. I'd said goodbye to Takashi about a mile back up the road at the municipal (public) *albergue* where he was staying. I watched him gracefully disappear through the doors, appearing almost regal with the turquoise Native American blanket still draped around his shoulders and his fedora still squarely on his head.

There was no *Plaza Mayor* to speak of. Even worse, my hostel felt creepy. For the first time, I checked my mattress for bed bugs. Thankfully I couldn't see anything that looked like the pictures I had Googled before I left on my trip. I'd read horror stories of pilgrims dealing with bed bug issues and the thought completely grossed me out. This was not something I wanted to contend with. Despite my gratitude at finding a bug-free mattress, I wanted to spend as little time in my room as possible.

Luckily Debbie and I had made a plan earlier in the day to return to León that night to meet up with Laura for dinner. Laura's knee pain had worsened, so she was going to see a doctor in León later that afternoon and then take a few rest days there.

Since Debbie was in a town further ahead of me (and also staying in a less-than-satisfactory place), she offered to get a taxi, then swing by and pick me up on our way back to León.

"What is the name of your hostel horror house?" Debbie messaged me.

Fifteen minutes later, the taxi was in front of my place. We were on our way, both happy to be leaving our respective *hell holes*—and looking forward to reuniting with our friend.

Our taxi driver, David, dropped us off near the cathedral and promised he'd pick us up promptly at 9:00. He wouldn't take payment and insisted we just pay him for the round trip at the end of the evening. I marveled at the trust this kind Spanish man put in us. I was once again surprised at how this kind of trust and civility seemed to permeate the Spanish culture. I felt pretty certain that this wouldn't happen in most parts of the United States.

We met Laura at a nearby restaurant and it was wonderful to see her. Despite using her walking poles for support and clearly in pain, she looked bright, cheerful and happy to see us too.

We found a quiet table in the back of the restaurant. Since it was early, not even 6:00 yet, the place was practically deserted. Perfect. We had a lot to catch up on.

Debbie and I asked Alfie to join us later in the meal. We wanted him and Laura to meet, since we knew he was still in León. Alfie said he'd like to join us and was looking forward to finally meeting Laura. We felt like this was our little Camino family.

The doctor had given Laura a cortisone shot in her knee earlier in the day, so she hoped she could start walking again after resting for a few days. The pain had become so unbearable that she'd only been able to walk for short stretches each day. She then had to take a taxi or bus the rest of the way to her hotel for the night. This was not how she had intended or wanted to walk the Camino. Like it or not, she simply had to make some serious mental adjustments.

But Laura was determined to make it work. She acknowledged that this was *her* Camino—for whatever reason, this was how it was supposed to go. This was *her* struggle and she was going to embrace it wholeheartedly. Nothing was going to stop her from walking into Santiago on July 8th—her 60th birthday—with her family and friends.

I could feel her pain and disillusionment. But I could also sense her tremendous strength of spirit and determination. She was putting on a brave face, and I admired her courage and positivity in the face of her setbacks. She was a remarkable woman. And seeing her wrangle with this issue made me respect and like her even more than I already did.

The three of us talked for several hours, trading stories and laughing often. I felt like I was sitting with two dear longtime friends—even though we'd only met *13 days ago.* Once again I was struck by this powerful feeling of connection. *It's a Camino thing.*

Sadly, a little before our 9:00 pick-up time, we had to say our goodbyes. Alfie never showed up to the restaurant, so we were disappointed that he and Laura didn't have a chance to meet. It wasn't like him to just not show up. He knew I didn't have a data plan on my phone, but Debbie did. And she hadn't received a text from him. We hoped he was okay.

Debbie and I helped Laura hobble outside. Just as promised, David was waiting for us in his taxi. We asked him if he could give Laura a ride to her hotel, a few minutes away in the *Plaza Mayor.* "*No problema,*" David said, and we were on our way.

Debbie and I got out of the taxi to give Laura a hug goodbye. We said we hoped we could see each other at least one more time before reaching Santiago. We asked David to take our picture before we sadly climbed back into the taxi. Just as we were getting in, we noticed a group of young people sitting on a balcony overlooking the *Plaza Mayor.* We could hear loud music and it looked like some sort of party going on.

Suddenly I noticed Alfie sitting in one of the chairs, his long ringlets clearly outlined in the still light sky. I felt disappointed that he hadn't bothered to text us about his change of plans. At least we knew he was okay. And a *fiesta* with pilgrims his own age seemed like an entertaining way to spend the evening. Still, I was sad that I might not see Alfie again. I never got a chance to say goodbye. He was staying in León and I was forging ahead. This was part of the Camino that I found difficult—I disliked not knowing if I would see one of my friends again. And as much as I could appreciate the time we spent together, I still experienced a sense of loss when we moved on from one another.

On the drive back to Villadangos del Paramo, David insisted on taking us on the alternate Camino route so we could see the Pilgrim's Monument. We had told him that we'd walked the main route, so he didn't want us to miss seeing this architectural beauty. It was a large wall mosaic at the entrance of the tiny pilgrim-friendly village of Villar de Mazarife. The colorful scene depicted a group of pilgrims standing in front of a church, with three birds flying above and the town's name spelled out below. It was a true work of beauty and craftsmanship, and we were thrilled to have seen it. We thanked David profusely for insisting on this unplanned excursion.

David was also kind enough to find a small market for us so we could buy a few snacks for breakfast the next day. Despite the projected mid-30s morning temperature, Debbie and I had decided to leave early the next day. We knew it'd be near impossible to find food before we left. We also didn't want to stay at our *albergues* one second longer than necessary. We both hoped our lodgings would be better the next night. Debbie reserved a room in the same place as me, so at least we'd be together.

I said goodnight to Debbie and David and finally found my room—after searching in the pitch dark for a light switch, any light switch, to help illuminate my path. Once I finally found a button, I pressed it, triggering a great buzzing sound. Then the light would come on, but only for a few seconds. Followed by pitch black. Again. Leaving me to search for another button that might shed more light on my surroundings. And so on. I didn't see or hear another soul on the way to my room. I was ready to get out of this creepy place.

Day 22

True to my word, I was up and out of the *Hostel Libertad* by 6:30. The café wasn't open yet, and I couldn't find anything that indicated where I was supposed to leave my room key. In the other places I stayed there was a key drop or a sign saying to leave the key in your room. So after placing my bag on the floor in the entryway, I just left it on a ledge, hoping the check-in clerk would find it and the luggage transfer company would show up for my bag. I wasn't going to worry about this. I had a big day ahead of me—17.5 miles.

As I opened the door to the outside, a rush of cold air slapped my face. It seemed to be as chilly as the Spanish weather experts had predicted. For the first time on my journey, I was wearing my down jacket and gloves. It was an interesting look with my socks and Tevas. But I didn't mind. I was happy to leave this ghost town. And I relished the splendor and tranquility of the early morning.

About seven miles into my walk, I stopped in a quaint little town called Hospital de Órbigo for a *café con leche*. Within minutes of my arrival I spotted Debbie sitting at a table animatedly chatting away with another pilgrim. She seemed to be in good spirits and wasn't having any problems with her walk. We talked for a few minutes, but then she was ready to continue on while I stopped for rest. We agreed to meet up later that afternoon in Astorga.

Feeling refreshed, I prepared to cross the stunning 13th

century stone bridge over the *río Órbigo*. The Romans built the original bridge as part of the road from León to Astorga, and it had 19 beautifully constructed arches spanning over 200 meters, the longest on the Camino. I marveled at the architectural feat while I slowly made my way across.

It dawned on me how much more interesting my walk was today. The stark monotony of the *Meseta* was vanishing. In its place, I was seeing a more varied landscape full of hills, livestock and more colorful, visually arresting vistas. Astorga marked the end of the *Meseta*, as well as the place where the Via de la Plata and Camino Francés route met. So I was already seeing a difference in the terrain. I welcomed the change in scenery.

I arrived in Astorga a little after 1:00, passing by a life-sized statue of a *peregrino* on my way to the *Hotel Spa Via de la Plata*. Many such statues dotted the Camino, along with crosses made out of wood, stone or metal, plus makeshift memorials scattered with flowers, prayer cards or stones. I often saw a pilgrim or two stopped at one of these memorials, either taking the time to read some of the prayer cards or taking a moment for reflection. The spirit of the Camino could be felt in a myriad of ways, and I appreciated these symbols along my journey.

I was thrilled to find my hotel centrally located. Plus, my room was clean, bright and comfortable. And it had a tub. Hallelujah! What a difference a day makes. I took a long bath, soaking my blisters and massaging my knee. I seemed to be healing ever-so-slowly. But I felt grateful that, once again, my body somehow managed to carry me through an almost 18-mile day. Even though it had been a long walk, I was anxious to explore the town. From what I had seen so far, it looked lively and charming. And Astorga was also famous for its chocolate. I definitely wanted to do some tastings.

Debbie and I met in the lobby of my hotel and walked a short distance to the *Plaza Mayor*, where we sat at an outdoor table and enjoyed a refreshing drink—vodka and *agua con gas* for Debbie and a gin and tonic for me. The square was filled with people engaging in lively conversation, sitting under brightly colored umbrellas while they sipped on their drinks and enjoyed their meals. I felt uplifted by the buzz in the air, and I loved watching the bustle of activity around the many souvenir shops. As the hour struck, two mechanical figures—a man and a woman dressed in traditional *Maragato* costumes atop the historical building in the *Plaza Mayor*—struck the bell to ring in the new hour. I liked this place.

I learned that Astorga is the traditional market town of the *Maragatos*, a distinct ethnic group of unknown origin. According to the Camino Travel Center:

> The **Maragatos** are about 4,000 people who are believed to be the last Moorish people in Spain. They were descended from the Berbers of North Africa who crossed into the Iberian peninsula with the first Moorish incursions in the early eighth century. The **Maragatos** are spread over 40 villages in the greatly depopulated hills outside **Astorga** in **León**, northern Spain.

Shops throughout Astorga capitalized on this unique attribute. I saw all sorts of Maragato products, costumes and food items for sale. After visiting the *Museo de Chocolate* and the exquisite cathedral, Debbie and I happened upon one such delicacy in a nearby bakery. The smell beckoned us inside, where we asked to buy a few of the traditional offerings. Debbie pointed to a plate of circular shaped pastries called *Roscas Maragatas de Astorga* and asked the saleslady to pop a few of them into the bag for us. I thought they looked fairly unremarkable, but I was willing to try anything.

Outside the bakery, we dug into our bag of treats and started sampling. To my great surprise, the unexceptional looking little pastry was an absolutely delectable culinary creation. That little ring of sweetness was one of the most delicious things I have ever put in my mouth—light, airy and velvety smooth without being too sugary. Chocolate paled in comparison. I thanked Debbie profusely for adding it to our bag. This town just got even better.

On a sugar high from my chocolate tasting and bakery samples, I was feeling energized once again. Debbie and I wandered around town, poking in and out of a variety of shops until dinnertime. We found a restaurant in the *Plaza Mayor* and ordered their Pilgrim's Meal—salad, chicken, dessert, a bottle of *vino tinto* and, of course, bread. Basic, but satisfying.

Debbie regaled me with hilarious stories of her dating life. Being single in New York City could be challenging, she assured me. Navigating through the many dating sites proved tricky. As I listened to her, I tried to imagine myself in the modern dating world. I shuddered at the thought. It sounded exhausting—like weaving through a complicated obstacle course with a lot of booby prizes disguised as golden trophies waiting at the finish line. No thank you. I felt thankful to be married to a good, decent man.

Despite Debbie's humor, I sensed she often felt lonely.

She had experienced a lot of heartache throughout her life—especially the loss of her son, Philip, with whom she had been incredibly close. She worked hard, yet money seemed tight—New York was expensive. But she managed to make this trip work. In fact, she was taking advantage of her newly acquired passport and the Camino was her second big trip out of the United States. Her first trip had been to Costa Rica. Now the Camino seemed to really have ignited her love of travel and adventure.

I noticed that in the days since I first met Debbie, only a few short weeks ago, she seemed more confident and sure of herself. She seemed less reliant on help from others and her body language appeared stronger and more positive. I thought back to the morning after I met Debbie, when she sat at a table outside a café and tearfully confessed that she didn't think she could finish the Camino. This wasn't the same woman before me now. She was killing it. And I was thrilled for her. And even happier to think that we might reach Santiago together.

Alfie, on the other hand, probably wasn't going to catch up with us. He sent me a text earlier in the day apologizing for not showing up in León, saying he had a little too much fun with his friends and didn't want to meet Laura in his condition. Understandable, I thought. I told him that I would miss watching him spar with Debbie and promised that we would raise a toast to him, a member of our Camino family. I told him I was sad I wasn't able to say goodbye in person and wished him luck on the rest of his Camino.

Debbie and I commiserated over Alfie's absence during dinner, but I enjoyed my one-on-one time with Debbie and came away from our meal feeling like I had a deeper understanding of who she was. Exhausted after our long day, we said goodnight. We wouldn't be staying in the same town the following night, so we wished each other a *Buen Camino* for our walk the next day.

Day 23

I didn't want to leave Astorga quite yet. The bakery where Debbie found those yummy *Roscas Maragatas* didn't open until 10:30 this morning. But, alas, at 8:30, after eating a quick breakfast in the hotel dining room, I had to say goodbye to this charming little hamlet and start walking. I would look for more *Roscas Maragatas* in Rabanal del Camino, today's destination.

I was thrilled to be wearing my hiking shoes again for my 13.5-mile walk. My blisters were healing nicely and my knee was improving, too. And I was happy that I wasn't the only one on the mend. Earlier that morning, Debbie and I received a WhatsApp message from Laura:

Hey buddies—have woke this morning with no pain...
trying not to be too excited. OMG I could be walking
again Sunday no problem. Keeping fingers crossed.
Have a fab day both of you. Keep safe. Xx

I prayed this would hold true. Laura had been trying to stay positive, keeping up with her daily yoga practice, journaling and enjoying multiple *cafés con leche*. But I also knew she was anxious to be on her way again.

The weather today was sunny, with a chlorine blue sky and large cotton-white clouds dancing in the wind. It was warm enough to wear shorts—but not hot enough for me to walk without my long-sleeve quarter zip. The vistas were suddenly vastly more interesting now that I was out of the flat stretch of the *Meseta*. Every few kilometers I passed through a small village or hamlet and admired the modest stone houses, with their colorful kelly green or robin egg blue doors. I marveled at the rolling hills and the variety of foliage, happy to see the tapestry of landscapes once again after the monotony of the *Meseta*.

Almost eight miles into my walk I entered the tiny town of El Ganso. Directly in front of me stood the tiny *Mesón Cowboy*, a bar offering *bocadillos, empanadas, tortilla Española* and *café*. Bright blue doors adorned the entrance and the bar's offerings were painted on the doors in bright yellow lettering. There was an outdoor patio crowded with pilgrims, always a welcome sight. And the food looked delicious. I definitely had to stop and experience this place for myself.

I ordered a *bocadillo* of *jamón serrano*—my usual. My mouth watered as I watched the man behind the counter cut into a thick slice of fresh bread and carve a generous helping of the cured ham for me. The *bocadillos* here were all made to order and the freshness was worth the wait.

With my food in hand, I stepped outside to find a table on the patio. Lo and behold, there was Debbie—but, of course—sitting with a few pilgrims, talking a mile a minute. She greeted me with a huge smile and I was soon thrilled to hear that she was having no issues walking that day. Debbie was going to end up in a town a little further ahead of me that night—she was feeling *that* good—so I was glad I got to accidentally bump into her here in El Ganso. Especially since she was leaving in a few minutes.

So I found a table nearby, took off my pack and soaked up the sunshine while savoring every bite of my sandwich. I also struck up a conversation with a few young women sitting at the table next to me. They both looked to be in their mid-20s and I learned that Page was from Florida and Talley lived in the Bay Area, not far from my home in California. We even discovered that we had a few friends in common. I knew several of the families she grew up with in Piedmont, a tiny city about 15 miles east of San Francisco. What a small world!

Talley told me that she and Page were also going to be in Rabanal del Camino tonight. They'd found a place to stay that they were really excited about. Apparently the innkeeper was American and had walked the Camino a few years ago. When she passed through Rabanal del Camino, she saw the inn for sale and decided to buy it. So now the woman runs *The Stone Boat*, which Talley and Page strongly encouraged me to check out when I arrived.

About five miles later I reached Rabanal del Camino. The Camino path was the main street through town, which made for a semi-dramatic entrance. As I climbed my way up the gentle slope of the thoroughfare, I admired the ancient stone buildings, many of them adorned with bright royal blue or kelly green painted doors and window boxes filled with colorful flowers. What a sight.

Minutes later I looked to my right and noticed a particularly attractive stone building. Next to the front door, hanging on the wall, I saw a simple slate sign with white chalk writing: *The Stone Boat*. Here it was. Of course, I had to stop and take a look.

There in the window I saw another slate sign with chalk writing. It was an excerpt from a poem by David Whyte, Jackson's favorite poet. And the poem was from the book *Pilgrim* that Jackson had given me for my birthday just a few months ago. He wanted me to have it before I embarked on my journey.

Santiago

The road seen, then not seen, the hillside
hiding then revealing the way you should take,
the road dropping away from you as if leaving you
to walk on thin air, then catching you, holding you up,
when you thought you would fall,
and the way forward always in the end
the way that you followed, the way that carried you
into your future, that brought you to this place,
no matter that it sometimes took your promise from you,
no matter that it had to break your heart along the way:
the sense of having walked from far inside yourself
out into the revelation, to have risked yourself
for something that seemed to stand both inside you
and far beyond you, that called you back
to the only road in the end you could follow, walking
as you did, in your rags of love and speaking in the voice
that by night became a prayer for safe arrival...

I was absolutely stunned. Had I not struck up a conversation with Talley and Page, I may not have noticed this window. I wouldn't have been keeping my eye out for *The Stone Boat*. But I *did* talk with them—and I even found out I had friends in common with Talley! Seeing this poem by David Whyte only reinforced my belief in the whole *It's a Camino thing*—those random encounters with a stranger who's somehow connected to you, the signs you see along the path that have a special, almost mystical, resonance with you, the song that suddenly pops up

189

on your playlist with lyrics that perfectly fit what you've just been contemplating.

When these experiences start piling up, it can't help but feel magical. And at that moment, as I re-read David Whyte's poem, I felt Jackson with me, lifting me up and encouraging me. My body shivered, chills running through me.

Feeling newly energized, I continued my walk until I reached the edge of town, where I found my hotel. *La Posada de Gaspar* was a charming little inn. And despite having to lug my duffel bag up the steep staircase, I was thrilled with my large, brightly lit room. It was spacious enough for a small family, as it was equipped with two double beds and a twin pushed up against a wall. Crisp white linens, attractive wrought iron headboards and rich hardwood floors gave the room enormous appeal. I happily unpacked my things, showered, then headed downstairs to the hotel's outdoor patio to enjoy the sunshine.

I connected to the Wi-Fi and saw I had a WhatsApp message from Dan. I'd messaged him before I left this morning to see how he was doing and to find out if he'd heard from his boss about getting the extra days off of work to reach Santiago. He replied:

> *Emi and I decided to go for it! Work said no, but there's no sadness here. I found my way before I got to the end.*

Dan certainly sounded happy. Meeting Emi seemed to take the sting out of not being able to reach Santiago. But I still felt sad for him. I knew he wanted to finish.

Later that afternoon I was ready to explore the town. I couldn't stop thinking about those *Roscas Maragatas*. I was on a mission to find them again. I weaved in and out of the narrow streets of Rabanal del Camino—there weren't many—seeing some familiar pilgrim faces and noting that the town was not yet abuzz with activity. *Siesta* time was not quite over.

But I found a market that was half the size of today's hotel room. And they were open for business. I walked in, hoping I would find my treats. But the place had very minimal inventory. I was out of luck. I asked the shopkeeper where I might find some *Roscas Maragatas.* Her answer left me crestfallen. She told me that those bakery treats are only found in Astorga—and unique to that particular bakery. I would have to return to Astorga if I ever wanted to taste them again. How unbelievably sad!

As shops began opening their doors again, the streets started to fill up with people. The small town became alive. As I walked back towards my hotel, I saw Talley and Page sitting at an outdoor table drinking a glass of wine. They motioned for me to join them and I happily accepted their invitation. I enjoyed a glass of *vino* with them and raved about my experience at *The Stone Boat.* But I left once I finished my wine because I wanted to hear the singing at the vespers service in the tiny Catholic church around the corner.

I loved this particular church. It was plain and unadorned—a stark contrast to all the ornate churches I'd come across so far. I found great beauty in its simplicity and I felt soothed listening to the mellifluous sounds of the music. After another long day of walking, this was a restorative place to end my day.

Eventually I became hungry again. My *bocadillo* from earlier had filled me up for hours. But I was ready to eat dinner, so I returned to my room, grabbed my Kindle and headed downstairs. The dining room was closed until breakfast the next morning, but the innkeeper directed me to a small area with a few scattered tables in front of the hotel bar. A young Asian man who appeared to be a fellow pilgrim was sitting by himself at another table nearby. I nodded hello. He responded by sticking his head back into his book.

I ordered my pilgrim's meal—*ensalada, pollo, postre, pan y vino tinto*—salad, chicken, dessert, bread and red wine. I'd finished *Where the Crawdads Sing* a few days ago, so I opened my Kindle and started a new book. I decided to dive into Takashi's favorite book, *Siddhartha*, since I'd never read it before. I also knew Jackson loved it.

Once my meal arrived I was enjoying my book in the relatively quiet setting when, out of the corner of my eye, I noticed a man enter the hotel. He saddled up to a barstool, his back directly in front of my table. I heard him order a whiskey with an accent I didn't recognize. I looked up to peer at him more closely and could see that he was in his late-30s, early-40s. Just as I was looking at him, he turned around to survey his surroundings. He was attractive, with close-cropped medium brown hair and a light facial scruff. It looked like he hadn't shaved for a few days. Our eyes met and he acknowledged my gaze with a friendly smile. Then he returned to his drink as I resumed my reading.

A few minutes later, I sensed that he was looking around the room again. Was he looking for company, I wondered? Maybe he was a pilgrim looking to connect with a fellow traveler. As I was contemplating whether or not I should say anything, he promptly got up and left the bar. Oh, well. Back to *Siddhartha*.

To my surprise, the man returned to the bar a few minutes later and ordered another whiskey. Once again he turned to look around the room. It was still just the Asian man and me at our lonely tables. But this time I spoke up. I soon found out that indeed he was a pilgrim. I asked if he'd like to join me at my table. And this is how I met Florian, the handsome man from Austria.

He asked if I'd also like a whiskey. Being more of a tequila lover, I rarely ordered whiskey. But why not? Plus, Spain wasn't known for their tequila, and I hadn't been able to find a decent tasting one since I arrived.

We ended up talking for several hours, deeply engrossed in conversation. Florian was charming and easy to talk with. He listened attentively and intently as I spoke, his eyes fixed on mine with a warmth that I found both exhilarating and unsettling. I learned that he had walked part of the Camino 14 years ago and was just now coming back to finish it. He told me he thought the Camino had changed dramatically since then. He found it far more commercial and crowded. He also noted that he'd encountered very few Americans and no Asians on his first trip. This time, he'd met several Americans and had seen large groups of Asians walking together.

"You don't seem American," Florian remarked.

"What do you mean?" I asked, somewhat confused.

"So many Americans are loud and abrasive."

Florian certainly didn't hold back his opinions. And he didn't seem concerned that his observation just might offend me, even though he didn't lump me in with the masses. How would he like it if I made some gross generalization about the characteristics of Austrian people?

We talked about the various ways that pilgrims walk

the Camino and Florian seemed to have disdain for those who didn't carry everything on their backs. I listened and didn't comment. He was entitled to his opinions and I was interested to hear them. Florian would surely consider me a *plastic* pilgrim, a term I first heard from Debbie. She learned about this from a group of pilgrims who told her these types of *peregrinos* aren't *real* pilgrims because they don't carry all of their possessions on their backs and often opt to stay in private rooms. They are missing out on all the things one might encounter with shared lodgings—the good along with the bad. From sharing a pleasant meal together and feeling a sense of community, to putting up with loud snoring and unpleasant body odors.

As I listened to Florian rail against *plastic pilgrims*, I realized that no matter where we are in this world, even on this glorious Camino, we all have to deal with judgment. It's human nature. Our job is to learn how to not internalize it. I was okay with my decisions. But I was not eager to get into a conversation justifying those decisions. So I simply chose not to engage.

Instead we started talking with the three older men sitting at the table next to us. They'd arrived at some point without me noticing and soon let us know they were locals. They encouraged us to try a drink found only in their little town and offered us a shot glass of some unknown concoction. Not wanting to offend them, Florian and I obliged. And it wasn't bad. It tasted similar to limoncello, but markedly stronger and not as sweet. But I definitely didn't need another. Besides, it suddenly felt late and I needed to get to bed in preparation for a long walk the next day.

Florian looked at his watch and jumped up. He didn't realize how late it was. He said he only had a few minutes before curfew and he'd be locked out from his *albergue* if he didn't return in time. The night had flown by. What started out as a quiet, uneventful night turned into a memorable chance encounter with someone who I connected with immediately. In some ways, I felt like I was back in college, meeting a handsome man in a bar and enjoying a night together. Florian somehow made me feel young, attractive and carefree again. I thanked him for a lovely time and we said goodnight, before he rushed back to his *albergue*, hopefully without missing his curfew.

Day 24

I awoke to another brilliant blue sky, ready to attack my 16-mile day. The air was crisp and cool when I departed a little after 8:00, but I warmed up quickly as I made a steady climb for the first eight miles or so. My hiking boots didn't irritate my blisters yesterday, so I went back to them again today—while also packing my knee brace, just in case. I was feeling excited to reach the famed *Cruz de Ferro*, a simple iron cross located at the highest elevation point on the Camino Francés. It was about a mile past the town of Foncebadón, which was just under four miles from Rabanal del Camino, today's starting point.

Many pilgrims bring a stone from home or find one along the Camino and carry it with them on their journey. Then when they finally reach the big rock mound at *Cruz de Ferro*, the pilgrim is ready to offer their stone contribution to the sacred hill. Why do pilgrims do this? I've read many accounts, but I think the website *dothecamino.com* sums it up best:

> *Some carry stones (traditionally that they brought from home) along the Camino as a symbol of the burdens they bear in life. Others carry the stone as an act of penance for the sins they have committed (by making their backpack heavier and therefore making the walk to St. James more difficult). Still others will carry a stone in remembrance of a deceased loved one.*

Some choose to never reveal why they are carrying their stone, because of the deep emotional significance it holds.

As I prepared for the Camino, I wanted to select a stone from a place that was meaningful to me. Having spent many happy family times in the La Quinta, California area, I decided I would look for a stone from that corner of the world. I found the perfect stone on the picturesque Painted Canyon trail, a hike featuring ladders, slot canyons and gorgeous views of the Salton Sea. My purpose for carrying the stone was to leave a little tangible piece of myself on the Camino. For me, the stone symbolized the realization of a long-held dream. I wanted my rock to share space with those left by *peregrinos* of the past and with those yet to be placed in the future.

But when I finally arrived at the *Cruz de Ferro*, I was slightly underwhelmed. Maybe my expectations were too high. After reading about it online and in my guide book, I pictured something more...*grand.* Maybe I'd been conditioned to think big by all the massive cathedrals I'd seen over the last several weeks. But the cross and mound of rocks surrounding it were much smaller than I had envisioned. Knowing how many pilgrims walk the Camino each year left me wondering where all the rocks were. Did someone clean them up every few months? Would I ever be able to find my rock if I were to return a few years later? I'd marked it with my name, hometown and year. I wanted to believe that if I ever returned, I could find it once again.

I realized that it was the actual placement of my stone, the letting go, that was significant about this moment. Still, I somehow felt disappointed. Or rather, I didn't feel as emotional as I thought I would—or *should.* All around me I saw various pilgrims either praying in groups or kneeling by themselves, some crying softly as they placed their stones. I knew many pilgrims carried a lot of sadness with them—loss of a loved one, loss of a job, loss of self—and perhaps placing a stone at this cross stirred up deeper emotions for them. Whatever the case, I couldn't force myself to feel a certain way—I just had to recognize my reaction and move on.

As I continued on my way, I was struck by the gorgeous scenery. I was walking on a wide dirt path, with lush foliage on either side of me in candy apple reds, bright yellow and several shades of green. I passed mooing cows chewing on high grass and marveled at the majestic beauty of the *montes de León* in the distance, rising inexorably through the puffy clouded sky. I inhaled the sweet floral aromas as I listened to my unlabored rhythmic breathing. I was all alone. No pilgrims in sight, either behind or ahead of me. Pure joy.

I thought about last night with Florian. I could feel a mutual attraction—and it rattled me. On one hand, I liked the feeling of excitement and mystery of being with an attractive stranger who looked at me in a way that made me feel desirable and beautiful. Something about Florian sparked a flame in me. It was nice to have someone see me with fresh eyes—to notice me in a way that any husband of 30 years might not. For one innocent night, I vividly remembered what it was like to be Margarita 35 years ago.

After walking around five miles, I reached the tiny village of El Acebo. I wasn't far from my final destination of Molinaseca, only about four or five more miles, but I read that the descent was steep and could prove challenging. I decided to get a coffee and rest a bit before I forged on.

Outside the café, I recognized a pilgrim who I often saw on my daily walks. Mark invited me to join him at his table and I happily obliged. He was an older gentleman—late 60s, maybe early 70s—and he was walking the Camino for the second time. He appeared to be in excellent shape and often bypassed me with his brisk footsteps. As we were chatting about our day and our plans for the evening, I heard a familiar booming voice behind me. It sounded just like Arnold Schwarzenegger. I turned around to find Danish Big Michael jauntily walking towards me, a huge smile plastered on his face.

"Michael!" I yelled excitedly.

"Oh, hey, Margarita!" he called back, his huge dimples now even more pronounced.

I got up to give him a big hug.

"I didn't think I was ever going to see you again."

I hadn't seen him since Belorado two weeks ago. I knew he walked fast, often covering 25-30 miles in a day, so I didn't hold out much hope of a reunion. Big Michael explained that he had taken several rest days and was just now catching up. He, too, would be staying in Molinaseca that night. What a happy coincidence. I finished up my coffee and told him I'd hopefully see him later in Molinaseca before I continued on to complete my final stage of the day.

Just outside El Acebo, I noticed a sculpture of a bicycle. I stopped to read the placard below and saw that it was a memorial for a biker killed on the Camino. No surprise. The roads here looked steep, windy and treacherous. What a tragic loss. I decided to take an alternate, quieter, route of the Camino rather than walk on the one that hugged the road.

Brierley's Camino guidebook did not exaggerate the

difficulty of the descent on this alternate route. The terrain was exceedingly steep, brimming with large rocks that were a challenge for me to navigate. I had to focus intently on each step to avoid twisting an ankle or slipping and falling on the scrabbly pathway. Beads of sweat pooled at my neck and my breathing became short and ragged. This was not a relaxing, peaceful walk. Not even close. It was a far cry from the stretch a few miles back, when I was blissfully enjoying the picturesque scenery.

To make matters worse, my knee began to ache. I stopped to retrieve the brace from my pack and secured it tightly around my joint. Now I felt like I was walking at a snail's pace, seemingly making very little progress towards my destination.

Finally, at a little after 2:00, I was rewarded for my efforts when I arrived in lovely Molinaseca. The town of approximately 800 people sits on the banks of the beautiful río Maruelo, which sparkled in the sunshine as I crossed over the stone bridge above it. I noticed several people eating and drinking while basking in the sun at outdoor tables overlooking the river. I wanted to hurry up and unload my pack so I could shower and head back out to enjoy the idyllic setting.

I was staying at the *Hostal el Palacio*, located right next to the bridge and easy to find. I checked in, quickly ran through my unpacking/organizing end-of-the-day routine, showered and then made a beeline for the riverfront restaurant I spied on my way into town. As soon as I walked on the patio of the *Meson Puente Romano*, I saw Big Michael looking jovial and relaxed, sipping a large mug of beer. He waved me over, his bright blue eyes illuminated in the shimmering sunlight, and I happily took a seat beside him. I learned a little more about him as we soaked in the warmth of the sun.

Big Michael was retired and now spent his time traveling the world. He wasn't married and didn't have children, so he had the freedom to go wherever and whenever he pleased. He seemed to thrive on adventure and new experiences. I could sense his genuine sense of gratitude for being able to see so much of the world and meet people from all over the globe. Big Michael exuded warmth and positivity. Everyone he met seemed to like him immediately.

As we whiled away the late afternoon hours, a stream of familiar faces joined us at our table. First Florian appeared, his eyes twinkling as he said hello. My stomach did a little flip when he approached our table, but I tried to act calm and collected. Then came a family of three from England—Tom, his wife Adriana and their son John. Debbie briefly introduced me to this family back in León, and I'd seen them every now and then since. But I hadn't ever really had a conversation beyond hello. Then Debbie herself arrived. She was staying in Ponferrada, a city just over four miles up the road from where we were. But she messaged me earlier saying she didn't like it and wanted to take a cab back to join us for dinner.

Then, to my utter disbelief, Alfie turned up with Almandine, the young French girl I met in Terradillos. He must have walked some long distances during the last few days to have caught up to us. Just like Big Michael, I thought I might not see Alfie again. But time and time again, I learned that this is one of the beautiful surprises of the Camino—people weaving in and out of your journey all along the way. Before you know it, the Camino feels like an extended road trip full of friends, acquaintances and familiar faces.

So there we were, all nine of us—most of us complete strangers a few weeks ago. Sitting and laughing in the sun at this charming spot in Molinaseca. On another brilliant day in Spain.

We pushed a few tables together to make room for everyone, which led to a late afternoon filled with jokes, storytelling and lots of laughter. And cigarettes. Yes, it seemed like the majority of pilgrims I encountered enjoyed their *cigarillos*. I still had a hard time sitting amidst the plumes of smoke, but I was most definitely in the minority. So I withstood the discomfort, silently appreciating our no-smoking policies at the restaurants and bars back home in California.

Adriana told us how someone in their *albergue* peed on her backpack in the middle of the night. She wasn't sure if it was on purpose or accidental—maybe some disoriented *peregrino* got up in a sleepy or drunk fog and thought he was peeing in the bathroom instead of Adriana's bag. Either way, she was disgusted and horrified. And it prompted the family to look for private rooms for the remainder of the trek.

At one point, Florian pulled me aside.

"Are you having your bag transferred ahead every day?"

Somewhat surprised by his question, I answered, "Yes."

"I thought about our conversation last night. I noticed you didn't say anything when we were talking about this. I thought you might be doing that," he said with a slight smirk.

Not feeling like I had to justify my decision to him, I simply confirmed his suspicion. He smiled warmly at me, but part of me felt rankled by his implicit judgment. I got even more riled up when he mocked me for using a meal voucher for dinner, saying I should choose where I want to eat. Even though I could admit to myself that he had a point, I didn't like how he made me feel. Besides, for the first part of the Camino—back when I was getting my bearings and hadn't met any friends yet—finding a place to eat dinner was one less thing for me to contend with.

To add even more fuel to the growing fire in my belly, Florian questioned my *real* reason for walking the Camino.

"There *has* to be more to your story," he insisted. As if I needed a *story* to walk the Camino. He had a hard time believing that my husband would just *allow* me to go off on my own. *What?* Who was this guy to say my reasons for walking just didn't measure up? I told him exactly what I was thinking, and he could tell I was angry. He tried to laugh it off, saying he was only teasing. Maybe I didn't get his Austrian sense of humor. I told him his jokes didn't translate well and was relieved when our group got up to head to dinner together. Florian later told me he'd chosen to stay in a private room that night so he didn't have to deal with a curfew and could get a decent night's sleep. I guess he thought it was okay for *real* pilgrims to do this every now and then.

Despite this episode, dinner was hugely entertaining. It was wonderful to be surrounded by so many familiar faces. And I was thrilled to be reunited with Debbie and Alfie again, our little Camino family.

After dinner Debbie took a taxi back to her place in Ponferrada. Adriana said goodnight and returned to her hotel, just a short distance away. I walked with the rest of the group—Big Michael, Almandine, Alfie, Florian, English Tom and John—up the narrow main street to an outdoor bar a few blocks from the river.

I sat across from Florian, and he repeatedly tried to

catch my eye. He tapped my leg with his foot under the table and smiled warmly at me. What did he want, I thought? I needed to remove myself from this situation. Alfie, sitting at the end of the table in between us, noticed our interaction. Then *he* tapped my leg. I had a feeling Alfie didn't care much for Florian.

"I'm really glad I caught up with you Margarita," Alfie said.

Sweet Alfie. "Me, too," I replied.

I stood up. All of a sudden, I felt exhausted. And my emotions were swirling with confusion. Last night I found Florian attractive and interesting. But tonight, although he still looked handsome, he seemed smug and critical. I needed to leave. I said goodnight and headed back to my hotel. The next day would be the longest walk of the Camino so far.

Day 25

I awoke early and peered out my window. I could see the sun already shining brightly under a brilliant cloudless blue sky. It was supposed to be warmer today, so I slipped on my shorts and a few layered tops. I laced my hiking shoes, grabbed a banana from the hotel restaurant and set off around 8:00.

I had a 20-mile day ahead of me.

But I felt mentally ready and physically strong. My knee wasn't bothering me, despite the challenging descent yesterday. And my blisters were continuing to heal nicely. Fingers crossed.

The scenery during my walk today reminded me of California, with its rolling hills and acres of vineyards. As I took in the glorious sights, my mind wrangled with the *plastic vs. real* pilgrim topic. Was I a *plastic* pilgrim after all? Was I missing out on the *real* Camino? Since I was getting my bag transferred each day, was my pilgrimage a lesser experience? Was this some kind of competition for who has the most authentic pilgrimage? Would I choose to do things differently next time? Did this issue rankle me because Florian brought it up? How come I was letting what *he* thought bother me so much?

As I pondered these questions, I knew in my heart that, despite not carrying everything on my back and staying in shared lodgings, I was still experiencing all the things I hoped I would—a solo journey, time for self-reflection, an opportunity to connect with people from all over the world, a physical and mental challenge, and a chance to do all of this in *España*. I had to trust that I was doing what worked well for me. I just needed to figure out how to tune out the judgments of other people.

I also thought about how my Camino was about to change. Tom would be joining me in four days. Six days after that we'd be entering Santiago together before continuing on to Finisterre. That was the plan, anyway. And as much as I was excited to see Tom, I didn't feel ready to share my journey. I cherished this time on my own. I wasn't sure how I would feel about giving that up.

And I worried that we'd be in very different places on our first day of walking together. He was sure to be jet-lagged and dealing with the novelty and challenges of the Camino, just as I had several weeks ago. Was he going to take over and set the tone and pace for the remainder of my journey? I was feeling strong. I loved walking at my own pace, stopping or not stopping whenever I pleased. Soon I'd have to consider Tom's needs too. He might want to stop and rest or eat when I'd prefer to just keep moving. Of course I *would* stop.

But I wanted a little more time to be selfish and just think about myself. I was enjoying not worrying about anyone else's needs but my own. I didn't want this forever. I loved Tom and my life with him. And I felt lucky to be with a man who loved me enough to support my dreams.

And yet, I still wanted more alone time.

I'd also have to share my room. I'd gotten efficient with my daily unpacking/packing routine. And I liked to spread my stuff out. Now I'd have to share my space. How was *that* going to work?

I was excited to introduce Tom to my new friends. I knew they were going to love him, with his larger-than-life personality, his engaging smile and his quick wit. He had a hysterical way of saying things that people often think in their heads but wouldn't dare speak out loud. He's a master of shock humor—but good-natured and always with a twinkle in his eye. His ability to make me laugh was a huge reason I fell in love with him. And underneath all of his humor, he has an enormous, sensitive heart and generous spirit.

And Tom is an excellent storyteller. He can remember jokes and tell them with perfect timing. He captivates his listeners and parties are always more fun when he is around. I often avoid telling a story when he's around because he tells it so much better.

But here in Spain I felt like I was finding my voice. It felt good. I could tell a story and not feel like I was fighting to be heard. It's not like I thought of myself as a quiet little mouse, afraid to speak up. But I have a soft voice and it can be tough sharing a stage with a man with such a strong, dynamic personality.

Maybe most importantly, I wondered how we would mesh psychologically. Having experienced multiple moments of Camino magic and meeting so many remarkable people along the way, I felt like I was fully immersed in the spirit of the Camino. I was looking forward to reaching Santiago with many of the people who shared these experiences with me from the beginning. Would Tom be able to understand the emotional significance when we entered Santiago? It wouldn't be fair of me to expect him to completely comprehend my range of emotions. But I wanted him to *get it*—to get *me*. In a matter of days I'd have the answers to many of my questions. In the meantime, I wanted to savor every moment I had left by myself.

I strolled into Villafranca del Bierzo at around 2:30 in the afternoon. For the first time since I'd started the Camino, I lost my way and overshot my hotel by about a mile. I had to turn around and backtrack, making my long day even longer. Despite my challenging day—21 miles was my longest walk yet—I didn't feel tired. After 25 days my body had clearly adjusted to walking lengthy distances. I loved how strong I felt. I checked into the *Parador de Villafranca*, where Debbie was also staying. The room was pleasant enough, but the hotel was outside of the main part of town. The place seemed quiet and dull, especially after last night's reverie. Today there were no pilgrims in sight. This wasn't the sort of place I loved. At least Debbie was down the hall from me.

We met in the lobby a little after 6:00 and walked into town to find an appealing place for a cocktail before dinner. We ended up at *La P'tit Pause,* a tiny outdoor café run by a charming French man who offered us delicious homemade *sangría.* Alfie soon joined us—what a pleasant surprise!—and our little Camino family was together again. We talked about how much we wanted to reach Santiago together and I felt hopeful that we'd make this happen.

After dinner at the nearby *Plaza Mayor,* we all headed back to our hotels, ready for some rest after a long day. It was still light out, so it was hard to fathom that it was nearly 10:30. I realized this was why I could never manage to get to sleep much earlier than midnight every night. By the time I got back to my room, read about the next day's hike, prepared my pack, laid out my clothes for the next morning and caught up on my blog writing, it was past 1:00 a.m. when I finally turned off my light to get some sleep. What was I thinking? I had another huge day ahead of me and prayed I wouldn't be too tired in the morning.

Day 26

Thanks to my late night, I slept in a little longer than usual today. I needed the rest. I had a 19-mile walk ahead of me, the last part of which was apparently a monster uphill climb. I'd mentally prepared for this day though, ever since I realized it would be my last long, tough walk before I reached Santiago. By now I was only a little over 115 miles away. I couldn't believe how far I'd come already.

I left my hotel around 8:30, after a quick breakfast of bread and cheese. Later that day I wrote the following on my blog:

> Looks like my 21-mile day yesterday didn't do any favors for my left heel blister. As good as I felt yesterday, I winced in pain as I put my boots on this morning and thought I better take my Tevas just in case. Good thing I did, as I couldn't bear the pain after the first six miles. I changed shoes and continued on my way for what was going to be my second longest day of walking.
>
> The weather was warm enough for shorts, and the first part of the walk ran alongside a road. At times we had to walk on the road itself with cars whipping by at great speeds, and I intentionally opted not to use my headphones so I could listen for oncoming traffic. I wouldn't say this was the most relaxing way to walk.
>
> I eventually joined in rhythm with a Korean man

who spoke very little English—just enough so we could generally communicate. He commented that I walked very fast. Then I had to laugh because, out of the blue, he asked me how old I was. Age seems irrelevant on the Camino, and people don't generally ask this. So being somewhat surprised by the question, I asked him to guess. He took a close look at me and scanned me up and down. Finally, he said, "Old face, strong body— 45." You gotta love the bluntness that comes with language barriers. The whole interaction made me smile.

About 12 miles into my walk, I met Debbie at the albergue where she was staying for the night to say a quick hello before my climb to O Cebreiro. She'd decided to do the climb the next morning, as she's an early riser and thought she would have more energy then.

When I first met Debbie, she gave me the impression that she was going to do the Camino at a much slower pace than me. But she's been amazing every day, and she's absolutely killing it. And she hasn't gotten one blister! Incredible! It's been such a blessing to meet her, and I'm so happy that we can share the Camino together. She is absolutely hysterical, fun, thoughtful and kind. I can't wait to walk into Santiago with her as she and I have shared this crazy journey all the way from Day 8 in Nájera.

After saying goodbye to Debbie, I mentally geared up to attack the climb to O Cebreiro. It ended up being seven miles of extremely vertical and mostly rocky terrain, with an elevation gain of almost 2,000 feet. One way to make this trek is to go on horseback. Many *people opt to do this, and after making the climb, I can see why it's an appealing idea. So not only did I have to navigate around rocks, I had to avoid stepping in the several mounds of horse dung all along the way. It was definitely an exercise in focus and determination. But the reward was worth the effort.*

The views from above were absolutely magnificent. The light and the mist from above made the vista look like an impressionist painting, too hard to adequately capture with my iPhone. And the little town of O Cebreiro was enchanting. It was cold at the top of the mountain, and my room was like a cabin you might find in Tahoe—wood floors and furnishings, big blankets and warm lighting...

I checked into the *Hotel O Cebreiro* around 3:30, feeling elated that I had made it through my last long, challenging walk. I was now in the region of Galicia, the region known for its *pulpo* (octopus) and *Albariño* (white wine), as well as a delicious dessert—the *torta de Santiago*, an almond tart with caster sugar sprinkled on top in an outline of the cross of the Knights Templar.

I thought about the seven-mile uphill climb I'd just completed. I was struck by the fact that, despite the challenges of rocks and horse manure, I had trucked up that mountain. I felt strong, nimble and energetic. No heavy breathing. I focused on finding a good foothold, then just seemed to glide up the ascent. I marveled at how far I'd come since Day 1. And I said another prayer of thanks for my trusty Tevas. There is no way I could've walked without them.

My room thankfully had a bathtub, so I once again attended to my blisters. It was looking like I'd have to resume my first aid/bandage routine. Not fun. I showered, changed into my non-hiking evening uniform and decided I was too tired to deal with laundry in my room. I was relieved to learn there was a place a few doors down from my hotel where you could leave your laundry and pick it up cleaned and folded a few hours later. Perfect.

After dropping off my clothes, I headed back to my room so I could get Wi-Fi and try to FaceTime with my son, Charlie. I'd texted with Tom and all of my children every so often throughout my trip, and I FaceTimed with Tom, Mia and Jackson once or twice. But Charlie's work schedule was demanding and we had difficulty finding a time when we could do a phone call. I missed hearing his voice and seeing his handsome face. We decided this would be a good time to try, so I attempted to place the call. But my room's Wi-Fi was practically non-existent, and the call kept dropping. I didn't have a phone plan during my time in Spain, so I needed to make this work.

I decided to walk outside the hotel to see if it was any better there. But the call still kept dropping. Frustrated and disappointed, I looked up from my phone. To my happy surprise, I saw Alfie just entering town. When he found out what I was trying to do, he offered me his phone, telling me not to worry since he had an international calling plan. Sweet Alfie.

After I dialed the number, I handed the phone back to Alfie so he and Charlie could catch up—it had been a few years since they'd seen or spoken to one another. Charlie couldn't believe that Alfie and I had met halfway across the world.

Once the two old frat brothers were finished talking, I happily chatted with Charlie until I felt like I got my motherly fix.

After hanging up, I thanked Alfie profusely for making my day. He made me one happy mama! With a big smile, he set off to find a room for the night. Before he left, I asked him to join me later for dinner.

While I waited for Alfie to get settled and showered, I joined a group of Brazilian pilgrims for a drink at an outdoor table in front of my hotel. It was cold at this higher elevation. I needed to pull out my down jacket as an extra layer to keep me warm enough. But the magnificent views were worth the slight discomfort.

The Brazilians were eventually ready to eat and invited me to join them. But I declined and said I was going to wait for Alfie. So by the time he arrived, it was just the two of us for dinner. Being alone with Alfie for the first time gave me a chance to learn even more about him. Having already formed a close connection, our conversation bypassed any surface chatter and delved into deeper, more revealing exchanges.

I told Alfie about my *plastic pilgrim* conversation with Florian and how it rankled me.

"I wouldn't let that bother you, Margarita. There was something about him I didn't like," Alfie confessed.

"Oh, yeah? What didn't you like?"

"He seems to be quite judgmental. Not like other pilgrims. I don't know—I can't tell you exactly what it was."

"Hmmm. That's interesting. I know you seem to be able to read people well." I let Alfie's comment sink in. "Fuck Florian then," I said resolutely, relishing the sound of my crass alliteration.

Alfie smiled at this, happy to see me move on from the issue. I then turned my attention back to Alfie.

214

Clearly a sensitive, creative and soulful young man, Alfie yearned to live his life as an artist through his writing and music. But as with so many artists, the struggle was figuring out how to do this in a financially sustainable way—a situation that was complicated by the fact that he was the son of a highly success-ful businessman who, I gathered, found it challenging to have a son with such different aspirations.

Alfie divulged his past struggles with feeling *unseen* by both of his parents—not being recognized for his genuine self and being encouraged to follow a more conventional path. It sounded like he had a tumultuous and complicated relationship with his parents. I didn't get the sense that he felt particularly close to either one of them. Although his parents were appar-ently coming around and learning to embrace Alfie for his many gifts and talents, I could see that the experience had taken a toll on him.

I learned about his history of depression and his family's attempt to help him when he would dive deeply into months of paralyzing darkness. I pictured his parents desperately search-ing for answers and trying *anything* they could do to help re-lieve their beautiful son's pain. But as much as they tried, these waves of depression would suddenly emerge, a force too great to easily overcome. Alfie struggled with questions of self-worth and I found it painful to hear his vicious self-criticism. He was clearly a kind, genuine, intelligent and wise young man. I want-ed him to see what I saw.

The cycle seemed to continue in irregular, unpredictable patterns. Life seemed uncertain. Alfie could be rolling along, feeling good—then, without warning, his depression would rear its ugly head. He'd suddenly withdraw and isolate, no longer able to connect with the outside world as he dealt with tortuous self-loathing and a hateful internal chorus. He spoke of his time at USC, admitting that he should have chosen a smaller, liberal arts college. The highly-magnified, image-conscious atmosphere—teeming with ambitious Type A go-getters, Division 1 athletes and Greek life activities—was, in retrospect, clearly not the ideal setting for Alfie.

In fact, the experience propelled him into a downward spiral. He shuttered himself inside his off-campus apartment and completely fell off the radar. He stopped going to classes. He stopped answering texts and phone calls. His concerned friends didn't know how to help. Other people he'd been close to, busy with their own lives, had no idea where he'd disappeared to. Eventually Alfie withdrew from school without any goodbyes. He headed back to London in hopes of figuring out a Plan B. Meanwhile, his younger sister—outgoing, fun-loving and embracing all that USC offered—seemed to be thriving.

Before coming on the Camino, Alfie lived in many places, including South Africa where he focused on his music, performing his freestyle rap with abandon. He loved adventure and the Camino would surely provide a perfect dose of inspiration for his writing and music.

From what I could tell, the Camino was doing wonders for Alfie. He seemed happy, laughing easily as pilgrims shared their funny stories. He seemed at peace. He met other pilgrims effortlessly. And from what I observed, thanks largely to his kindness and acceptance of others, he was well-liked by all those who met him. Most importantly, I think Alfie felt *seen* and appreciated for his genuine self. The Camino appeared to be working its magic on him.

The Alfie I knew on the Camino was starkly different from the troubled soul in the grips of depression—the dark Alfie he told me all about. I worried about what might happen to him when we finished the Camino. I hated the thought of this sweet, caring young man possibly getting swept away into the unforgiving grips of darkness again. I let him know that I cared about him and would only be a phone call away once we eventually went our separate ways.

Despite our obvious age difference, Alfie and I seemed to enjoy each other's company. I rarely thought about the disparity in our age. Instead I appreciated connecting with this old soul, listening to how his mind worked and hearing his observations and reflections about life. There was something about Alfie that felt familiar. Jackson is also an artist who expresses himself through poetry and music. I know he, too, has struggled to navigate his way through our family of hard-driving Type-A personalities. And thankfully, after some rough years, I feel like Jackson has found firm footing within our family, feeling accepted and appreciated for the beautiful human he is.

As for me, I felt like Alfie saw me as *Margarita*—someone other than a wife, mother and caretaker. And somehow I seemed to make Alfie laugh, and we had fun together. Maybe Alfie enjoyed talking with me because he sensed that I saw him for who he truly was and supported who he wanted to become. Whatever the case, we shared a powerful connection.

After dinner, Alfie and I walked the length of the tiny town of O Cebreiro, picking up my clean laundry along the way. We stopped to admire the magnificent sky, streaked with hues of pink and lavender above the mountains all around us. I convinced him to take a picture with me to capture the moment. And with a little good-natured poking, I even managed to elicit a smile from him as a passerby snapped our picture. It was a perfectly lovely evening.

Day 27

I awoke feeling relieved that my long, arduous days of walking seemed to be behind me now. I left my hotel a little after 8:00 and later posted this on my blog:

Galicia is lush, green and gorgeous. Of course, it's that way because of its huge amount of rainfall. Today was no exception, as the rain fell steadily throughout my steep climb down the mountain from O Cebreiro to Triacastela. Thankfully my rain jacket kept me dry. And even though I still couldn't put my hiking shoes on, my Tevas worked great and somehow my socks never became soggy and uncomfortable. I meandered through beautiful tree-lined paths listening to my Spanish guitar playlist. I felt so good that I never even stopped during the 13-mile walk.

I'm staying in an adorable pensión, Casa Simon, right on the Camino. The owner, Natalia, who lives on the top floor, greeted me with a huge smile and a very warm welcome. She then asked if I could please take my shoes off and leave them downstairs, and she gave me paper slippers to use. The place is absolutely spotless, so I can appreciate her wanting to keep all the dirty shoes out of her house. She showed me to my room, and she had already brought my bag inside...I then noticed that there was a little note welcoming me next to a box of cookies made in Galicia. What a warm and thoughtful touch. I love this place!

As I'm writing this, I'm sitting in my cozy bed, the window is open with the diaphanous white curtains swaying in the breeze, and I can hear the rain pouring down. It's lovely. And peaceful. And perfect. I need to remember this feeling when I get home, as I rarely take the time to sit and reflect and write. I find I get easily distracted at home. My to-do list is too long, without leaving enough time for uninterrupted contemplation. This has been one of the greatest gifts of the Camino—the time and space to think and reflect without distraction, interruption and obligation. I know I'm currently living in a little glorious bubble, but I am trying to soak up every second before I return to reality.

My early arrival into Triacastela a little after noon allowed me the luxury of enjoying one such lazy, relaxing afternoon of contemplation. But this was only after my trip to the town's pharmacy to consult with the pharmacist about my blisters. Seems I was all too familiar with first aid offerings in these small town *farmacías* and now fluent in my newly acquired Spanish vocabulary words describing blisters, bandages, needles and ointments. But this was all part of the Camino experience. Or at least it was part of *my* Camino experience.

Undeterred by my blister issue, I happily explored the narrow streets of Triacastela before returning to my room for a few hours rest before dinner. Alfie and I had made plans to meet again for our evening meal, and I was looking forward to more laughter and in-depth conversation.

We met at the *Complexo Parrillada Xacobeo*, a lively restaurant and bar just down the street from my *pensión*. The restaurant name reminded me that I was now in Galicia and would be seeing signs written in the regional dialect of Gallego. I soon learned to pronounce the letter *x* as *sh*. This was a dialect very different from the Spanish I knew.

Alfie and I both seemed to be savoring every moment of the remaining time we had left before reaching Santiago. We had less than 85 miles to go. Even though we both intended to continue on to Finisterre, the flavor of the Camino would surely change after Santiago. Many pilgrims either finish their journey there or opt to ride the bus rather than walk to Finisterre. Plus Tom was showing up in three days, so our group dynamic was bound to change.

Alfie and I talked about the book he was writing about the summer he spent in Florence. He hoped to return to Florence after the Camino and finish it.

"Would you be willing to read my first draft? Can I email it to you? I still have a lot to do on it, but I would love to hear what you think."

"Of course, I would be honored to. When I get home from the Camino and have time to focus on it, I would love to read it."

"Thanks. So Margarita, how are you feeling about seeing Tom in a few days? I can't wait to meet him. I know I'm going to like him."

I shared some of my mixed feelings of sadness about ending my solo Camino and of excitement about being together again after such a long separation. Aflie seemed to empathize with my myriad of emotions.

Not wanting the evening to end, I suggested we walk through town after dinner. Apparently only two bars were open in this tiny town. The first one we entered looked dull and practically empty. We found our only other option, and thankfully the place was lively and filled with a number of what appeared to be local townsfolk.

We ordered two *tintos de verano*, a popular drink in Spain made with red wine and a fizzy soda—most often with *Fanta Limón*. It's also sometimes referred to as the poor man's sangria. I must admit, when I heard the drink is made by simply adding fizzy soda to wine, I thought it sounded pretty gross. But I loved the concoction. And after ordering several of these refreshing Spanish specialities on my trek, I discovered there were some markedly better than others.

Our tiny bar in Triacastela did not disappoint. Alfie and I sipped our drinks leisurely while enjoying light conversation and more laughs. I found it easy being with Alfie and appreciated our alone time together. I liked that he felt he could open up to me.

After an hour or so, it was time to head back to our respective accommodations—each of us lost in thought, comfortable with the silence between us as we strolled slowly in the misty darkness, the rain falling softly all around us.

Part Three

Endings & New Beginnings

Day 28

I awoke today feeling melancholy. This would be my last day walking alone. This part of my Camino, my solo journey, would end when I arrived in Sarria this afternoon. Tomorrow I'd have my first rest day while awaiting Tom's arrival. Then we'd take off the following morning, embarking on our journey to finish the Camino together.

I still felt mixed emotions about his arrival, for all the reasons I had contemplated a few days ago. While I was excited to see Tom and introduce him to my new friends, I knew I would have to make a mental shift and prepare myself to consider someone else's needs and wishes besides my own. And how would his presence affect my now well-established daily rhythm? The dynamics would surely change and I prayed that it would be a smooth transition.

Part of me felt guilty for feeling this way—Tom had been unbelievably supportive of my desire to walk the Camino alone. He had also continued to support me with texts of encouragement along the way. I knew he was looking forward to experiencing part of the journey with me, so I didn't want my concerns to mar our time together. And I didn't want to hurt his feelings, especially knowing how excited he was to join me on this adventure. Our daughter, Mia, had texted me several times saying how much Tom missed me. He wasn't used to being alone—especially for four weeks. Not much of a phone person, he was now calling Mia every other day just to check in. He didn't seem to crave or enjoy solitude the same way I did. Mia had flown up from Los Angeles a few days ago to be with him for Father's Day. She sounded concerned.

"Mom! Dad is eating frozen dinners. He's even eating his gross cream chipped beef."

The "gross cream chipped beef" was something Tom ate as a kid. The nasty dried beef came in a can, to which Tom would add a roux of flour and milk—all of it piled atop a toasted English muffin.

When Jackson, Charlie and Mia were little, I used to go on an annual girls' weekend away with college friends. Tom would inevitably make this for dinner, telling the kids what a treat it was. For years they played along, not wanting to squelch his enthusiasm. Maybe they also didn't want to risk losing their special meal routine when Mom was gone. Dessert for dinner and dinner for dessert. In any case, they didn't care much for the meal these days and it horrified Mia to imagine Tom eating the infamous "gross cream chipped beef" dish now.

I knew Tom missed me. But I also joked that I wasn't sure if he actually missed *me* or just my cooking and general management of our home. Maybe it was a little bit of both. But I wasn't ready to return home to that life yet. I wanted to hold on to *this* piece of my life—an experience I could have all on my own, without sharing with anyone else. I liked that it was all mine. I liked doing exactly what I wanted, when I wanted.

But that part of the journey was ending today.

I noticed I had a message from Alfie. He'd sent me a poem by Khalil Gibran titled *On Marriage*. It perfectly echoed my feelings I shared with Alfie last night about wanting to be independent within the bond of marriage:

Then Almitra spoke again and said, And
what of Marriage, master?
And he answered saying:
You were born together, and together you
shall be forevermore.
You shall be together when the white
wings of death scatter your days.
Ay, you shall be together even in the
silent memory of God.
But let there be spaces in your togetherness,
And let the winds of the heavens dance
between you.

Love one another, but make not a bond
of love:
Let it rather be a moving sea between
the shores of your souls.
Fill each other's cup but drink not from
one cup.
Give one another of your bread but eat
not from the same loaf.
Sing and dance together and be joyous,
but let each one of you be alone,
Even as the strings of a lute are alone
though they quiver with the same music.

Give your hearts, but not into each
other's keeping.
For only the hand of Life can contain
your hearts.
And stand together yet not too near

together:
For the pillars of the temple stand apart,
And the oak tree and the cypress grow
not in each other's shadow

I brought my bag downstairs, found my Tevas and swapped them for my paper slippers before departing the *Casa Simon*. It was a little before 8:00 when I returned to the restaurant from last night. I took my time eating a hard boiled egg, cheese and a large hunk of bread, along with my *café con leche*. I had a short day of walking ahead of me, so I wanted to take my time. I needed to savor every last minute of my day. Sarria was only ten miles away.

I began my walk a little after 9:00 in a light rain. Dressed in pants and my rain jacket, I felt warm and comfortable. I was hyper-aware, ready to relish the sights, sounds and events of the unfolding day. Later I wrote on my blog:

> *...I set out on my short 10-mile walk today and took my time, taking in all the sights around me as the rain fell intermittently throughout the day. I thought about my frame of mind on the first day of the Camino and how it was all so new and exciting and how I didn't know a soul and had to get into a rhythm of walking each day, changing accommodations every night. And how now, 28 days later, it has become such a wonderful routine and way of life: walking for hours every day, taking in the beauty and splendor of the Spanish countryside, running into pilgrim friends, enjoying a morning coffee, relaxing during siesta time and then meeting up with friends at night for cocktails and dinner. I really love*

this lifestyle. I'm not ready for this to end and will be savoring every minute of the last few weeks I'm here.

One of the highlights on my walk today was coming upon a magical oasis for pilgrims, a place where food and rest are offered freely, and people can donate as they wish. The space was filled with comfy couches and a garden full of slate boards with various messages written on them. I spent a long time taking it all in and it moved my soul reading all the beautiful words filled with love and self-empowerment.

Rounding the corner of the Camino's path and suddenly finding this special *donativo* before me was a magically memorable way to mark the last day of my solo journey. I snapped a photo of a few of the slate signs that resonated with me:

Camino

For the highs and lows
And mountains between
Mountains and valleys
And rivers and streams
For where you are now
And where you will go.
For I've started this journey
and I'm feeling the glow,
for blisters are forming
and things have gone wrong.
It's here in this adventure
you will learn to be strong.
You will get where you're going,
Landing where you BELONG

you'll strengthen your body,
soul and mind too
its friendships on the way
that are certainly
TRUE

And this one was on a heart-shaped slate stone, painted bright red:

Of all the amazing things
that I discovered on my Camino
journey, the most important
and my favorite,
is myself

As I left the *donativo*, I turned another corner and headed back on the path to Sarria. To my utter surprise I was suddenly face-to-face with a herd of cows—and they were walking directly towards me on the flagstone path. I instantly stopped, not sure who was going to make the first move. I'd never been so close to a cow, let alone a group of cows. There must have been 15-20 of the moo-dy bovines. I convinced myself they wouldn't be aggressive as I gingerly weaved my way through the crowd. A little excitement for the day!

For the remainder of my walk, I tried to slow my pace and just appreciate all the beauty around me. I took pictures of the lovely tree-lined paths, the robust and colorful pink and light blue hydrangeas, the lush foliage lining the Camino and the little family of ducks swimming in the river near my hotel in Sarria.

I arrived at around 12:30 and found my lodging for the next two nights—the *Hotel Alfonso IX*. Debbie had also booked a room here for the next two nights. She had decided to take a rest day, too, so we could spend more time together.

Since I checked in early, my bag still hadn't arrived. I decided to explore the old part of the city, across the river from my hotel and up a steep flight of stone steps. The steps led to a narrow street, flanked on either side by hostels and *albergues*. The street ran uphill, leading to a small square with a few restaurants busy with outdoor tables filled with customers, many of whom were fellow pilgrims enjoying food and libations. It was also a perfect place to sit and people watch. The street I had just climbed was part of the Camino and it ran smack in the middle of the lively square. I definitely wanted to return here later with Debbie.

Once my bag arrived, I settled into my large room. Not only did it have a nice king-size bed, it also had an adjoining sitting room—without a single chair to sit on, oddly enough. Plus, not one but *two* bathrooms. I chuckled to myself thinking that Tom wasn't really going to get a good sense of Camino life with this fancy room. But he was barely going to spend any time in our room, since he wasn't due to arrive until late tomorrow evening. The plan was to hit the road and start walking early the following morning.

Even though Tom insisted he wanted to walk the next day and didn't want a rest day after his interminably long travel day, I worried that he might have been overconfident in his ability to bounce back after such a grueling trip. He was flying from San Francisco to Paris, Paris to Madrid, Madrid to La Coruña—then an hour-and-a-half drive to Sarria. It sounded *exhausting*. Then to get up and walk 14.5 miles on his first day of the Camino? That could definitely prove challenging. Especially since the longest distance he'd *ever* hiked was just under 10 miles. But he was determined to make it work. And I prayed he would hold up.

After a nice long hot shower, I met Debbie in the lobby of our hotel at around 5:30. We walked to the square I found earlier, since we had learned that many of our pilgrim friends were also staying in Sarria and thought this would be an ideal meeting place. Debbie and I were both ready for a festive evening. For the first time since we began our adventure across Spain, we didn't have to get up early to walk the next day.

We found a table at the *Mesón O Tapas*, the more crowded of the two restaurants at the top of the hill. We ordered *tintos de verano* and they soon arrived in enormous goblets garnished with bright, juicy orange slices and multi-colored straws sticking out of each drink. The festive drinks immediately put us in a celebratory mood.

We were soon joined by Alfie, sporting his usual evening uniform of rolled jeans and the red and navy plaid shirt Charlie's friend had given him back at USC. And accompanying Alfie, to our great delight, was Big Michael, a.k.a. Arnold Schwarzenegger. The two of them had arranged to share a private room that evening at a nearby *albergue*. During the next hour or so, more and more of our pilgrim friends joined the festivities. To keep the party going, we kept pushing tables together to make room for the growing crowd. Among others, we were joined by Almandine from France; Joey, a Canadian man with a zillion tattoos who I'd seen infrequently on the Camino; plus Tom, Adrianna and their son, John, from England. We ordered a bazillion tapas, several rounds of *tintos de verano* and we chatted with several other pilgrims stopping by our table to say hello.

During all the commotion, both Debbie and I noticed the proprietor of the restaurant. He was a short, gray-haired, bespectacled old man, with a paunch protruding from his drab olive green v-neck sweater. He stood outside the restaurant, a frown firmly etched on his face. Debbie became agitated simply looking at him. She proclaimed that she *really* wanted to make this miserable-looking man smile. Fortified by several *tintos de verano*, she accepted my challenge to see if she could elicit even a closed mouth grin from the local curmudgeon.

Alfie heard our exchange and watched with me as Debbie sauntered over to the man, greeting him in her discordant Spanish accent. But her vocabulary didn't extend much beyond *hola*. So she simply began speaking to him in English, acting out her words like a bad game of charades.

It was clear the man didn't speak English. But Debbie's earnest attempt to get through to him—combined with her smile and warmth—did indeed tickle the man. In no time he was grinning from ear to ear. And just like that, Manuel became our friendly, exceedingly attentive host for the evening. Every time he walked by our large table, we all yelled *"Manuel!"* And every time his face lit up with a huge smile.

As the evening progressed and Manuel warmed up to us even more, he offered to let us try his top secret, homemade liqueur. He told us he owned the adjoining hotel and proudly gave us a quick tour, clearly pleased to show off the fruits of his labor. He became our best pal of the evening and I marveled at the outcome of the innocuous challenge Debbie accepted. With her big heart, she made us a new friend.

I was feeling good—happy, energetic and ready to let loose, knowing it was my last solo night on the Camino. I even subjected Alfie and Debbie to my silly *palms down* move I tend to make when I'm in this elevated mood—a little dance I do with my hands when I'm feeling particularly happy.

"Oh no, there go Mom's hands," my kids would say with a smile on their faces. "Watch out!"

Shortly after midnight, Manuel sadly told us we had to leave. He needed to close for the night because he had to get up early the next day to prepare for another long day. But several of us weren't ready to call it a night. So Debbie, Alfie, Big Michael, John and I walked down the steep stairs heading towards our hotel and found a bar that was still open. And, amazingly, the place had a dart board. Perfect. Rematch time. I challenged Alfie and Debbie to another game. But once things began, not one of us seemed to be able to hit the target very accurately—which may or may not have been due to the copious amounts of Spanish wine we'd consumed up to that point.

Once we ditched the darts, we sat on our barstools and someone got the harebrained idea to do tequila shots—since they knew I liked tequila. But as I've already mentioned, good tequila was hard to find in Spain. At least, it had been in the towns we traveled through. Nevertheless, someone ordered shots. And they tasted just as horrible as I suspected they would.

By this time, it was getting late. I knew I needed to get to bed. I didn't want to feel lousy when Tom arrived. It was time to go, but Big Michael seemed pretty drunk. In fact, surprisingly, he seemed to be in the worst shape of all of us. I had assumed that with his size, he might fare the best. But I had no idea how much he had to drink tonight. I just knew that he was more than tipsy.

A slurring Big Michael claimed he was too tired to climb

the steep steps back to his *albergue*. He tried to convince either Debbie or me to let him stay in our room, since the hotel was only steps away from the bar. Debbie was the obvious choice, since Big Michael knew that Tom probably wouldn't appreciate me sharing my bed with him. He didn't ask this in a creepy way at all. Instead he just moaned about how tired he was. He didn't think he could make it up the super steep stairs, then climb the uphill street back to his *albergue*.

It was rather comical. Here was this big, strong man— with his huge smile, deeply-etched dimples and bright blue eyes—who'd clearly hit a wall of extreme fatigue and honestly didn't think he could make the trek back to his place. He pleaded with us in his Arnold Schwarzenegger voice, begging us to save him from making the arduous walk.

Thankfully Alfie convinced Big Michael that he indeed could make it and offered to help him along the way. It was a little after 2:00 in the morning when we finally said goodnight.

Debbie and I returned to our hotel, laughing about all the festivities of our night together. It certainly had been an entertaining evening. But I knew I would not have been able to function well if I'd had to walk the next day. I definitely overindulged with cocktails, and that tequila shot wasn't the best idea. But what a fun night! I felt a deep sense of relief about the fact that I could sleep in as late as I wanted tomorrow. I wanted to feel fully rested. The next evening I would be reunited with Tom after being apart for over a month.

Day 29

It was an odd sensation to sleep in and awaken without any plans of walking to a new destination. I felt strangely off-balance. But I took advantage of my first rest day and lounged around in my room until almost 10:00 this morning. Debbie, ever the Energizer Bunny, had already been awake for hours, eaten breakfast and was waiting for me to text her to make a plan for the day. I picked up my phone and saw that Laura sent a WhatsApp message to Debbie and me:

I am setting off for Molinaseca—depending on how I feel, I may come over. Is that cool? Xx

Laura messaged us yesterday saying she was walking very slowly. The whole process with her knee was exhausting. My heart ached for Laura. I could tell she was trying to put on a brave face, despite her frustrating situation. I loved the idea of us meeting up one last time before Santiago. So I texted back right away to let her know I'd be thrilled if she felt up to it and hoped we'd see each other later that day.

Then I made a plan to meet Debbie and Alfie in the hotel restaurant, where we got some coffee and a bite to eat before exploring Sarria together. We asked Alfie how Big Michael was feeling this morning and were astonished to hear that he was up early. Apparently he didn't seem to be showing any ill-effects from last night. Amazing.

Debbie, Alfie and I spent the rest of the morning walking

the streets and exploring the tiny shops of Sarria. We noticed a huge influx of pilgrims we hadn't seen before. Many of them looked fresh-faced, with shiny new walking poles and unscuffed hiking boots. They walked with a bounce in their step and a look of excitement and anticipation that screamed of their recent arrival.

But, of course, this made perfect sense. We knew that thousands of pilgrims begin their Camino journey in Sarria, since it's only 100 kilometers from Santiago—the minimum distance required to walk in order to earn a *compostela,* the Camino certificate of completion. It felt strange to see so many new faces though. I almost felt resentful that these new pilgrims would be crowding the remaining path to Santiago. I knew that sentiment wasn't very *Camino-like* and welcoming. I reminded myself that Tom was one of those pilgrims. I needed to change my frame of mind and do my best to be as kind, accepting and hospitable towards these newcomers.

The three of us eventually made our way back to the same plaza we were at last night. We decided to try the restaurant across from Manuel's place, just to do something different. Then I felt guilty when I saw Manuel shortly after we sat down. We should have given *him* our business.

"Manuel!" I shouted to get his attention.

"Hola, Margarita!" he smiled back. He waved his arms to his patio tables, encouraging us to sit there.

I assured him we would return to his restaurant that evening. Seemingly mollified, he returned to keeping the food and beverages coming for the patrons in his crowded dining area. Alfie ordered us some sort of ice cold non-alcoholic beverage and we plopped ourselves down at a roadside table, an

ideal spot to watch pilgrims as they rolled into town. Alfie—
Mr. Social—seemed to know a huge number of them, and as
soon as they saw him, they'd stop by our table to chat. We saw
Sophia and Phoebe, sisters in their early 20s, traveling together from Rhode Island. Debbie and I met them in León and saw
them again in Astorga, insisting that they *must* try the delicious
Roscas Maragatas. I happened to see them again the next day on
the Camino, just as they were sitting down to enjoy a coffee and
round two of these amazing treats. They thanked me profusely
for the delicious tip.

We later met another charming young pilgrim who I described in my blog:

> *At one point Alfie recognized David, a young engag-*
> *ing South African who Alfie had met several days ago,*
> *and we invited him to join us at our table. He regaled*
> *us with an incredible story of him trying to have an im-*
> *portant job interview via Skype while on the Camino.*
> *He had the challenge of being in a place that had de-*
> *cent Wi-Fi (often a very difficult task) at the proper New*
> *York City time, and dressed presentably. Camino attire*
> *isn't exactly the kind of clothing that screams* profes-
> sional, *but David was going to make the best of his sit-*
> *uation. But as so many of us pilgrims have experienced,*
> The Camino provides. *Miraculously, David was able to*
> *find a place with strong Wi-Fi, a private room for his*
> *interview, AND a local woman who overheard his story*
> *turned up just in time to lend him her son's perfectly*
> *pressed button down shirt, tie and suit jacket. With this*
> *kind of luck, I have to believe that David will get the*
> *job. In any case, it makes for an amazing Camino story.*

I really enjoyed talking with David, a guy who has been on a quest since 2017 to meet 1000 strangers in 1000 days. He is outgoing and friendly, with a clear intelligence that makes it very interesting to hear his thoughts and perceptions about life and the unique attributes of the Camino that make it such a positive experience.

As David talked more about his 1000 strangers in 1000 days challenge, he explained that he asked the same question to all of them: What's the meaning of life? He then posted the answer each day on Instagram, plus a picture of him with the new stranger holding a tiny chalkboard sporting the stranger's name and number scribbled on it.

Alfie sheepishly looked at David and apologized for not saying yes a few days earlier, when David had asked him to be his stranger-of-the-day. It was the same night Alfie didn't show up to our dinner with Laura in León. David asked if he might like to be today's stranger, even though technically they'd already met days before. So Alfie became stranger number 892 and this is what David would later post:

Everyone deserves a second chance!
I met Alfie in León a few days before. We were in a little pilgrims' social, in a flat above one of the beautiful León open squares. I approached Alfie, who was sitting on a couch in the corner of the room, to be my stranger for the day. Alfie agreed and wrote on the board, but when it got to having to take a photo, he backed out. And so my stranger got away!
Eight days later, walking into the beautiful town of

Sarria, I saw Alfie sitting at a table. Joining him and the two American ladies, Alfie said he had to confess that he regretted not being my stranger for the day when I initially asked him.

Good thing I believe in grace and so I gave Alfie another opportunity. :) Alfie is an interesting young man from England who has travelled extensively and lived in various countries before. He is an artist in heart and soul, rapping and writing his way towards expressing his deepest thoughts.

Alfie believes the meaning of life is to express oneself in the way most natural and passionate to you. Great meeting you Alfie...again :)

Watching David take the picture with Alfie made me smile, knowing how much Alfie hated having his picture taken. I could see his discomfort as he attempted to put on a happy face for the photo. But he seemed pleased to have been given the opportunity to make good on his agreement to be one of David's strangers.

After watching the stream of pilgrims pass by our table for an hour or so, Debbie, Alfie, David and I decided we wanted to try *pulpo*, a delicacy in the region. Alfie searched on his phone for the best reviewed place in Sarria for octopus. After a short walk, we arrived at *Pulpería Luis,* not far from my hotel. I described the scene later in my blog:

The place was absolutely packed with locals, not a pilgrim in sight, and the food looked and smelled incredible. We watched as a man pulled out an entire octopus from a steaming cauldron behind him and then quickly chopped it all into bite-sized pieces on circular wooden plates. Another person then seasoned it with salt, olive oil and paprika before whisking it off to customers sitting at long narrow wooden community tables. We soon learned that the man doing the chopping was the owner, and he told me he had been running the restaurant for the last 25 years. Our pulpo *was served with huge hunks of crusty bread,* vino tinto *and water. It was definitely the best meal I've had since I've been in Spain.*

We asked Luis to pose for a photo with us to commemorate our incredible meal. Debbie, David and I congratulated Alfie on his fantastic find before we all went our separate ways, off to enjoy the bliss of an afternoon *siesta*.

I returned to my hotel to get some rest and a hot shower before Tom's arrival around 9:00 tonight. I saw I had a WhatsApp message from Dan.

Margarita! I'm already back home in Vancouver, got in today, and it's quite a shock to be back. Time to adjust. It would've been great to meet your husband and see Debbie at least one last time. I hope we keep in touch and hope to see you again:) Take care for now.

Again, I felt a twinge of sadness for Dan since he wasn't able to finish his Camino. I hoped he would return one day so he could walk into Santiago. I also looked forward to seeing him again whenever his WestJet flight attendant work schedule brought him out to San Francisco.

In the meantime, sweet Laura had decided to take a more than two-hour cab ride to Sarria to meet Debbie and me for dinner. I was looking forward to reuniting with her and pleased that she and Aflie would finally meet. But it was a shame she'd miss meeting Tom, since she had to leave before he arrived. And she wouldn't be in Santiago until her birthday on July 8th. By that time, Tom and I would already be home in California. But I felt sure that one day Laura and Tom would meet one another.

Debbie and I met Laura at our hotel, then set off to climb the steep steps back to Manuel's restaurant. Laura insisted she was fine walking, but I could see that it was a bit of a struggle. She was determined to make the climb though.

Manuel seemed delighted to see us again. He greeted Laura with a warm smile and showed us to an outdoor table. Debbie, Laura and I ordered a few *tapas* and enjoyed the next few hours together, talking about how far we had come since the first day we met back in Nájera. Debbie and I were extremely touched by Laura's effort to come see us one last time, and we promised we'd keep in touch after the Camino. When Alfie finally appeared later, Debbie and I loved seeing two of our favorite people finally meet one another. This was our little Camino family.

Eventually it was time for Laura to make the two-hour cab ride back to her hotel. So after many hugs, we said goodbye and wished each other a *Buen Camino*. It was also time for me to return to my hotel to wait for Tom. I said goodbye to Alfie and Debbie, and we made a plan to meet the following evening so I could introduce them to Tom.

Finally, at a little before 9:00, Tom strolled through the hotel entrance, looking amazingly bright and energetic after an almost 24-hour travel day. We hugged each other tightly, and I felt happy to be in his warm embrace after such a long time without him. We went up to our room so he could freshen up a bit before getting a bite to eat. We were surprised to find that the hotel had sent up a bottle of champagne with a note welcoming Tom. But he was more interested in eating, rather than drinking, after his long travel day. So we spent the next hour catching up over dinner in the quiet hotel restaurant.

I was struck by how much he seemed to have missed me. I felt a surge of love for this man who traveled all this way so he could be a part of my Camino experience. He clearly just wanted to go along for the ride, without any agenda of his own. I could feel my worries begin to evaporate. I breathed a sigh of relief and looked at my handsome, charismatic husband with a deep sense of appreciation while I laughed at one of his funny stories. Oh, Tommy Dogs. He could always make me laugh. Feeling connected and happy, we returned to our room, excited for our joint adventure to begin the next day.

Day 30

Tom and I were up and out of our hotel by 8:00 after dropping our bags in the lobby and eating a protein-rich breakfast of eggs, yogurt and cheese. The weather was warm and sunny, and we were both dressed in shorts and light layers on top. And we each wore baseball caps and similar blue quarter zips. After nearly 30 years together, apparently you instinctively start dressing like one another. And as many of our friends noticed, our entire family seems to wear the color blue *a lot*. I never realized this until a few people pointed it out. Now it's kind of a family joke. No one is surprised when we all show up to family gatherings wearing our favorite color.

I was able to wear my hiking shoes today. My down time yesterday gave my blisters a chance to heal slightly. Amazing what a single day can do for the healing and regeneration process. Tom, meanwhile, was surprisingly energetic, without any signs of jet lag. More than anything, he seemed excited to start his first day on the Camino. And he appeared undaunted by the 14.5-mile walk ahead of him. This was a positive start.

We climbed the steep steps that led up to the Camino path, and made our way to the now-familiar small plaza ahead. I wanted to see if *Meson O Tapas* was open so I could say goodbye to Manuel. To my great delight, we saw him, still in the same drab olive sweater, hard at work serving his customers their morning coffees. *Did this man ever go home?!*

I greeted Manuel with a hug and introduced him to Tom,

before taking one last picture together. I thanked him for making our time in Sarria so happy and memorable, then we were gone, waving goodbye as we set off on the first leg of our new reality. *This* was the real beginning of my Camino with Tom.

And I'm happy to report that the morning flew by. I was astonished at how well Tom was doing. He walked as if he'd been on the Camino for weeks and had no problem keeping a good pace and positive energy. He walked with a bounce in his step, and I loved hearing him constantly admiring the beauty and splendor of the lush countryside, the brilliant blue sky filled with dancing clouds and lush green canopied paths adorned with ancient-looking stone walls. He was impressed with how well the Camino was marked with arrows and distances to Santiago. He was seeing the Camino with fresh eyes, just as I had 30 days ago.

However, the vibe was different than it had been on my first day. One difference was in the amount of people walking the Camino. Several large school groups now crowded the narrow paths, making it difficult to get around them. At one point we passed a group of 50 or so Spanish high school students who were busy chatting, laughing and playing their music loudly. This was definitely different from the more spiritual vibe of earlier days. I wasn't a fan. But it was all part of the Camino experience, so I tried not to let it discourage me.

The other difference was we now had to get our pilgrim passport stamped two times each day (only one was required before Sarria) before reaching Santiago—a requirement if we wanted to obtain our *compostela*. This meant that many cafés (as well as a variety of other places on the Camino route) would leave a stamp out so that pilgrims could stamp their passport themselves.

With this in mind, Tom and I stopped at a little café, collected our stamp and ordered two cups of coffee. We also bought a Camino shell to hang from Tom's backpack—he was now an official *peregrino*.

As we enjoyed our break and watched the pilgrims passing by, I recognized a familiar face. It was the older South Korean pilgrim who I walked with briefly on my way to O Cebreiro—the man who tried to guess my age. Mr. Old Face-Strong Body himself. He smiled when he saw me and came over to introduce himself to Tom. Struggling to find the correct words in English, he told Tom he was a lucky man to have such a strong wife. Then, winking at me warmly, he was on his way again.

It was around 1:00 when we arrived in the picturesque town of Portomarín, a small (population around 2,000) but exceedingly charming place overlooking the *rio Miño*. We climbed yet another steep set of stairs to cross over the river bridge and reach the center of town, where we were greeted by a huge metal art piece, maybe 10 feet tall, of letters—each an individual bronze sculpture spelling out *Portomarín*. Nearby we found the *Hotel Vistalegre,* a clean and modern-looking place where we happily found our bags and dropped them in our room, before heading to the *Plaza Mayor* to meet Debbie for lunch.

The main part of town was idyllic—a tapestry of bright multi-colored buildings, abundant bubble-gum pink flowers hanging from balconies and attractive arched doorways lining the narrow stone street. On either side of the road, shops were bustling with activity. As we made our way up the slight incline towards the *Plaza Mayor,* we admired the massive stone church directly ahead of us. Its bright green wooden door was surrounded by an ornately carved stone archway.

We saw Debbie as soon as we reached the plaza. And just as I predicted, she and Tom hit it off right away. She connected to his sense of humor immediately. Within minutes, Tom was already bantering back and forth with Debbie, ribbing her affectionately just to make her laugh.

"Scusie!" Debbie called to the waiter, trying to get his attention to order a drink.

"Is that even a Spanish word?" Tom asked Debbie. "What kind of Spanish did you learn in New York? Sounds like you're just making up words!"

It made me happy to see the two of them together, acting like old friends.

Not long after we ordered *bocadillos* and cold beers, we saw David walking towards us—a sight that made Debbie and me very happy. We introduced him to Tom and invited him to join us for lunch. Within no time, David asked Tom to be his stranger-of-the-day. Here's what he would later post on his #haveyoumetdavid Instagram account:

I had the privilege of meeting a very special American woman through Alfie, Stanger 892 in Sarria yesterday. We had an incredible heart to heart conversation ovr a glass of red wine and the local delicacy...pulpo (octopus). There is something very special about her which resonates with her experience in family counseling.

A day later, I had yet another privilege in meeting

her husband when I passed their table at a restaurant in Portomarín. He jumped up with bright eyes and a joyous smile, gave me a fresh handshake welcoming... introducing himself as Tom.

Tom is an energetic, vibrant man with a heart for people. In his commercial real estate business, Tom loves mentoring his younger employees and takes pride in seeing them systematically growing their lives sustainably.

Tom says the meaning of life is his family. To look after and care for them. To live in a way that offers a positive example to each of them. What a man! It's no surprise he and his wife initially fell in love and have been married for 28 years. Great meeting you Tom!

After a long *siesta*, Tom and I planned to meet up with Debbie and Alfie for dinner. I was looking forward to Tom meeting another member of my Camino family. Alfie asked if a new friend could join us, and we soon met Marina, a young Italian woman with shoulder-length dark curly hair. She was wearing a brightly colored Hawaiian shirt and ripped jeans, smiling warmly as she introduced herself in halting English. Within minutes of meeting her, it was clear she had a crush on Alfie.

Tom greeted Alfie with a big bear hug, and they talked about Charlie and USC for a bit. They both marveled at Alfie's connection to our son and my it's-a-small-world-after-all happenstance Camino meeting with this old soul from London. We found a restaurant near our hotel called the *O' Mirador*, a lively establishment lined with huge windows overlooking the river below. We were seated at a window table in a prime spot—middle of the restaurant, with sweeping views of the river, rolling hills and lush verdant countryside.

We ordered a bottle of *Albariño*, one of my favorite varieties of wine introduced to me by my father many years ago. It's a fond memory for me and I always think of him when I drink it. Since *pulpo* was also native to the region, we convinced Tom that he had to try it—even though he disliked any kind of seafood beyond ahi, shrimp and crab. He certainly wouldn't be described as an adventurous eater, with a willingness to try any kind of new food. Anthony Bourdain, he was not.

But Tom was definitely up for new adventures on the Camino. So he agreed to try the *poo poo,* as he called it. His Spanish skills were on par with Debbie's. Of course, we needed to videotape his reaction as we all watched him gingerly cut a tiny piece, pop it into his mouth and chew slowly. His face was miraculously unreadable. All he could say was how good it was.

Laughing, Alfie asked him, "Do you actually *like* it?

Tom shook his head, nearly spitting out the octopus, and cried, "No!"

At least he tried it. That was, in itself, a shocking thing to witness. For me, anyway. And it made for some good laughs at Tom's expense. Even Marina, who clearly had trouble following our conversation in English, seemed delighted watching Tom's antics.

After dinner, our merriment only continued. I would later post the following on my blog:

We were not ready to go back to our rooms. But the sleepy little town was completely shut down, except for one bar. Many albergues *have curfews and lock their doors anywhere from 10-11:00 at night, since pilgrims get up early to walk. So the one bar would have to do. And to my surprise, John, the guitar playing Irish guy who I hadn't seen since Logroño, was there! I was so happy to see him. We were lucky enough to hear him sing a beautiful Irish love song, and then he strummed his guitar while Alfie did an amazing freestyle rap. It was incredible to witness and I am in awe of Alfie's creative talent. But we had to end our festivities as the bartender said we were too loud and he sent us on our way. Definitely one of my favorite nights so far!*

My first day with Tom had exceeded all of my expectations. We climbed into bed together feeling happy and content, ready for whatever adventures awaited us the next day.

Day 31

Knowing that Tom's jet lag might catch up with him, I suggested we leave a little later in the morning. I also wanted to avoid walking with the throngs of pilgrims now on the Camino. The hotel receptionist told me that the bag transfer company arrived sometime after 8:30 a.m., half an hour past the usual pick up time, so we were pleased that we didn't have to rush downstairs. We took our time eating breakfast before heading out around 9:30.

Turned out to be a good decision. We often walked with no one around us, and Tom was able to appreciate the peaceful serenity of the Camino. It was easy to become mesmerized by the sounds of birds chirping, cow bells ringing and roosters crowing as we ambled along the tree-lined path.

But for a while, my mind was consumed with thoughts about a text Alfie sent me early this morning:

I am really shocked. I just got a message from the Rhode Island girls that an Italian guy peed on Sophia and her stuff and she woke with his privates in her face. Then he continued to try and go into Phoebe's bed. Apparently they freaked out but no one did anything or cared. I think they are pretty traumatized. It's horrible.

Alfie told me he was going to walk ahead to Palas de Rei so he could be with them and see how he could help. Those poor young girls. Sounded awful. I found it very un-Camino-like that no one would help them. I also wondered if this was the same person who peed on Adriana's bag. Was this a thing? Or was this just the same drunk guy who got disoriented and mistook a backpack for a urinal? Whatever the case, the whole situation was disturbing. I was glad Alfie was going to help Sophia and Phoebe sort things out.

We had a shorter, relatively easy 13-mile hike, and Tom ascended steep hills and navigated rocky descents with ease. He seemed to be acclimating just fine. I felt grateful that he kept himself active and in shape so he could jump right in. But most of all I appreciated that he recognized and respected that I was well into my Camino experience. He was sensitive to the fact that he was just now joining me, and he didn't want to disrupt my rhythm and routine. He understood and acknowledged the significance of reaching Santiago and shared in my rapidly-building excitement. We would be there in four days.

In Brierley's Camino book, he outlines the route from Sarria to Santiago in five stages. But for some reason unbeknownst to me, the travel company arranged my itinerary for this route in *six* stages. So it was going to take us one extra day to walk—which didn't make any sense to me. Suddenly, I would be walking shorter distances each day. Even though I was over a month into my trip and I'd built up my endurance. I was feeling strong. And I was itching to get to Santiago—why would I want to slow my pace down now? Plus, the majority of pilgrims I'd been walking with from stage to stage would all arrive a day earlier than me. *No bueno.*

All I could think of was maybe the travel company wanted to give Tom an extra day of walking on the Camino. Or did they try to make sure he wouldn't have extremely long walking days after his arrival? Whatever the case, I told myself to remain *tranquilo* and enjoy the last few days at a more leisurely pace. Plus, I was back in my Tevas—better for slowpokes—since my blisters still weren't fully healed.

I certainly wasn't disappointed when we reached Lestedo, our stopping point for the day, at around 1:30 in the afternoon. As we rounded a tree-lined bend in the path, we came upon a stunning stone structure surrounded by nothing but brilliant green grassy pastures. A white horse stood next to a brown horse as they both lazily peered at the passersby. The sign outside the structure announced that we had arrived at the *Casa Rectoral de Lestedo*. This was our lodging for the evening.

Although the building stones appeared ancient, it looked like the place had been modernized. The grounds were immaculate. As we followed the sign directing us to the entrance, we walked through an attractive outdoor patio filled with pilgrims enjoying *tapas*, coffees and cold beers. Amazing. This lovely oasis just appeared smack in the middle of the Camino—*with nothing else surrounding it*. Just lush green fields with gorgeous pastoral views. From the looks of it, many pilgrims were pleased to have stopped for a snack and/or drink in this delightful place.

We followed the path to the reception area, where we met the man who was running the hotel. Anderson was a young Spaniard with perfect English. When he checked us in he explained that the hotel used to be a monastery in the 17th century. It later became abandoned and was in complete disrepair until a man walking on the Camino fell in love with the area, bought the place and completely remodeled it. He created a gem with seven private rooms, plus a separate little house that could accommodate six people—perfect for a family. The story reminded me of the woman who bought the *albergue* in Ribadiso and created *The Stone Boat*. After a month in Spain, I could certainly understand the appeal of such an endeavor.

Anderson pointed us to our bags, which we hauled upstairs to our room. The walls were various colored old stones. Huge wood-framed glass doors led out to a small balcony overlooking the verdant pastures below. The bed linens and room accessories were crisp white, while the console serving as the headboard and the bedside tables were painted a bright candy apple red. The bathroom featured an enormous built-in white rectangular tub that sat below a wide window. The bathroom walls were white, with one accent wall in bright red. The combination of the old stone with the modern touches made for a funky, inviting space.

After lazily downing a tall mug of ice cold beer on the intimate patio, Tom and I enjoyed a *siesta* in our cozy room before heading down to the dining area. With only seven rooms in the hotel, the dining area was small—but comfortable and tastefully decorated with light-wood floors, white tablecloths and modern-looking rattan chairs. A wall of windows lined the area, giving every diner an unobstructed view of the bucolic setting.

Anderson proved to be the ultimate host, attending to our every need. We felt like we were in a multi-star restaurant rather than in a refurbished monastery in the middle of a tiny *pueblo* on the Camino. Tom and I soaked up every moment, every detail. I couldn't help but feel a surge of happiness, grateful to be sharing this experience together.

Meanwhile, I heard from Alfie. He was with Sophia and Phoebe and they were both feeling better.

This is the first night without Margarita in a while. I will miss your palms down *move. Give my best to Tom.*

Yes, it *was* the first night without Alfie or Debbie in quite a while. It was a new chapter in my Camino. And thankfully, so far it was going well.

Day 32

There is one major advantage in staying in a town not designated as the end of a walking stage in Brierly's Camino book: the road is much less populated with pilgrims when starting your walk in the morning. We were staying about five kilometers behind the end of the next stage. If we planned our departure time just right, we could hopefully avoid the crowds.

With that in mind, we left the lovely hamlet of Lestedo a little after 8:30 in the morning. A light rain fell as we walked a full three miles before seeing another soul. It was a marvelous way to begin the day. And I was elated to see Tom experience the Camino in this peaceful state, away from the noisy crowds.

It was Tom's first day walking in the rain, and I assured him that because we had good rain jackets—plus water resistant pants and shoes and rain covers for our packs—we would be totally comfortable. I told him I actually thoroughly enjoyed walking in the rain, listening to the steady thrumming of the drops all around me. I'm not sure he was totally convinced he'd feel the same way. But to Tom's credit, he bundled up and didn't complain.

About an hour into our walk we came upon a small church in Palas de Rei. The doors were wide open and inside was abuzz with activity. Curious, we stepped inside to see what was going on. Several people were meticulously laying down pink, red, yellow and white rose petals to create a carpet up the center aisle of the church. Each square of the carpet was inlaid with these rose petals in various designs of hearts, crosses, candles and other religious symbols. We learned the workers were preparing for the celebration of Corpus Christi later that afternoon. Their handiwork was dazzling.

We walked the rest of the way at a leisurely pace, stopping in several small churches along the path, as well as a tiny jewelry shop which was tucked under a grove of trees on an otherwise deserted part of the Camino. Colors of the Camino arrows adorned the shop with the jeweler's creations affixed to swatches of bright blue and yellow fabrics. I found a simple wire-wrapped *tree of life* pendant and decided this would be a perfect memento of my journey, since it symbolizes positive energy, strength and rebirth.

After walking 13 miles, we reached Melide, the city where the Camino Primitivo joins the Camino Francés, a little after 1:00 in the afternoon. As we entered the bustling little city (pop. 7,500), we walked past a lively-looking *pulpo* restaurant called *Pulpería Garnacha*. A bald man with bright green eyes and a dark beard and moustache stood behind an open window of the restaurant. He was busy chopping bits of steaming hot and delicious-smelling *pulpo,* offering samples to passersby. I gladly accepted the tasty looking treat, but Tom shook his head vigorously, making a face of utter disgust. This seemed to amuse the man and he began teasing Tom, saying he needed to be *fuerte*—only strong men ate *pulpo.* This tactic sadly didn't work. Tom could not be persuaded. One *poo poo* tasting was enough for him.

Check-in at our *alburgue* was at a bar around the corner from the entrance to *Pensión Esquina*, a spartan building with 20 or so small private rooms. It was the first night Tom would be experiencing bare bones accommodations. The room was barely big enough to place our packs on the floor without tripping over them. From our tiny window we looked across a narrow alleyway to another tall gray stone building, which obstructed our view of anything else. The bathroom was barely big enough for one person, so we carefully sidled by one another as we cleaned up before heading out to eat lunch and explore the city.

Debbie was staying down the hall from us, so we met in the bar where we had checked in. We headed back to the *Pulpería Garnacha,* hoping to enjoy another delicious meal of the local delicacy. Well, at least Debbie and I were. Tom was game to come along, but insisted he'd find an alternative selection for his lunch.

Tom, Debbie and I spent the rest of the afternoon walking through the busy town. An open-air market—selling clothes, toys, household items and various other local goods—was in full swing. Outdoor tables were filled with people smoking, drinking coffee and enjoying their mid-day meals on this gorgeous sunny Sunday afternoon.

In contrast to this *tranquilo* vibe, I noticed I felt extraordinarily antsy. Santiago was now only about 36 miles away—but we were taking three more days to walk this short distance, when we easily could have covered it in two. I also wanted to reach Santiago and see familiar pilgrim faces—my Camino family—all around me. I feared I would miss seeing them, since they'd surely be ahead of me now. Only time would tell.

After dinner in a quiet, nondescript restaurant that offered a basic pilgrim's menu, Debbie, Tom and I took one last stroll to walk off our meal. We found the path of the Camino, where we'd begin our walk the next day and climbed a slight incline towards a small stone church at the top of the knoll.

Surprisingly, the doors were locked. So we poked around the grounds as we surveyed the grand vistas from our perch above the city. Debbie insisted on taking a picture of Tom and me to capture the moment. We both smiled dutifully, but she immediately chided us for looking too posed.

"What kind of smile is *that*? That looks totally fake. You guys can do better."

And with that, she launched into another hilarious Debbie rant, making Tom and me explode into fits of laughter as she snapped more photos. We ended up with one of my all-time favorite candids of Tom and me—in our matching lightweight hiking vests, long pants and Allbirds athletic shoes. Both of our faces consumed with pure joy. And, of course, each of us decked out in our beloved blue.

Day 33

I was anxious to get going in the morning, even though we had a short 9.5-mile walk ahead of us—the second shortest distance of my Camino so far. I was starting to get reminders of just how close we were to completing our journey. Bearded Michael from San Diego sent me pictures of his arrival into Santiago yesterday with Sean and Jenny. It was wonderful to see them looking so happy. But I also felt sad that I would miss seeing them when we arrived.

We left shortly after 8:00, well after Debbie's early morning departure. Thankfully, we seemed to avoid the crowds. We were rewarded with a serene and peaceful walk under a soft pale blue sky as we glided over the undulating hills and through thick, lush tree-lined expanses. I was back in my hiking boots, feeling good in just some light layers and long pants.

We were scheduled to stay in Arzúa that evening, the city where the Camino del Norte joins the Camino Francés. But when we arrived into town a little after 11:00 later that morning, the directions to our hotel on my paper map appeared to be taking us far from the center of town. I found myself feeling aggravated. I didn't understand why the travel company selected a hotel in a remote location, far away from the places where other pilgrims might be staying. This was not part of the Camino experience I envisioned.

I wanted to be staying in the heart of town. Amongst my fellow *peregrinos*.

With every step forward taking us even further from town, I could feel my irritation growing. I began to walk at a clipped, furious pace. I was now several yards ahead of Tom. Now, I'm normally pretty even-keeled. And I knew perfectly well that I was not exhibiting my usual behavior. But that still didn't stop me. Tom didn't understand why I was so irritated. He just patiently let me vent and walk ahead.

After walking another 30 minutes—which felt like 30 hours—we finally arrived at the *Pazo Santa María,* an absolutely stunning stone and wood structure built on a hill overlooking a valley below. An old wood wagon filled with bright pink and white flowers greeted us at the entrance. A series of stone buildings lined with perfectly manicured hedges were encased by the outer stone wall. We felt as though we were entering an enchanting compound. A magical place found in childhood fairy tales.

Wood arrows stacked one on top of another and nailed to a stake were artistically lettered with various locations and the distance to each place, including: *Madrid 540 km, Finisterre 128 km* and *Santiago de Compostela 39 km.* In the distance we saw a pond surrounded by lush foliage, featuring a majestic swan followed by a bevy of baby swans. Seeing the fairy tale surroundings and my lucky number 39 next to Santiago immediately melted away all of my frustration.

This place was a little paradise.

I knew it was a far cry from your typical *peregrino* lodging, but its charm won me over. I put aside my earlier disappointment over not having a typical pilgrim experience and embraced our out-of-the-way surroundings with open arms. We learned that the manor (*pazo*) house was originally built in 1742 as a private home and still retained many of its original structures. The lobby and adjoining library were tastefully furnished with comfy looking chairs and couches upholstered in pale yellow and soft red-patterned fabrics. Richly colored rugs dotted the tile floors, and pleasing landscape paintings in gilded frames hung on the exposed stone walls.

The innkeeper welcomed us warmly and showed us to our magnificent room on the second floor. The room exuded old world charm with its exposed-stone walls, wood-beamed ceilings, hardwood floors and canopied bed. Antique furniture filled the spacious room, complete with a French blue chaise lounge and khaki and white striped couch. The view from our window overlooked the garden grounds below, with rolling hills reaching out into the distance. We were in heaven.

Thanks to our early arrival, we had nearly a full day to explore Arzúa. Since the city was known for its cheesemaking, we knew we wanted to do a cheese tasting at some point, including the popular *queixo tetilla,* a simple soft cheese made from cow's milk. And we read about a local museum of honey—*Museo Vivente do Mel*—and thought it would be fun to learn about beekeeping while tasting some yummy honey.

We called Debbie and invited her to join us on the patio overlooking the swan-filled pond. She was staying in a modest *albergue* in the center of town and seemed pleased to leave, since the city seemed pretty dead on this Monday afternoon. Apparently there had been a big *fiesta* of some sort over the weekend and the locals were still recovering.

Debbie arrived after a short taxi ride and we lounged lazily on the patio, admiring the sweeping views of our beautiful oasis as we shared a delicious cheese platter and cold bottle of

Albariño. Tom, ever the entertainer, held Debbie's rapt attention with a series of funny stories and jokes, including his well-told *Timbuktu* joke. (For those of you who want to hear the joke, you'll have to trust me when I say it's long and probably doesn't translate as well on the page.) I watched in delight as he would deliver each punch line with perfect timing, expertly accomplishing the desired effect of peals of laughter.

Later in the afternoon we took a taxi to the nearby honey museum, where Debbie got more amusement from Tom—while I was slightly embarrassed. Tom seemed more interested to find out why our attractive young female tour guide wasn't married yet than learning about the art of honeymaking. In Tom's typical way of saying things that most people wouldn't dare utter aloud, he disarmingly probed and prodded the young woman with charm. She seemed amused and played along, without appearing to be offended by Tom's curiosity. Debbie laughed at the entire interaction, while I apologized for my husband's brazenness. I was used to this. I had nearly 30 years of experience. It didn't make it any less embarrassing, but I knew his teasing was harmlessly good-natured.

We enjoyed the remainder of the day by taking a long nap in our beautiful room. Debbie went back to her *albergue* for her own rest time and agreed to join us back at the intimate hotel dining room for dinner.

That night we were excited to eat something different than a typical pilgrim's meal. The resident chef used fresh local ingredients incorporating all organic meats, fruits and vegetables in his creations. As the wait staff attended to our every need, we felt like we were in a five-star resort while we talked excitedly about reaching Santiago together in just two more days.

I got a text from Alfie later that night saying he would be in Santiago the next day—one day earlier than us. He wanted to spend time with some of his pilgrim friends before they had to catch their flights home. But he promised to stay in Santiago an extra day so we could all celebrate together.

He also updated me on Sophia and Phoebe. Turned out the Italian guy was blackout drunk and didn't remember a thing about the incident. Apparently he was incredibly embarrassed and apologetic. Most importantly, the girls were doing much better and seemed unscathed.

I couldn't wait for our little Camino family to be together in Santiago.

Day 34

We had another short walking day ahead of us, so we took our time in the morning, soaking up the splendor of our surroundings. We set off on our 12.5-mile hike a little after 9:00 on a bright, sunny day. This morning was the first time in several days that it was warm enough to begin the day in short sleeves, shorts and sunglasses. It felt glorious. My knee and blisters weren't an issue, so I was walking comfortably in my hiking shoes without a brace. Life was good.

On the other hand, Tom was beginning to develop some blisters. I was convinced that his attempt to keep up with me during his first few days didn't do him any favors. He hadn't had the chance to ease into the walking routine like I did when I began. He didn't want to slow me down and jumped right in at a pace his feet probably weren't ready for. But he didn't complain. He simply applied bandages and Moleskin—*not* Compeed—to his sore spots and soldiered on.

We were fortunate to avoid huge crowds of pilgrims for the first hour of our walk. But after stopping for our morning coffee, we got sandwiched between several huge groups of junior high and high school Spanish students. With their spirited chatter, loud music and hurried pace, I found it difficult to get into a peaceful state of mind. Yet again I was reminded how different this stretch of the Camino from Sarria was. I really hoped I would rediscover the tranquility of my earlier Camino days when Tom and I walked from Santiago to Finisterre.

Despite the crowds, I thoroughly enjoyed the scenery today. We walked on tree-lined dirt paths, past charming village homes with lovely gardens, one of which was surrounded by a stone wall with a message for all of the Camino's weary travelers to see: *BE KIND*.

At one point we turned a corner in O Outeiro and came upon the *Casa Tia Dolores*, a crowded, noisy outdoor beer garden. The entrance was adorned by hundreds of empty beer bottles stuck into large wooden posts. Apparently pilgrims scribbled a date or name or message on a bottle, then were encouraged to place it where they could find a free spot within the spacious beer garden. As we looked around, we saw literally thousands of bottles scattered throughout the restaurant. And it was abundantly clear that the many pilgrims in attendance were thoroughly enjoying themselves. But we weren't in the mood to stop so we continued on our way.

A few yards ahead, we walked past a shop selling all sorts of Camino souvenirs. The path narrowed and the crowds made it difficult to navigate the bottleneck. The Camino suddenly started to feel very commercial and touristy. Tom and I made the decision to quicken our pace and try to get ahead of these large packs of school-age kids.

For the next several miles, we hurried ahead. We were finally rewarded with some peace and serenity as we neared our destination of A Rúa, a hamlet just outside of O Pino. We walked through a huge grove of Eucalyptus trees, so massive that it blocked the sky above and made us feel like we were walking through an enchanted forest. Tom took a picture of me from behind. I looked miniature next to the giant trees, with my Camino shell hanging from my pack and my arms outstretched in a show of respect for the grandeur around me.

We arrived at the *Hotel Restaurante O Pino* a little after 1:00 in the afternoon. Our room was small and simple, up a short flight of stairs from the restaurant below. Tom was happy to get off his feet—his blisters were becoming painful. But I wanted to walk ahead to O Pino, where Debbie was staying for the night, so I could check out the town and determine a meeting spot for the next morning. Debbie and I planned to walk into Santiago together, step by step. We had been together since the 8th day of my Camino, sharing our many ups and downs in solidarity. I wanted to experience this momentous occasion with her.

After showering I was ready to head off and suggested Tom rest his feet. But he insisted on walking with me, despite his nagging blisters. So he wore flip flops and gingerly walked beside me as we made our way in the hot sun to Debbie's *albergue*, a longer walk—nearly two miles—than we had expected. As the road stretched on, I kept encouraging Tom to turn around and return to the hotel to rest his feet. He was now griping, clearly tired and overheated. But he stubbornly carried on, limping along at a snail's pace. I felt a rising impatience and told myself to hold my tongue—I didn't want to get into a spat at this point on the Camino. And I didn't want anything to spoil my feelings of excitement and anticipation.

We finally found Debbie's *albergue* and located a good spot where we planned to meet the next morning at 6:00 a.m. We wanted to leave early enough to avoid the large crowds we dealt with on today's hike.

Tom and I decided to have dinner on our own. But before we said goodbye to Debbie, we agreed to find a bar nearby where we could enjoy a *tinto de verano* together on this blistering hot day. Debbie began walking us back and we nearly reached our hotel before we finally found a rustic bar with outdoor tables on a small patch of grass.

One drink later, we said our goodbyes to Debbie. Before long we were back at our hotel and Tom was finally able to plop himself on our bed, instantly falling asleep for a much-needed *siesta*. Meanwhile, I checked in with Alfie to see how his arrival into Santiago went. He sent me a picture of him sitting in the square in front of the famous Santiago de Compostela Cathedral with Sean and Jenny, happiness etched on each of their faces. Alfie said Bearded Michael was already in Finisterre or on his way there. Sean and Jennie would be leaving the next day to join him. Sadly, it looked like I was going to miss seeing them. But I was thrilled that Debbie and I would be reunited with Alfie.

Feeling refreshed from his nap, Tom showered before we headed downstairs for dinner. The restaurant was packed with *peregrinos* and I could feel a buzz of excitement in the air as pilgrims discussed plans for their walk into Santiago the next day. Tom and I talked about my journey and how far I'd come since that very first day in Saint-Jean-Pied-de-Port. Tom seemed awed at my accomplishment and I could feel how proud he was. He was clearly excited for me.

After our meal—despite *my* excitement—I forced myself to turn the light off before 10:00. I needed to get a good night's sleep before our 5:15 a.m. alarm sounded. I wanted to feel ready and well-rested for our big day.

Day 35

I was already awake by the time the alarm sounded. I could feel the adrenaline coursing through my entire body. I was ready to attack the day—our final 14-mile push to Santiago.

Tom and I dressed and packed up quickly. We left our bags at the bottom of the stairs, in front of the locked entrance to the restaurant, where they'd be picked up hours later by the luggage transfer company. It was 5:40 in the morning and still dark outside.

As luck would have it, I forgot to transfer my headlamp from my bag to my day pack. So we were forced to rely on our phone flashlights to lead the way. We had a mile or so to walk before we reached the spot where Debbie would be meeting us at 6:00.

The Camino was eerily quiet on this pre-dawn morning. But as we neared the designated meeting point, we began to notice flashes of light in the distance. As we got closer, we realized it was our fellow *peregrinos* who apparently had the same early departure plan as us.

Debbie greeted us excitedly, anxious to begin what would be her last day of walking on the Camino. Her flight home to New York was in two days. So as we set off for Santiago, the three of us huddled together on the densely forested path trying to share the light from Debbie's headlamp, not wanting to misstep and twist an ankle or injure ourselves in the darkness. The plan was to walk for a few miles, then stop for our morning coffee and breakfast.

It was a little before 7:00 when we arrived in Amenal and parked ourselves at the *Kilometro 15* bar. We found a table outside, where the sun was now rising. The sky was streaked and striated in glorious shades of pink, white and pale blue. And yet, none of us felt like lingering at our table to lazily admire the morning sky. We were anxious to reach our destination. So after a quick bite, we collected our pilgrim passport stamps and continued on our way.

I envisioned arriving in Santiago on a brilliant sunny day. I dressed in shorts and light layers, hoping my optimistic fashion choices would somehow help realize that vision. But the sun had other plans that day. Instead, we soon found ourselves walking in the rain. Tom and I stopped to put on our rain jackets and secure the rain covers over our packs. Debbie, dressed in a non-water-resistant jacket and leggings, didn't have any extra clothing with her. She was only carrying a fanny pack, yet seemed completely undeterred by the rain.

Debbie preferred a quick pace, her arms swinging wildly by her side. Tom was doing his best to keep up, despite his nagging blisters. Meanwhile, I was back in Mama Bear mode, trying to find a medium pace that we could all manage together. This was the first time I'd walked with Debbie for an entire stage, and it took me a while to get used to her constant chatter—it left little room for me to get lost in contemplative thought about this momentous day. Debbie was bursting with excitement, talking animatedly about finally reaching Santiago. I was excited too, of course. But I seemed to internalize those feelings, preferring to keep my talking to a minimum.

A few hours later, on the outskirts of Santiago, we came

upon a colorful array of discarded items left by passing pilgrims. Pairs of shoes, bandanas, hats, maps, Camino shells and other objects were tied on to a swath of chicken wire propped against a large bush—an apparent shedding of items no longer needed by pilgrims about to end their journey.

The simple yellow Camino *flechas* were soon replaced by ornate brassy gold shells embedded into the sidewalks, marking the distance left to Santiago. As we neared the city, we noticed many of these shells were missing—evidently some pilgrims wanted to take them as a keepsake. Seemed very un-Camino-like to me.

Finally, after four hours of walking today, we spotted it in the near distance, jutting through the mist of the thick gray fog—the Cathedral of Santiago. A chill went through my entire body. I had to catch my breath as my eyes teared up. We knew we were close now. Our excitement palpable, intoxicating. My stomach lurched with anticipation and my steps quickened. A light rain continued to fall.

The narrow cobblestone streets were now filled with locals hunched under their umbrellas, as well as a parade of pilgrims moving briskly ahead and behind us. Our early departure turned out to be a good decision. Although we saw other pilgrims, the Camino wasn't too crowded. We even managed to avoid seeing any of the big Spanish student groups from the days before. We all agreed that we'd take inclement weather over walking in the sun with zillions of other pilgrims any day.

As we descended some wide stone steps—now only a mere few yards away from our final destination—we heard a bagpipe nearby playing beautiful, soul-stirring music. It was as if the gods were heralding our arrival, instantly heightening our emotions. Tom walked ahead so he could video our arrival. Debbie and I stopped to savor this moment. We hugged each other tightly, recognizing the significance of what we were about to do.

And then, a little after 10:00 in the morning on Wednesday, June 26, 2019, we entered the famed square of Santiago de Compostela, the *Praza do Obradoiro*. Tom's video shows us in stark contrast—Debbie jumping up and down, swinging her arms and joyously exclaiming, "We're here!"—while I'm caught calmly walking in silent awe, my head tilted up to catch a glimpse of the famed Cathedral. A big, unmistakable smile illuminates my face.

Someone viewing the video might mistake my quiet calm for a lack of enthusiasm. But I distinctly remember feeling completely overwhelmed by the moment. With the haunting bagpipe music supplying the soundtrack on this gray misty day, I was now peering up at the imposing Cathedral of Santiago. Its magnificent baroque beauty absolutely took my breath away. I had walked *500 miles* to get here. And despite my various ailments, my 55-year-old body didn't betray me. It carried me through. I felt an overwhelming sense of gratitude. It all felt surreal.

As I swiveled my gaze ahead, I suddenly saw Alfie standing before me, waiting to welcome us. Debbie and I ran over and hugged him tightly, thanking Alfie for celebrating this moment with us. It was impossible to hide our joy as we took a bunch of pictures to capture our arrival—there was the one of just me, my arms spread out wide in jubilation, the one of Debbie and me, the one of Alfie, Debbie and me, and finally the one of Tom and me. We all felt a rush of joy and elation—we made it!

Then it was over to the *Oficina del Peregrino*, where the line wasn't long, thankfully. We received our official *compostela*—as well as a *certificado* showing the distance we traveled—within a half hour after showing our stamped pilgrim's passport.

As I stood at the counter, waiting for the clerk to write my name on the certificate, I overheard the conversation next to me. A fellow pilgrim was talking to the clerk helping her. He was studying her pilgrim's passport.

"You realize you have to walk at least a 100 kilometers in order to get a *compostela?*" the clerk asked her.

There seemed to be a bit of a language barrier. The young Korean woman pointed to the stamps in her passport, indicating that she had begun her Camino in Sarria and had the necessary stamps required.

"Yes, I see you have these stamps. But you're missing some," the clerk said. He looked at her questioningly.

"That's the part where I took the bus," the woman said in halting English.

The man handed back the woman's pilgrim's passport. "You can't take the bus. You have to walk all 100 kilometers. I'm sorry."

The young woman took her passport, a look of extreme confusion and discouragement clouding her young face. I felt a surge of sadness for her.

But I could see that it was serious business in this office. Clearly, the clerks were checking passports for the required stamps and only dispensing the coveted *compostelas* to pilgrims who earned them.

Now it was time to celebrate. Tom and I had booked a room at The Parador, also known as the *Hostal dos Reis Católicos*, a historic five-star hotel. The Renaissance facade was originally built in 1499 as a royal hospital to accommodate pilgrims traveling to Santiago. Located in the same square as the Cathedral, it's also famous for being one of the oldest hotels in the world.

After checking in, Tom and I invited Debbie and Aflie to join us in our room to celebrate with a bottle of champagne. We were staying in the Cardinal's suite, a fantastically ornate, luxurious and gigantic room, complete with not one but *two* king beds canopied with deep red velvet. The room also featured wood-beamed ceilings, a large and handsomely furnished sitting area, a raised second sitting area overlooking a giant balcony and a spacious, modernized bathroom. With our champagne glasses in hand, we joyously toasted one another and relished the moment.

But as nice as our room was, we all wanted to return to the magical *Praza do Obradoiro*, find a comfy place to sit and watch the constant stream of pilgrim arrivals. It was only noon, so we were sure to see many more pilgrims enter the square throughout the day.

Feeling hungry, we bought some snacks and drinks before finding a spot in the square directly in front of the Cathedral. The rest of the afternoon was a blur of euphoria, joy, laughter, singing and elation. I watched pilgrims enter the square and fall to their knees in tears of unbridled joy. Some kissed the ground beneath them. Bikers hoisted their bikes high above their heads with cheers of jubilation. Groups of school-age kids ran in, noisy and boisterous. Other groups of friends jumped high in the air, trying to synchronize their leaps for an Instagram-worthy photo.

Pilgrims were greeted by waiting friends and family members. Tearful hugs were exchanged. Other pilgrims just laid down in the middle of all the activity, heads resting on their packs while soaking up the experience of finally arriving at their destination.

I watched all these scenes before me, riveted and enthralled. The unmistakable heightened emotions were addicting to witness. And then a stream of familiar faces began entering. First Big Michael and his radiant smile. Then Takashi in his fedora, that familiar turquoise blanket still wrapped around his shoulders. Then came David, looking fresh and energetic. Before long I saw Irish John, his twinkling eyes and kind smile lighting up his face. I hugged each one, in disbelief that we were all together in Santiago—and entirely ecstatic at the same time.

By now it was close to 4:30 in the afternoon and the sky had changed to a brilliant shade of blue above the Cathedral. Irish John whipped out his ukulele and began playing, his achingly beautiful voice making this day even sweeter. He soulfully crooned Bob Dylan's *Girl from the North Country*, a song I will forever affectionately associate with my Camino experience.

The hours slipped away that afternoon as we sang and celebrated, took pictures, and watched all the activity around us. I sent Laura a photo of our arrival and wished her a *Buen Camino* for the rest of her journey. I told her how excited I was for her to enter this magical place on her birthday. I would have liked to have been in Santiago together, but I felt sure I would see her again. I introduced Tom to Big Michael and Takashi and we said goodbye to Sophia and Phoebe, who were leaving Santiago. At around 6:00 Tom and I crossed the square and headed up to our suite. It was time to shower and get ready for dinner.

A few hours laters we met Alfie and Debbie at *El Papa-*

torio, a *tapas* bar and restaurant not far from the Cathedral. I invited David and Takashi to join us, then a few other pilgrims I just met rounded out the group. David had previously heard me talking about Takashi, but hadn't met him yet. So, of course, David chose to sit next to him—and before long he had his stranger-of-the-day. He later posted the following:

Takashi — stranger #899

A friend I made on the Camino once mentioned this great guy she met while walking. She told me about his positively calm and peaceful personality. A mere one week later, I had the opportunity to find myself sitting next to this gentleman at a final celebratory dinner in Santiago. Takashi! Japanese born and raised, been living in Spain for the last two years and without a doubt has a positively calm and peaceful personality :) He met his wife on his previous Camino and decided to make the move from Japan to base his life here in Spain. "What? The meaning of life? Everyone knows the answer," Takashi told me in a gentle voice. I almost felt a bit silly for asking :) "Love! Everyone knows the meaning of life is love."

What a legend! Couldn't agree more. Great meeting you, Takashi.

I found it satisfying to see people I connected with on the Camino meeting one another. Alfie and Taskashi also met earlier that afternoon after both hearing of one another through me.

We continued our post-dinner festivities at a nearby bar, where we sat outside at a long narrow table. The English father and son, John and Tom, joined us as well. So did Big Michael and Irish John. More music and singing. And cigarette smoking by almost everyone at the table except the Americans. Irish John led us in a boisterous sing-along of *Stand by Me*. Lots of laughter ensued. Especially by Big Michael. His warm, infectious laugh was like a spark that got others to chuckle alongside him. Then Alfie spontaneously entertained us with another heartfelt and brilliant freestyle rap, while Irish John strummed along.

It was a magical night and a perfect way to end this leg of the journey.

At around midnight, I sadly said goodbye to Takashi and David. They were both leaving Santiago in the morning. We promised to keep in touch and hoped to reunite one day in the future. Debbie wanted to head back to her hotel to get some sleep before an early wake-up call. She had booked a bus trip to Finisterre and back for her last day. Thankfully I didn't have to say goodbye, since we planned to meet for dinner tomorrow night with Alfie in Santiago. One last celebratory dinner with our Camino family.

But I still wasn't ready to call it a night. So a group of us—including Tom, Big Michael, Irish John, Alfie, English Tom and his son John—headed off in search of a lively late night bar. We seemed to walk for a good mile before we finally found a place. And while the others ordered a drink at the bar, I scooted into a booth to wait for them and found myself next to a German pilgrim in his early 30s. I'd seen him across the table at the previous bar, but I hadn't met him yet.

The German man looked and acted as if he'd chugged one or 10 beers too many. His eyes were glazed over. As he began speaking to me, his words were slurred and heavy. He was lamenting his return home. Nearly in tears, he confessed that he feared going back to a place where no one talked to him—a place where he didn't feel seen. He wanted to remain on the Camino, where he felt accepted. Where he was invited to be part of a community. He wasn't ready to let go of the magic of the Camino.

It was heartbreaking to hear the anguish in his voice. I tried to comfort him, but he seemed inconsolable. And the alcohol clearly wasn't helping his mood.

I suddenly felt inordinately tired. It was time to end this magical day.

As Tom and I walked back to our hotel, it dawned on us how lucky we were to be going home to our family and friends when we finished our journey. Not everyone had this to look forward to. And some pilgrims, as in the case of the German pilgrim, dreaded the end of the Camino. It meant returning to a life they were trying to escape as they walked across Spain.

We finally got to bed in the wee hours of the morning having almost pulled an all-nighter—21 hours of exultation, celebration and joy. A day I will cherish forever.

Tom and I felt drained the next morning. Turns out walking nearly 15 miles before celebrating all night will do that to you. I was feeling a few other mixed emotions, as well. Part of me felt an emotional letdown after achieving this major goal of reaching Santiago. I also knew this meant I'd be saying goodbye to Debbie and a bunch of other familiar faces I'd grown fond of. *This* part of the journey was now over.

But the other part of me knew I still had 50 miles to walk

before finishing my Camino in Finisterre. I was happy that I still had a few days left. I wasn't ready to leave the Camino just yet.

Despite our fatigue, Tom and I wanted to explore the charm and splendor of Santiago. But before we started poking around the city, I wanted to find the travel office responsible for making all the changes to my Camino itinerary. I wanted to thank Nuria in person for all her help. We soon found her office not far from our hotel and I didn't hesitate to give her a huge hug, thanking Nuria profusely for rearranging my trip. She wished me a *Buen Camino* for the reminder of my trip, and we said our goodbyes as she smiled warmly at us.

Tom and I knew we couldn't attend the pilgrim's mass in the Cathedral. It was undergoing major renovations. But we still wanted to walk inside and see the heralded *Botafumeiro*, an enormous incense burner swung from the central nave. Purportedly this was originally used to mask the pungent smell of the great unwashed masses of pilgrims descending upon Santiago. I'd seen a video of it swinging and it looked phenomenal. I was sorry to miss it in action. But at least Tom and I got a look at it secured safely amidst the construction.

We met up with Alfie and walked to the church that was serving as the temporary site of the pilgrim's mass. It was crammed with people—standing room only—and hard to find a place to stand without an obstructed view. I felt claustrophobic. After a few minutes of craning my neck to see over the crowds, I decided I was ready to leave. Tom and Alfie felt the same and followed me out. Instead we found a nearby empty church, where we each sat by ourselves in the peace and quiet. I realized I wasn't ready to be thrust into huge crowds just yet.

Alfie kept us company over the next few hours during

lunch and a trip to a sportswear store. Tom bought a pair of open-toed sandals for our long walk the next day. His blisters were still painful and he worried he wouldn't be able to walk in his hiking shoes. Better to have a backup plan if that was the case. We would soon find out.

On our way back to the hotel, I ran into Big Michael sitting in the square in front of the Cathedral watching the pilgrim arrivals. When he saw me he greeted me with his usual big bear hug and huge smile. But I could tell he was struggling with his emotions. He hated saying goodbye. And in the last few days, he'd already said many goodbyes to pilgrims he cared about, strangers-turned-friends with whom he shared a multitude of magical experiences on the Camino. When we came upon him, he'd just said goodbye to yet another beloved pilgrim. It was too much for him. He looked close to tears.

In that moment, as I looked at Big Michael's imposing physique—combined with his booming Arnold Schwarzenegger voice—it struck me what a teddy bear he was. A softie with an enormous heart. I felt his pain. This was absolutely one of the hardest aspects of the Camino—saying goodbye to all of our new friends from all over the world, most of whom we may never meet again. I sensed Michael needed some time alone to grieve, so I hugged him and said I hoped to see him later that evening. Sadly, we never got a chance to say goodbye—probably just as well, since he hated this ritual.

Then Alfie tapped me on the shoulder. "Look who I found?"

It was Bearded Michael, just back from Finisterre! He was in Santiago to pick up his girlfriend at the airport later that night. I gave him a warm hug and introduced him to Tom. We talked about the Camino-to-Finisterre route, since he was one of the few people I knew who walked it. Most pilgrims I met either ended their Camino in Santiago or took a bus to Finisterre. Very few opted to keep walking to Finisterre. We chatted a while, but then had to say our goodbyes since Tom and I were scheduled for in-room massages. I had booked them as a surprise for Tom. We were both looking forward to some much-needed restorative work on our bodies.

Our masseuse, Petra, was short and petite. But her size didn't stop her from giving a satisfying deep massage. With her strong hands, she kneaded every tired and overworked muscle in a way that left me feeling completely rejuvenated. And Tom looked content and refreshed, ready for our last night in Santiago.

Dinner was spectacular! Petra recommended we try a restaurant just down the street from our hotel. Alfie, Debbie, Tom and I showed up at *Casa Marcelo* just as they were opening for dinner. The place served delicious Galician-Asian fusion and had earned a one-star Michelin rating. A few long community tables ran through the center of the tiny restaurant. It wasn't long before the place started filling up. With no reservation, we were doubtful about our chances. But by some stroke of luck, the host said he had just four seats left and pointed us to the empty chairs. Tom and Alfie sat across from Debbie and me, smack in the middle of the long table.

We watched as small plate after small plate arrived on either side of us, each looking more mouth-watering than the last. We asked our tablemates what we should order. They said that wasn't how it worked at this restaurant. We were supposed to let the chef just bring us things. He would decide what to serve us. This sounded like fun!

When our waiter appeared to take our drink orders, Tom explained that he didn't like seafood. Could he have anything other than seafood? Within minutes, the chef appeared and implored Tom to just try what he brought. He promised Tom he'd bring him something else if he didn't like it. And he didn't let us down.

Each dish was more delicious and creative than the last—from exquisitely seasoned sea bass sashimi to frozen cucumber sorbet over tomato salad, from spiky pork bao buns to crab dumplings and spicy ahi tuna tartare. To the chef's delight, Tom ate every single thing and loved it all.

Later on my blog I wrote:

The dinner was perfect in so many ways. The food was incredible, the atmosphere was fun and festive, and my stomach hurt from laughing at the exchanges between Tom and Debbie. You would think they've known each other for years the way they tease each other. Tom giving Debbie a hard time for her lack of Spanish speaking skills, imitating the way shes says "Scusie" (her unique way of saying excuse me in Spanish) followed by a pouring out in English in her fast New York accent, often resulting in a completely blank look by the Spanish person who doesn't understand any English. And then Debbie, quickly picking up on the reason why our family gave Tom the nickname "Michael Scott" from The Office, *giving him a bad time for his incredibly inappropriate comments. Alfie and I just laughed, thoroughly enjoying the entertainment of their banter. I am going to miss this.*

Afterwards we walked to the garden terrace above the restaurant and enjoyed a delicious Albariño *and met Grace, a sorority sister of Mia's. Unbelievable that I have now met three people on the Camino who each know one of my children. Grace has been traveling and decided to walk part of the Camino a few weeks ago. She and Alfie met randomly and they figured out their USC connection. That's how I came to meet beautiful Grace!*

Soon it was time to say goodbye to Debbie. She and Alfie said their goodbyes, while Tom went back to the hotel to rest up for his biggest walk yet tomorrow. I walked Debbie back to her hotel. It was so sad to say goodbye and to close this chapter of my Camino journey. I know we will see each other again, and I feel so blessed to have met Debbie, someone who made me laugh every single day. What a gift!

On the way back to my hotel, I ran into Alfie, Bearded Michael and his girlfriend, Sarah. We decided to have a final final. When in Santiago, right?! It was past midnight and the streets were filled with people laughing and enjoying the nightlife. This is one of the things I love most about Spanish people—such amazing energy and lust for life. My kind of people. But I knew I couldn't stay up too late again. I had a 30+ kilometer day ahead of me tomorrow. So I finally had to say goodbye to Bearded Michael and Sarah—and hopefully only goodnight to Alfie, as he may be in Finisterre when we arrive. Both he and Irish John are planning on taking a bus or taxi there. I have 50 more miles to walk before I complete my journey across Spain, and I am ready to go!

Day 36

We awoke to a sparkling, clear blue sky. Not a cloud in sight. With warm weather predicted, we happily dressed in shorts and short-sleeve shirts. Tom spent several minutes taping his ankle and bandaging his blisters, before slipping on his socks and open-toed sandals. The socks-and-sandals look was one we weren't likely to be seeing Tom sporting back home—at least, not until he's 80. He wasn't convinced he'd like walking in his new footwear, so he added his hiking shoes, plus a massive bag of first aid products, to his pack. I could tell he was feeling apprehensive. We had a 19.5-mile walk ahead of us.

Tom and I stood in front of the cathedral for one last picture on this glorious sunny day before we headed out. It was a little before 9:00. Leaving Santiago was bittersweet. I'd said goodbye to many friends, including Debbie, my constant companion. And I'd closed the chapter on reaching this famed city. But I felt excited to continue on to Finisterre, where I would end my journey.

Within 20 minutes, we were out of the bustling heart of Santiago and walking on an uncrowded, peaceful stretch of the Camino. We were rewarded with vistas of wide-open fields, wildflowers in bright pinks and purples, and graceful trees swaying in a slight breeze as we plodded along the dirt path. What a refreshing change from the crowds we encountered since Sarria. Tom would finally get a sense of my earlier Camino days.

A few hours later we stopped for a coffee break and

snack. The temperature was rising. We needed to make sure we kept our bodies fueled for our long day of walking in the heat. After I went inside to order for us, I soon came back out with our food and drinks to find Tom rummaging through his pack. I watched as he pulled out his enormous first aid bag and proceeded to meticulously rebandage each of his blisters.

He said he didn't like walking in his sandals. He wanted to try his hiking boots again.

I had serious doubts that he'd be able to finish our walk today. But I kept those thoughts to myself. I continued to watch him, his brows furrowed in deep concentration, tongue poking out as he carefully fashioned each Moleskin piece and gingerly placed it on the beleaguered blister.

When it looked like Tom was finally ready to go, I suggested we get moving before the heat became too oppressive. He began walking slowly and tentatively.

"You go ahead," he said. "I don't want to slow you down."

After a few more steps together, he insisted I walk ahead. He would catch up. I knew he meant it, so I quickened my pace. He was quickly falling behind. Several yards later I saw a huge sign posted on a tree:

24 HOUR TAXI

Below was the number to call. I stopped and considered the sign. I knew Tom was really only walking the Camino for me. He didn't have a huge desire to do it on his own. And it seemed crazy that he would need to walk in pain and discomfort for the rest of the day. There was no shame if he wanted to take a cab to our hotel. I could easily meet him there at the end of the day. I decided to wait for him in front of the sign.

"Hey," I said as he finally hobbled up. "I saw this sign. I thought maybe you might want to take a picture of it. Just in case you change your mind about walking today." I tried to sound casual, aware that his pride was at stake.

Looking slightly offended, Tom whipped out his iPhone and snapped a photo.

But then we both kept walking. Once again, he urged me to go ahead. I told Tom I'd walk for a bit, then wait for him to catch up. So for the rest of the very warm, very long day we walked just this way—navigating several miles of steep up and down elevation changes as Tom continued to plod forward in his floppy sun hat, determined to reach our destination.

Finally, a little after 4:00, after walking up a steady incline along a narrow tree-lined stretch, I saw a bright red sign posted on a tree in front of me. It had the Coca-Cola logo on top of the name of our final destination: *Albergue Cafeteria Alto Da Pena*. An arrow below indicated it was only 300 meters away. I stopped and waited for Tom to catch up, watching as he staggered towards me. I pointed to the sign. A huge look of relief washed over his flushed, sweaty face. He couldn't wait to plop himself down and drink an ice cold beer.

After climbing a ridiculously steep set of stairs just off the dirt path, we finally arrived at the *Alto Da Pena*, a small *albergue* in the middle of nowhere. I sat down at one of the outdoor tables and recognized a young pilgrim with bright blonde hair. I'd talked with her briefly on the Camino and learned she was from South Africa and traveling by herself. Here we were in the middle of nowhere, having barely seen any other pilgrims the entire day and I sat down next to a familiar face. Crazy. She was talking on the phone with her parents, so we just waved hello and found a table. Time to enjoy those refreshing drinks.

The plan for tonight was to meet a driver at the *albergue*, who would then drive us to a hotel about 20 minutes away. The same driver would then pick us up the following morning and return us to the *albergue*, where we would resume our walk.

Our friendly cab driver dropped us off at the *Hotel Gastronomico Casa Rosalia* in Brión, A Coruña. The exterior of the hotel was a nondescript stone building with a huge *Hotel* sign affixed above a doorway. It didn't look particularly promising and I questioned the need for our 20-minute cab ride.

However, the interior was a different story. I felt as if I were entering someone's home. The lobby and adjoining rooms were cozy, welcoming and furnished with comfy-looking chairs and couches. Our room was spacious and bright, with hardwood floors and a large window overlooking the hotel's expansive lawn, pool area and patio, which was filled with people enjoying libations and *tapas*.

We wandered out to the patio and found a table near the pool. Children were splashing about, clearly happy to find relief from the heat. I looked around and noticed several families. The hotel appeared to cater more towards vacationers, young families in particular, than to *peregrinos*.

As we relaxed with a glass of wine and a few *tapas*, Tom and I rehashed our day. I told him how impressed I was that he overcame his blister challenges and walked all 19.5 miles. He grinned at me sheepishly.

"You know that taxi sign you showed me?"

Nodding my head, he continued. "Well, I saw that sign way before you said anything. I'd already decided I better take a picture of it. I wasn't sure I was going to make it today."

"Oh, so you just pretended to be offended by my suggestion?"

"Yeah," he said. "In my mind I saw that sign as 1-800-taxi-for-Tom."

We ended the evening in a small conference room at the hotel. We'd explained to the hotel manager that we were hoping to watch the Women's World Cup soccer quarterfinal game between the U.S. and France. He led us into a tiny room, saying apologetically that this was the only room with a TV. He then found the channel for us, treated us to a bottle of wine and some dessert and left us to enjoy the game. The U.S. team prevailed over France 2-1. It was a perfect way to end the day.

Back in our room, I saw I had a message from Alfie:

Feeling pretty low today...think I'm just stressing about reality coming back.

I felt sure this was a pretty common reaction for many pilgrims finishing their journey. I could understand the roller coaster of emotions, especially since the Camino seemed to be more about the journey than the actual destination. Once we reached the end, we'd all have to return to our own lives and our own realities. We would have to leave this Camino bubble and deal with the responsibilities of our daily lives, and we would have to say goodbye to our Camino friends.

This gift of time and magic on the Camino would end.

I knew my time was coming in just a few days. I wondered how I would feel. I also worried about Alfie—I hoped the end of the Camino wouldn't mean the beginning of another bout of depression. But I was optimistic that the Camino had changed something in him.

Day 37

Our driver picked us up promptly at 8:30 this morning. About 20 minutes later, he dropped us off at the *albergue* where we met him yesterday. By 9:00, Tom and I were on the road on this cold, windy day. I recorded the day on my blog later:

Today was much cooler weather, and several times we had to walk on roads rather than pathways. It was still beautiful scenery, and we didn't have to deal with a lot of cars on the road, so I enjoyed our 16.5-mile walk.

Tom seemed to be feeling much better, just preferring to walk a little slower. We decided to meet up later in the morning so we could both walk at our own pace. I wanted to enjoy one of my last days of walking, listening to music while getting lost in thought and reflecting on all I've experienced so far on my Camino.

I'm feeling sad that I only have two more days of walking until I reach Finisterre. I've become accustomed to this routine and I'm not sure I'm ready for it to end. And I still have questions I'm seeking answers to—perhaps they will come after I've had time to absorb everything I've experienced. Or maybe I'm meant to continue searching for answers in this crazy life journey. Only time will tell...

When we reached our pensión (Pensión Rústica As Pias) in Olveiroa around 2:30 in the afternoon, the sun was out and the sky was a brilliant blue. Our little accommodation was run by Paco, a man with kind eyes and a warm smile. He helped us settle in, then after lunch I wanted to catch up on my blog. I found a nice table outside my room and was happy to be sitting in warm weather. Listening to the sound of clinking glasses, laughter and singing emanating from the large group of people enjoying a Saturday lunch in Paco's restaurant directly below me.

But my mood slowly shifted from feeling content to feeling exceedingly frustrated. The tiny town where we were had incredibly weak Wi-Fi, so it was a painstakingly long process to try to get my pictures uploaded. Not really a big deal in the scheme of things. But it made me think about the difference between my life at home and the life in this little village. There is something so appealing about living a simple life in a place where you are not always connected to the barrage of news headlines, social media, entertainment and content. Paco radiated happiness and seemed to take great pride in running his pensión and restaurant, providing good food for the locals as well as pilgrims like us. It's amazing to me how disconnected his little village is from all the things I take for granted at home. I have to imagine that stress is not a huge health hazard in Olveiroa. Not a bad way to live.

By 9:30 it was still completely light out. And even though it was early for most Spaniards, we were hungry for dinner. Paco encouraged me to try a local dish called percebe, *known as the goose neck barnacle. I thought Tom was literally going to throw up when I started eating it. He could barely gaze at my food and the look of disgust on his face was priceless. Unlike the night in Santiago when the chef encouraged him to try fish, he was not going to be convinced to even touch my dish. Oh, Tommy Dogs! Some things never change!*

Day 38

Today Tom and I were walking to a town called Cee. We started our 12-mile stroll this morning a little after 8:00 in cool, comfortable weather. And with no other pilgrims in sight, we had the Camino to ourselves.

As we ambled along the path, we admired the many old stone *hórreos,* granaries raised above ground by pillars to keep rodents out. We climbed a steep tree-lined ridge overlooking the river valley of the *río Xallas* as the Camino path alternated from dirt roads to stone pavers through open fields and dense forests.

About an hour into our walk, just beyond the hamlet of Logoso, we came upon a highlighter-yellow tiny building. The bright, new-looking structure seemed out of place amongst the old stone buildings surrounding it. We were somewhat surprised to discover that it was the *Centro de Informacion Peregrino*—the Pilgrim Information Center. It seemed like a random place to have this tiny office. But by now, I was used to seeing some of these random sights along the Camino. We simply stopped to take a look at the map of our route painted on the building facade and continued on our way.

Ten minutes later we reached the crossroad of the Camino, where pilgrims can choose either Muxía or Finisterre. Two cement posts—both emblazoned with the yellow and blue Camino shell emblem at the top—stood side by side, with arrows pointing north to Muxía or south to Finisterre. Each post also marked the distance to each destination. We only had just under 30 kilometers—about 18 miles—to go before reaching Finisterre. I could feel my excitement building.

At this point, we were about 1,300 feet above sea level and about to start a steep decline. After walking together all morning, Tom and I decided to walk separately for a stretch. So I forged ahead, once again savoring my fleeting moments of solitude on the Camino. And I appreciated that Tom seemed to understand my desire to be alone without taking offense.

I walked along lovely forested, stone-walled paths as I made the steep descent. And then, three hours into the day's walk, I caught a glimpse of the ocean below for the first time. What a rush to see the magnificent sea! Something about seeing a great expanse of water, with the horizon line in the distance, always brings me a rush of joy, peace and gratitude for nature's magnificence. But today, after walking over 500 miles to get here, something about this particular ocean seemed particularly impressive.

As I strolled further along the path, I could see the Cape of Finisterre in the distance. I now had a visual of my final destination. I knew I had several more miles to go, but I loved that I could actually see the place I was heading.

I waited for Tom to catch up and we admired the stunning scenery together. He could feel my growing excitement and he seemed to be just as enthusiastic about me reaching my final destination as I was.

It was just after noon when we arrived in Cee, a sleepy seaside town with colorful buildings built on a hill in front of a picturesque bay. The town was bustling with activity on this Sunday afternoon, with a flea market and farmer's market both in full swing. We sampled some local cheeses and snacked on fresh, melt-in-your-mouth *churros* before finding our lodging for the night. The *Hotel Insua* was a sterile-looking, multi-story structure and our room was simple and somewhat drab. But, hey, at least it was clean.

We spent the remainder of the day walking around town, grabbing a bite to eat and doing laundry at a nearby *lavandería*. We washed our walking clothes for the very last time—the first in a series of *lasts* for me on this unforgettable journey.

After a *siesta* and shower, we headed out to dinner around 8:00. Tom found a well-reviewed local family-run restaurant, after we decided to forgo our dinner voucher at the dreary-looking hotel dining room. A short walk later, we arrived at the *O Recreo da Costa da Morte*, where we sat at the bar. The bartender, Julio, made us delicious, finely-crafted gin and tonics, delivered in beautiful clear goblets, with lime wedges artfully affixed on each rim.

Having arrived on the earlier side of the dinner service, the restaurant was still quiet. So we had a chance to strike up conversations with both Julio and the owner, Ernesto. Both men enthusiastically recommended their favorite restaurants in Finisterre and showered us with warm hospitality. Ernesto escorted us into the dining room, checking on us often once we were seated.

After I told him I loved *Albariño*, Ernesto excitedly insisted that we try a bottle from the Rías Baixas region, where the *Bodegas Lagar de Pintos* produced the hard-to-find *Cepas*

Albariño. The winery was known for producing only 3,000 bottles a year, making it highly unlikely that we would ever get the chance to try it back home in the United States. So when Ernesto presented us with bottle number 2,661, we joyfully sipped the crisp, aromatic wine, happy that we had discovered this local gem of a restaurant.

Feeling energized after dinner, we walked around town to see if anything was going on. But it was Sunday—a slow night just about anywhere in the world. This place was no different. Cee was quiet and uneventful, leaving us little choice but to return to our dreary hotel.

Time to rest up before my very last day of walking.

Day 39

My alarm sounded at 7:00 and I popped right out of bed, beyond excited for the day ahead. I was thrilled to open the curtains to see some blue sky peeking out from behind a few wispy morning clouds. After the cool and cloudy weather we endured yesterday, I welcomed any signs of the sun and warmer temperatures.

Tom and I dropped our duffel bags at the front desk, grabbed a few snacks from the hotel dining room buffet and stuck them in our packs. We were on the road a little after 8:00, with only a short walk ahead of us today—a mere 10 miles to the famed lighthouse on the Cape of Finisterre. I wanted to take my time today. I needed to savor every last moment of my Camino experience.

We began our day walking at a leisurely pace, stopping 20 minutes later in the charming town of Corcubíon for coffee and breakfast. We sat at a tiny outdoor table at a bistro just off the Camino, with a stunning view overlooking the Atlantic Ocean. We watched as a few small groups of pilgrims walked past us, disappearing up the narrow medieval cobblestone streets. I was going to miss this ritual—sitting down for my morning *café con leche*, taking in the sights and waving hello to passing *peregrinos*.

It was soon time for us to head up those same streets. The reassuring appearance of the yellow arrows pointed us up a steep, windy, narrow path—stone steps encased on one side by a lovely moss-covered stone wall, on the other side by trees and lush greenery. Every so often Tom and I stopped to turn around and admire the view from our ascent. We were always rewarded with stunning views of the sea below and the emerging shining sun above. It was turning into a beautiful day, with a promise of clear blue skies ahead.

My senses were on high alert. I took in every vista with extra pleasure while we walked on dirt paths and through forests. At times we had to contend with oncoming cars as we walked single-file on roadside stretches of the Camino. It was still early morning—around 9:30—when we reached the region of Fisterra, the Cape of Finisterre in our sights, but still several miles away. As we wended our way along the path, the clouds continued to clear, rewarding us with azure skies and a sun-kissed glistening blue sea. My heart felt full, grateful for the magnificent views to enjoy on my last day.

Less than two hours later, we spotted Langosteira Beach, the gorgeous white sand paradise not far from Finisterre's center of town. I reminded Tom that this was the beach Jackson told us about when he did the Camino four years ago. Upon seeing the inviting crystal white sands, Jackson commemorated his arrival to Finisterre by throwing his pack off, stripping down to his boxers and plunging into the cool blue water, an overwhelming sense of joy and elation washing over him. He described it as a powerful baptismal experience, a moment of rebirth and rejuvenation. I joyfully pictured the scene in my mind's eye and looked forward to hearing Jackson retell the story once again now that I'd seen the beach.

The Camino path led us through the bustling seaside town of Finisterre. We passed by several restaurants, *albergues* and tiny shops selling clothes, hiking gear and Camino souvenirs. Plenty of pilgrims like us were making their way up to the lighthouse on the Cape of Finisterre. While others, apparently finished with their Camino, were celebrating or relaxing with friends at several of the seaside restaurants.

A few minutes outside of town, we began climbing the steep incline to reach the cape. We noticed a sign announcing the *Costa da Morte*—the Coast of Death—below. It was so named because there have been a number of shipwrecks on this treacherous stretch of the Atlantic. As we trudged *up, up, up,* the wind became fierce, constantly whipping my pony tail across my face. The waves crashed against the rocks below. I understood how ships could be battered in this unforgiving sea.

Nearly halfway up we stopped and took a picture by the famed pilgrim statue. The man is wearing a brimmed hat, with a Camino shell emblazoned on the front. He's wrapped in a simple long robe, a cape covering his shoulders, a staff in hand and a small pouch tied at his waist. His eyes are fixed ahead, a look of grit and determination etched on his face. His gear is in sharp contrast to many of the pilgrims of today in their bright clothing, slick backpacks and shiny walking poles. The pilgrim statue is a powerful reminder of the Camino's long, rich history.

Tom and I continued our climb up. We were finally approaching Cape Finisterre. I began to pick up my pace as I neared the lighthouse. Tom urged me to walk ahead. By now, miraculously, only a scattering of clouds appeared in the brilliant blue sky. I could see the final Camino distance marker only steps away. And I could hear—yet *again*—the melancholy strains of a bagpipe. At last, I had reached the final marker—*km 0,000*—on Monday, July 1, 2019 just before noon on a magnificent sunny morning. I had just finished *walking across Spain.*

The moment felt surreal.

I turned around to see Tom, tears streaming down his face. He hugged me tightly, saying over and over how proud he was of me. I was proud of him, too, for fighting his blister pain and completing *his* Camino. And I appreciated how he seamlessly dropped into my journey, supporting me every step of the way.

After several celebratory pictures by the final distance marker, Tom and I walked further ahead towards the solo bagpiper, who stood barefoot in front of a waist-high stone wall with the sea as his backdrop. His achingly beautiful music only heightened our emotions, creating a magical soundtrack and unforgettable scene on this final day.

We passed the lighthouse and made our way out to the rocky outcrop below. We stepped carefully across the rocks until we were as close as safely possible to the edge of Cape Finisterre—*the end of the Earth.* We dropped our packs and I found a place to sit by myself to take in this moment. I wrote the following on my blog:

> *I had a hard time grasping the reality that my body had carried me 550 miles across the entire country of Spain. I had taken over one million footsteps to reach my destination. At that moment I experienced so many emotions. But most of all, I felt grateful for the resilience and strength of my body, the opportunity to experience this decade-old dream of mine, the amazing friends I met along the way—and most importantly for the support and encouragement of my family*

and friends back home. That support was the anchor throughout this journey. I realize more than ever how lucky I am to have that in my life.

After celebrating with a glass of champagne while overlooking the ocean, Tom and I walked back to town to get our Compostela *of the Camino Finisterre before heading to our hotel, the* Hotel Mar Da Ardora. *On the way we stopped in the* albergue *where Jackson told us he'd stayed when he was here four years ago. He asked us to see if something he made was still hanging in the reception area. Sadly, I couldn't find it. I enjoyed imagining Jackson in the welcoming and bohemian* albergue *(more like a* zen den*) that had colorful artwork and cozy seating everywhere—even a meditation room adjacent to the dining area. The innkeeper said he remembered Jackson's face. Amazing. I can't wait to trade Camino stories with Jackson when I get home, now that I have a deeper understanding of this unique experience.*

Later in the evening we met Irish John and Alfie for drinks, then had a quick dinner in time to get to the beach to watch the sunset after 10 p.m. The circle around our campfire continued to grow as people came by asking to join us. At midnight we sang happy birthday to Alfie. I was so glad we could be there to celebrate with him. I know Debbie was with us in spirit. We stayed until the early morning hours, sitting around the fire listening to Irish John, Alfie and a few others share their musical talents with us. It was a perfect way to end the day. And a perfect way to end my Buen Camino.

I met the end of my 550-mile journey with joy and sadness. I felt a remarkable sense of strength, satisfaction and
accomplishment. I had finally completed this dream trek.
But I also felt melancholy about saying goodbye to this way
of life and the reality of closing this chapter. I also hated saying goodbye to dear Alfie, who had shared so many special
Camino memories with me. I hoped we would one day see
each other again and I promised to keep in touch. Later he
messaged me:

> You are such a bright light. I consider it an honour
> and privilege to have shared time with you in the
> way I have. You have become and will remain a part
> of my heart. I love you Margarita. Safe travels.

Sweet, sweet Alfie. I will always have a special place in
my heart for him, too.

But it was time to go. Time to leave the peace and tranquility of the Camino. Time to head to the lively, boisterous
city of Madrid for a few nights, before flying home to California. Tom and I packed all of our belongings, happy to stuff our
hiking clothes at the bottom of our bags—and eager to retrieve a few pieces of clothing we brought for the big city. I
mentally geared up to leave the Camino, to begin the process
of letting all my experiences marinate and take shape during
the months to come.

I was ready.

Afterward

Returning home after nearly seven weeks in Spain was much more difficult than I'd anticipated. Especially after an unforgettable, Camino-ending, three-day trip to Madrid.

We hit the city smack in the middle of Gay Pride Week. So, of course, the city was ablaze with celebration—rainbow flags, free outdoor concerts, sangria-soaked partiers and crazy costumes everywhere. This was Tom's first trip in Madrid, so it was extra special for me to show him all around the *ciudad* that had been my home city so many years ago during my junior year at UCLA. We walked for hours each day exploring everything from *Parque del Retiro*, the *Prado* and the Royal Palace, to the high-end Salamanca district, the *Plaza Mayor* and the *Plaza del Sol*.

I took Tom to a fabulous food market—*Mercado de San Miguel*—where the displays of fresh fruits, cheeses, charcuterie, seafood, chocolate, *tapas* and various cold beverages served up a staggering visual feast. We weaved our way through the lively crowd, squeezing into a sliver of space at one of the counters. When it was our turn to order, we pointed to several appetizing-looking *tapas* behind the glass case and ordered two glasses of bubbly rosé, the perfect drink on a hot summer day in Madrid.

And with the scorching heat, it was a perfect time to take Tom to a few rooftop bars. We ate lunch at a rooftop garden restaurant called *El Jardín Secreto*—The Secret Garden—so named because it's above a retail store off of the *Plaza del Sol* and not easy to spot. In the evening we enjoyed cocktails at the *Círculo de Bellas Artes,* a place that drew Madrid's beautiful, cool crowd. Elegantly dressed men and women lounged in comfy couches or sat at high-top tables, sipping craft cocktails while we all soaked up the stunning, sweeping views of the city below. What a night.

The highlight of our short stay, though, was reuniting with Javier and Vicente, the Spanish brothers I befriended during my year abroad in Madrid 35 years ago. I hadn't seen Vicente for over three decades. But he was still every bit as warm, kind and funny as I remembered him. And Javier, who I'd seen four years ago when I visited Jackson in Madrid, welcomed me again with a warm embrace. They seemed delighted to finally meet Tom and we laughed our way through lunch, trying to communicate as best as possible. Javier didn't speak English and Tom didn't speak Spanish so Vicente and I translated as best we could—with big gestures and exaggerated facial expressions filling in when language failed us.

Vicente and Javier presented us with a few gifts right before dessert. Knowing how much Mia and I like Manchego cheese, they gave us an enormous wheel—already wrapped airtight and airline-ready. Next I opened a beautifully-wrapped smaller gift. It was a picture of Tom and me in front of the Cathedral right after we arrived in Santiago. Our hands are outstretched in joy, our faces beaming with happiness. Vicente printed the photo from my blog and had it framed in time for our arrival. Sweet, sweet Vicente. My eyes welled with tears. I was touched deeply by this act of thoughtfulness. These brothers were such good men. And I felt blessed to have met them, lucky to have had the opportunity to reconnect with them all these years later.

After our leisurely *five*-hour lunch, I hugged them tightly as we said our goodbyes. We promised to see one another in the not too distant future and I hope it happens.

Tom and I left Madrid for home the next afternoon.

I knew re-entry would be an adjustment. I'd experienced this after returning home from my year abroad in Madrid. But this felt different. I had a tough time acclimating. As I would find out in the ensuing weeks, the difficulty of re-entry was not un-common amongst returning pilgrims. I just don't ever remem-ber reading about this phenomenon or hearing people discuss it on the Camino.

My arrival back to U.S. soil started out brilliantly though. Mia and Jackson had flown in from Los Angeles and Denver to surprise me at the San Francisco airport on a Saturday night in early July. Charlie was visiting a friend in Washington, D.C., so he couldn't join them. In fact, he was visiting his friend Matt, the same friend whose red plaid shirt Alfie had been wearing daily on the Camino. But I was absolutely shocked, thrilled and over-joyed to be greeted by two of my children.

When we arrived home later that night, I was surprised with fresh flowers and welcome back notes and signs. Mia and Jackson had gone out of their way to make my homecoming special. I was so happy to be able to share some of my stories with them in person and give them big hugs. And after over 40 days of sleeping in a different bed every night, I was ecstatic to sleep in my own bed.

We were all able to enjoy the next day together. But then Jackson had to return to his home in Boulder, Colorado.

Mia had to get back to her internship in Los Angeles. It was time for me to get resettled. But I missed my routine of waking early, walking for several hours, seeing new sights and meeting interesting people along the way. So I tried this at home.

But it wasn't the same.

"Where did you go today on your walk?" Tom asked me one evening.

After telling him my route, he exclaimed, "Wait, what?! How many miles did you walk?"

"Fifteen," I whispered, somewhat embarrassed. I knew this wasn't normal.

Yes, I was walking. But I wasn't meeting any pilgrims. People around me seemed to be operating at a frenetic pace, too busy and distracted to make any human connection. Stress permeated the air. People's faces were buried in their phones or laptops. I felt a heaviness around me—the constant push for people to be productive and speedy in whatever they did. The expectation that they should be available 24/7 for their employers, friends and family.

The work/life balance felt completely out of whack. And it rattled me to my core.

Driving my car wasn't much better. I was struck by the road rage I witnessed—and felt—as I maneuvered my car around town. People drove dangerously fast, tailgated the cars in front of them, made unsafe lane changes, flipped off other drivers and honked if you didn't respond quick enough after a light change. I felt completely stressed out.

No wonder the United States is dealing with the problems of an overmedicated population and a record number of young people with anxiety issues. This fast-paced, productivity-driven lifestyle doesn't create happiness. We need to figure out a way to restore a more sustainable and realistic balance in our lives. That seems to be the surest path to finding joy and meaning in our lives.

I appreciate how the Spaniards take time to eat their meals sitting at a table—"to go" cups and containers were nowhere to be found in most of the small towns I visited. And the *siesta* in the middle of the day—what a concept! The afternoon nap gives people a chance to physically and mentally recharge for the evening. From what I could tell, people in Spain work to live—not live to work. The Spaniards I encountered seemed happy. Life seemed a lot less complicated.

Back home I also noticed how bombarded I felt by all the content floating around me: ads for upcoming shows on cable, network TV and streaming services, piles of catalogues appearing in my mailbox daily, ads on my Instagram feed urging me to buy the latest fashion or gadget, and social media postings with smiling happy faces, often in beautiful locales. How did the pre-Camino me manage all of this, I wondered?

The messages were strong and loud—"WATCH ME," "BUY ME," "TRAVEL HERE," "SPEND MONEY." The mighty U.S. dollar. Consumerism. Materialism. We get messages every day promising us happiness—but only if we spend our money on the right product or look a certain way.

It can all be too much to take in. Too many choices. I felt overwhelmed. I yearned for the peace, serenity and simplicity of life on the Camino: wake up, walk, eat, explore, connect with others, sleep, repeat. Bliss.

I was having a difficult time adjusting to life at home. Tom clearly noticed I wasn't myself and tried to give me the space I needed to reacclimate. But I felt that even though he had been on the Camino for nine days of walking, he couldn't really understand what I was going through. His experience was very different from mine. So I didn't expect him to comprehend all the various emotions I was feeling.

But it was straining our relationship. He was at a loss about how to help me transition. And I couldn't simply flip a switch and make myself return to the person I was before I left. I knew it would take some time for my re-entry to stabilize. Patience isn't a strong suit for either Tom or me, so we were both put to the test during this time.

About three weeks after I came home, I wrote the following in my journal:

Been home since July 6th and dealing with so many post-Camino emotions. Hard to make the transition home—so fast-paced and busy here. Traffic, people, bad moods, anger, stress all around me—I feel the negativity here. So different than the Camino, where I constantly felt love, peace, tranquility, happiness, inclusiveness. Camino people "SEE" each other, whereas here I believe people are suffering as they are not being seen or noticed. Everyone is working too hard—too myopic with their own lives and problems. Don't have the time nor the space for other people. How can we change this? How can I avoid getting sucked in? I don't want to live my life that way.

Also—so unique to the Camino—forming friendships with people of all ages. Age is irrelevant. If you connect, you connect. Would I ever have been able to form a relationship with Alfie here at home? Probably

not—too much judgment at our age difference. So sad.
We probably miss out on so many meaningful relation-
ships. If only we could remove the stigma, the social
norms and unwritten rules, things could be different.

Seems I wasn't the only one dealing with some of these issues. Debbie found herself yearning for these same things as she went out for daily long walks in New York City. She caught herself several times from shouting out *"Buen Camino!"* to fellow pedestrians and became distressed when failing to make eye contact or elicit a smile from strangers. People are busy and often in their own heads. They have jobs, bills to pay, responsibilities. Life can be stressful. Debbie and I both agreed how lucky we were to have had the experience of walking the Camino—a place where the majority of pilgrims are able to put their everyday worries and responsibilities on hold so they can be in the moment, enjoy their surroundings and connect with one another.

Laura was also dealing with the challenges of re-entry. She told me she constantly had to refer back to her journal to capture the feelings she experienced on the Camino. That Camino journal was her mood booster.

Alfie had flown to Florence to resume working on his book. However, he ended up meeting several new people and it sounded like their social schedule didn't leave much room for writing. He hoped to work on the book when he flew home to England later that summer. It sounded like he was in a good place and adjusting well after the Camino. I felt relieved.

As for me, getting over the post-Camino blues simply took time. I eventually settled into the rhythm of life at home and didn't feel the same urge to escape for a five-hour walk. I was able to appreciate what my life at home had to offer—most importantly my family and friends. And I was beyond grateful for the privilege of walking the Camino. I felt truly happy during my several weeks there. Despite dealing with nagging blisters and excruciating knee pain, I never once regretted my decision to embark upon this journey. I never once shed a tear (except when I was in Burgos trying to reach Nuria in the travel office). Or felt scared. Or wished I was someplace else. I felt happy in a way I remember feeling as a child—pure, genuine joy—the kind that pulses through every crevice of your body. Even my mother noticed it in the pictures she saw of me on my blog. "I've never seen you look happier" she told me when I came home. And my friend Beth commented on my blog: "The Camino definitely agrees with you. You are exuding peace and happiness."

At home I was finding a new balance though. The Camino had re-awakened my longing for travel and adventure. I wanted to figure out how I could incorporate these things going forward. I hadn't been able to answer some of the many questions I pondered while on the Camino—"What path do I want to take going forward?"..."How can I make a meaningful impact in this life?"..."What's important to me?"—but I hoped that, in time, some of these answers would become clear. And I felt at peace with the "not knowing" all these answers and just letting my life unfold. The Camino had taught me a little something about patience. You can't walk to Santiago in a day. But if you just keep taking those steps—asking the big life questions—eventually you'll get to your destination. As long as your mind is open, your heart is full and you're steadfastly curious.

I'm convinced that one of the reasons there's been a surge in popularity for the Camino is that people are longing for human connection. They want to be seen. And heard. And acknowledged. In our technology-driven world, the practice of connecting with people face-to-face, using sustained eye contact in conversation, is waning. Humans are social creatures. Multiple studies have shown we live longer when we have meaningful connections and interactions with others. The Camino is one of the greatest places on the planet for human connection. Why? Because the majority of pilgrims take the time to listen, to see and to bond with other pilgrims. Pilgrims break bread, sip *vino tinto* and share stories with fellow travelers from all over the world, each with a tale to tell.

Why is it so hard to recognize that we've each got a tale to tell when we get back to our real lives?

I realize that life on the Camino is like living in a bubble. It's not the *real world*. It's a temporary way of life that ends, in most cases, when pilgrims reach Santiago. But there are many elements of Camino life that we can incorporate into our lives back home. We can limit our intake of social media and learn to carve out time for ourselves every day to do something that brings us joy. We can take a moment to sit and enjoy our meals rather than eat on the go. We can pick up the phone and call a friend rather than communicate through text—or better yet, find time to meet that friend in person. We can smile at a stranger—you never know how this might brighten someone's day. We can create time to enjoy the outdoors, appreciate nature and explore new places. Put our phones away. Extend ourselves to meet new people and focus on *really* listening to what they have to say. Connect.

A few days after finishing the Camino, Tom and I walked to a restaurant near our hotel in Madrid to enjoy a late-night dinner. While waiting for our table, we sat at the bar, the air electric with buzzing energy. Well-dressed men and beautiful, elegant women surrounded us as the sounds of cocktail shakers and loud pop music filled the air. While Tom began talking with a guy sitting next to him, I struck up a conversation with a woman—early 40s, sitting alone—with long, wavy dark hair. She exuded confidence and sensuality in a subtle, but attractive, way. Her smile was warm and inviting. I liked her immediately. Within a few minutes, I discovered that she, too, had walked the Camino Francés a few years earlier.

From that moment on, Elizabeth and I talked non-stop until I paused and impulsively invited her to join Tom and me for dinner—which she accepted. I don't think the pre-Camino me would have invited a complete stranger to join us for dinner. But Margarita would. It felt good to extend myself and seize the opportunity to be inclusive. Thankfully, Tom went along with it without a second thought. We ended up having an amazing night—a delicious dinner, followed by dancing until 3:00 in the morning at the club below the restaurant. After exchanging contact info, I felt sure I would see Elizabeth again.

This is the kind of experience I hope I can recreate in my life at home. I want to remain open to meeting and connecting with new people—while continuing to strengthen the connections I have with my family and friends. I know my life will be richer and more fulfilling by living this way. I now have a greater understanding of what I need to achieve a better balance in my life. The challenge will be to figure out how I can sustain it.

After years of checking off to-do lists, spending the energy and time that's required to raise three children, managing a home and juggling a myriad of other activities, if nothing else, writing this book has given me something tangible to hold in my hands. Like looking at my children, I can see the fruits of my labor.

Now that I've returned from the Camino, I find that I am more fulfilled focusing my energy on things I can create—art, writing—anything tangible. I no longer want to fill up my days with tedious to-do lists. Of course, these tasks are part of my life and things still need to get done. But I am choosing to make more room for other, more fulfilling endeavors.

The Camino was one of the greatest gifts I ever gave to myself. It set me on a path of rediscovering who I am and what brings me joy. Thanks to the Camino, I was able to reconnect to the person I was before I married and became a mother. And I liked experiencing life as Margarita—carefree, adventurous and spontaneous.

About a month after I arrived back home, Charlie told me that as he read my blog, for the first time in his life, he saw me in a completely new light. I wasn't just his mother—I was a person with my own needs, wishes and dreams. Charlie said he could imagine what I must have been like as a young girl living in Spain, traveling with friends and enjoying life. This was an eye-opening revelation for him. I feel like it has deepened our already close relationship. He has a better understanding of who I am as a person now.

I also think Tom saw me in a different light after we returned. I think he, too, could see my former self emerge after being a mother to our children for so long. I felt like he could now truly appreciate my independent nature, as well as my yearning to travel, explore and try new things. For so many years, he saw me as someone who managed our three kids and household responsibilities, constantly checking off my long to-do lists. But on the Camino, I felt he could see *me*, the person he fell in love with so long ago, with my own aspirations, dreams and desires.

A few weeks after I got home, Jackson sent me a beautiful poem he wrote on June 12th, 2019—the 21st day of my Camino.

To My Mother, Walking the Camino
It is the still wind
that makes me think
of my mother;
the burning sun
a little more gentle;
a peace in the body found
from working hard
through the heat
of the day,

imagining her
trekking long hours
into the sunset
day after day
after day
deciding
again
and again
to say "yes"
to her life
to her journey
as woman
towards whatever
is waiting
towards whatever

she wishes
to cultivate
in her empowered
eldership
now that
her children
have left
the home,

and I think of her
hopefully enjoying
a cold beverage
in the shade
of some old
stone building
in a tiny
Spanish town
with that same,
tired
bodily feeling
of satisfaction
from having also
worked hard
today,

and I think of all
she sacrificed
willingly of herself
to be mother
to us children,
witnessing us, caring
for us, loving us,
supporting us
as we journeyed
from diapers
to young
adulthood
where we are
now,
bearing witness

for the first time
to Margarita's dream — free
of responsibility
to anyone
but herself
doing only
and exactly
what she desires
to do —

and I think
how much
she deserves this
and how
I could not wish
for anything more
for her
as a son
than for her
to be committed
wholeheartedly
to something
that is completely
and totally
for her own life's
path,

and I love her
so much
for who she has been,
for the mother
she will always be
to me, and also,
more importantly,
for the person
she is now
so bravely
walking
Into.

Mia also said how she admired me for following my dreams and having the courage to make them happen on my own, not waiting or relying on someone else to accompany me. I know Mia would do exactly the same thing, and I am proud of the strong, independent and capable young woman she has become.

Besides seeing how my Camino experience affected my family, I was surprised to learn how it affected other people. Many friends shared their desire to also walk the Camino, saying it had long been on their bucket list. And I had several female friends tell me that I had inspired them to follow through with something they wanted to do on their own.

My sister Sarah, a talented painter, had always wanted to do a plein air painting class in a beautiful locale, but for various reasons she kept putting it off. Despite her discomfort at the idea of traveling alone, Sarah insisted that my walking the Camino inspired her to sign up for a class on the gorgeous island of Capri. She told me she didn't think she would have gotten on the plane by herself otherwise.

Another friend told me that my walking the Camino made her look at her life differently. She is a dynamic woman who built her own successful business by employing her strong work ethic, determination and grit. But she said she was re-examining her life, looking at other ways to fulfill her life besides her business—and she came to the realization that she wanted to take time out from her busy work routine and do something for herself before life passed her by. She began with small steps—heading into the office late two mornings a week to carve out time for herself, and she hoped to make some larger, more significant changes as her job would allow.

Several other friends and acquaintances have also remarked that they want to embark on an adventure of their own or finally take the trip they've been talking about for years. My hope is that they all follow through on their wishes so they can experience the joys of doing something for yourself and realizing a dream.

I attribute these reactions to the power of the Camino. Not only do pilgrims benefit in a multitude of ways by walking, but people who witness others making this journey can also be profoundly affected to make changes in their own lives.

Maybe part of this is due to the unique traits of a *pilgrim* versus those of a *tourist*. A tourist's main objective is to reach a desired destination. The experience starts once the tourist arrives and tends to be outwardly focused on activities deemed worthy by the tourist. For the pilgrim, the journey *is* the experience. And the pilgrim often seeks self-enlightenment or spends time in deep self-reflection, hence making the trek more inwardly focused. Upon returning home, a tourist might inspire others to visit a particular place in the exterior world—but a pilgrim may spark a desire in others to take a journey into their inner world.

I noticed that many of the pilgrims I met were creative types—writers, musicians, artists. Many seemed to be searching for their place, their role in our tech-saturated world. Making a living in the creative arts can be challenging, especially when those skills don't hold the same value in our society as science and technology. But we need those gifts in our lives. The world would be a drab and monotonous existence without them. I wouldn't want to live in a world without these expressions of creativity. I often wonder what it will take for the world to bestow our artists with the value they deserve. I feel blessed to have a son who has a gift with words and music. But as much as Jackson would like to pursue his talents full-time, he knows, at least for the time being, he needs to supplement his income with other work.

I have been fortunate to remain in constant contact with several of the people I met on the Camino—including Laura, Debbie and Alfie. I believe we'll always share a special bond due to our shared experiences in Spain. In October of 2019, Laura traveled from England, and I flew from California to meet Debbie in New York City for a weekend together. Our little reunion was filled with sharing our fondest Camino memories, comparing our experiences of transitioning home and reflecting on the many gifts of Camino life. It was strange to see the three of us all dressed in something other than hiking clothes— wearing make-up even—and relating to one another in the *real* world. I felt happy that we all made the effort to come together for our Camino reunion.

Many of the other pilgrims—Takashi, Bearded Michael, Sean, Big Michael, David and Irish John—I either communicate with occasionally on WhatsApp or I follow them on Instagram, my one form of social media that I still check regularly. It always makes me happy when I see one of their faces pop up on my feed.

David, now living in Berlin, did in fact end up getting offered that job in New York City he interviewed for on the Camino. The job turned out not to be the right fit for him. But it's amazing that he was even able to secure an offer with the challenges he had to overcome to conduct the interview.

At the end of 2019, about five months after I returned from the Camino, Debbie texted me with some tragic news she'd seen on Facebook. Dan, the fast-walking Canadian pilgrim, had passed away unexpectedly—apparently from an accidental drug overdose. Debbie—who always said Dan reminded her of her late son, Philip—had been right to worry about him. And now she was experiencing another tragic loss. We all were. Dan also left behind Emi, the woman he met on the Camino and then married a few months later in November. She was pregnant with his baby and still living with her family in Japan. She and Dan had been working on the necessary paperwork to enable her to move to Canada. I couldn't believe it. I was rattled to my core.

I thought about my first long conversation with Dan over coffee. I remembered him telling me how he felt strong and healthy after rehab. His life was going in a positive direction and he felt optimistic about his future. He loved being on the Camino. He had to return to work at the end of the month, but Dan was trying to figure out a way he could delay his return so he could get to Santiago before his scheduled departure. He desperately wanted to finish the Camino. He hoped to have a family one day.

And now he was gone. Dan would never have the chance again to finish the Camino. Or meet his baby. The sadness was overwhelming.

I will always remember Dan's bright smile and his enthusiasm while trudging along the Camino with his loud clacking stick. And I cherish the joy-filled picture of us together with Debbie at the bar in León—the night I decided to stay for one last drink. It was the last time I would ever see Dan. It's a happy memory and I choose to focus on that rather than dwell on the sadness of his passing.

Connections made on the Camino can be brief—but intense. I encountered this many times on my own journey. Some of the friendships I made feel like they have been cultivated for years. That's how strong the bond is. In reality, we may have only spent a few days together—not much in the grand scheme of life. Yet somehow, the bond is strong and the connection is real.

And I met so many people that I may have never crossed paths with otherwise. What a joy to meet people of all ages from all over the world—some with vastly different backgrounds and others who seemed similar to me, some who I connected with effortlessly and others who I found I couldn't connect with either because of our language barrier or because we just didn't click. The power of the Camino is an amazing thing to experience and witness.

Perhaps the greatest gift of the Camino is providing a safe environment where pilgrims feel *seen, heard* and *accepted*. In this culture of connection, a solo *peregrino* is often invited to join others, an experience that many pilgrims may not get at home—especially those without a large social network. I often think about the crying young German man I met in Santiago, who desperately didn't want to return to his lonely life back home, where he felt utterly unseen. My heart breaks for him.

When I first began the Camino, I didn't understand why someone might want to do it more than once. I thought if I had that much time again, I'd want to do something new and different.

But now I get it.

Where else can you meet people from all over the world—fellow adventurers who are, for the most part, willing and interested to connect with others? Where in the world can you encounter a steady stream of strangers who are encouraging, inclusive, helpful, accepting and hospitable?

And while you're meeting all these interesting, big-hearted souls, you'll also have an opportunity to mentally and physically challenge yourself every day while enjoying gorgeous vistas. You have the chance to examine your life—your thoughts, your goals and dreams, your relationships. You have time to scrutinize your priorities, to figure out what things aren't worth spending your time worrying about. Walking the Camino is a chance to get rid of the unnecessary clutter and distraction—to live each day at a decelerated pace.

The Camino is a chance to *slow your roll.*

I was fortunate to be able to do all of those things. Would I do it differently next time? Probably. I'm not sure I would pre-book my rooms—maybe only a few in some of the bigger cities. I might like to leave a little more room for spontaneity. Maybe linger a little longer in some of my favorite places. But no matter how anyone chooses to walk the Camino, it's a magical experience under a unique set of circumstances. Now I understand why many pilgrims want to retrace their steps.

I hope I have the chance to return one day.

While You Still Can

Song by Brothers Osborne

Make amends with that old friend
You swore you'd never talk to again
Because you miss him
Call up your mom on the telephone
Talk a whole lot of nothing til the cows come home
And listen
Cross every T, dot most the I's
'Cause years grow wings and fly on by
And time slips through your fingers just like sand

Because everything you thought would last forever
Never lasts forever, like your plan
Don't let your night become another
So take life by the hands while you still can

Get your daddy to tell that same old joke
And laugh between the jack and coke
And hope one day you'll be half as funny
Count your blessings and your stars
It's in the air and who you are
It's about the wealth you give
It sure as hell ain't about the money

Because everything you thought would last forever
Never lasts forever like you plan
Don't let your night become another
So take life by the hands while you still can

You just imagine
Anything can happen if you live every moment like it's your last

Because everything you thought would last forever
Never lasts forever like you plan
Don't let your night become another
So take life by the hands while you still can

Note about the Ubuntu font used in this book:

I don't usually pay much attention to font styles, but a few days after I started writing this book my son, Jackson, posted one of his poems on his blog *The Early Morning Press*. I loved the poem, and I was also drawn to the font he used and wanted to use it in my book. Jackson asked me if I knew the meaning of the word "ubuntu." Since I didn't, I looked it up. This is what I found:

Ubuntu (Zulu pronunciation: [ùɓúntʼù]) is a Nguni Bantu term meaning "humanity." It is often translated as "I am because we are" or "humanity towards others," but is often used in a more philosophical sense to mean "the belief in a universal bond of sharing that connects all humanity."

And this:

Noun (SOUTH AFRICA) a quality that includes the essential human virtues; compassion and humanity.

What a fitting font for a story about the Camino, where compassion and humanity are on full display. The fact that I was suddenly drawn to this font for my book—well . . . *It's a Camino thing.*

Acknowledgements

First and foremost, I would like to thank my friend and editor, Bob Makela, who initially gave me the idea and then encouraged me to write this book. With his wisdom and ever present humor, he inspired me to stretch myself and take on this unfamiliar and challenging endeavor. I am forever grateful for his unwavering support, patience, brilliant guidance, sharp editing skills and, most importantly, his friendship.

Thank you to my gifted and artistic sister, Sarah Marcum, for saying yes without hesitation when I asked her if she would paint a Camino map to include in this book. And similarly, thank you to my extremely talented sister-in-law, Olga Arseniev, who designed the cover art and generously offered invaluable design consultation. These two women enrich my life and I feel lucky to call them sisters.

Thank you to my family and friends who supported and cheered me while I was walking across Spain and who championed the writing of this book. I appreciate each and every one of them.

Thank you to all of my Camino friends. They left an indelible impression on me, and I will always cherish the time we spent together on our magical journey.

Lastly, thank you to Tom, Jackson, Charlie and Mia for their unflagging support and encouragement and for their abundant love and affection. They are my pillars, my inspiration, my most ardent cheerleaders and the four people I love most in this world.

Live in the moment
Welcome each day—its pleasures and its challenges
Make others feel welcome
Share
Feel the spirit of those who have gone before you
Imagine those who will follow you
Appreciate those who walk with you today

(Spirit of the Camino)

About the Author

Meg S. Maloney holds a BA in English Literature from UCLA and an MA in Marriage, Family, Child Counseling from St. Mary's College. She has three adult children and lives with her husband in Northern California. This is her first book. And possibly her last. But hopefully not her last Camino.

Made in the USA
Middletown, DE
04 October 2020